WRITING AND PRODUCING RADIO DRAMAS

WRITING AND PRODUCING RADIO DRAMAS

Communication for Behavior Change, Volume 1

Esta de Fossard

Sage Publications
New Delhi ◉ Thousand Oaks ◉ London

First published in 2005 by

Sage Publications India Pvt Ltd
B1/I 1 Mohan Cooperative Industrial Area, Mathura Road
New Delhi 110 044

Sage Publications Inc
2455 Teller Road
Thousand Oaks, California 91320

Sage Publications Ltd
1 Oliver's Yard, 55 City Road
London EC1Y 1SP

Published by Tejeshwar Singh for Sage Publications India Pvt Ltd, phototypeset in 10.5/12.5 Century751BT by C&M Digital Pvt Ltd, Chennai and printed at Chaman Enterprises, New Delhi.

Second Printing 2007

Library of Congress Cataloging-in-Publication Data

De Fossard, Esta.
 Writing and producing radio dramas: communication for behavior change \ Esta de Fossard.
   p.cm.—(Communication for behavior change; v. 1)
 includes bibliographical references.
 1. Radio Plays—Authorship. 2. Radio—Production and direction. I. Title. II. Series.
 PN1991.73.D35   808.2'22—dc22   2005   2004025838

ISBN: 10: 0-7619-3326-3 (Pb)   10: 81-7829-454-0 (India-Pb)
       13: 978-0-7619-3326-7 (Pb)   13: 978-81-7829-454-4 (India-Pb)

Sage Production Team: Anamika Mukharji, Rajib Chatterjee, and Santosh Rawat

To my husband,
Harvey F. Nelson, for his tireless
and devoted help in reviewing all
sections of this book and for
taking the photographs for it.

Contents

List of Boxes   11
Definitions   13

Part 1
Introduction to Entertainment–Education Radio Drama

1 RADIO DRAMA FOR BEHAVIOR CHANGE   23

Radio for Social Development   25
Entertainment–Education Serial Drama   25
"Soap Opera" or "Serial Drama"   27
Using Serial Drama for Social Development and Behavior
   Change Communication   27
Characteristics of Serial Drama   28
Characteristics of Entertainment–Education Serial Drama   28
Characteristics of Radio   29
Creating the Radio Serial Drama for Social Development   29

2 THE DESIGN APPROACH: THE DESIGN DOCUMENT   33

Design of Serial Drama for Social Development and Behavior Change 35
The Role of the Writer   35
The Design Document   36
The Writer's Brief   52

3 THE DESIGN APPROACH: THE DESIGN TEAM   53

The Need for the Design Team   55
Advantages of the Design Team   55
Design Team Members and Their Roles   56

4   THE DESIGN APPROACH: THE DESIGN WORKSHOP   65

The Design Workshop   67
The Design Workshop in Progress   68
The Value of Change Agents   73
Changing Traditional Behavior and Encouraging Prevention Behaviour   74
After the Design Workshop: Completing the Design Document   75

Part 2
For the Program Manager

5   STARTING UP THE RADIO SERIAL DRAMA PROJECT   79

The Role of the Program Manager   81
Starting up the Radio Serial Drama Project   81
Preparing for the Design Workshop   85
Running the Design Workshop   88
Reviewing the Design Document   92
After the Workshop: Design Document Finalization   93

6   THE PROGRAM MANAGER AND THE WRITING PROCESS   95

Script Preparation   97
Selecting and Contracting with the Writers   97
Writing the Script   99
Script Review   110
Support Materials   115
Promotional Materials   117

7   THE PREPRODUCTION PHASE   121

Important Tasks to Complete before Production   123

8   THE PRODUCTION PHASE   129

Choosing the Audio Production House   131

9   GUIDELINES FOR RADIO ACTORS   137

Introducing Radio Acting   139
Preparing for the Role   140
Tips for Radio Acting   142
The Rewards of Entertainment–Education Serial Drama Acting   145

10 PILOT TESTING THE SCRIPTS — 147

The Importance of Pilot Testing — 149
The Purpose of the Pilot Scripts — 150
Questions that Can be Asked during Pilot Testing — 150

Part 3
For the Writer

11 WRITING ENTERTAINMENT–EDUCATION DRAMA — 155

Entertainment–Education Drama — 157
Challenges of Learning through Listening — 158
Fundamentals of Learning — 159
The Meaning of Drama — 160
Dramatic Conflict — 160
Components of a Drama — 163
The Structure of a Drama — 164
Types of Radio Drama — 170
The Multiplot Nature of a Serial — 171
The Structure of a Radio Serial Episode — 174

12 BLENDING STORY AND MESSAGE IN THE DRAMA PLOT — 181

The Ten Aims of Plot Development — 183
Combining Message and Story — 186
Creating Original Plots — 187
Steps in Full Plot Development — 189
Guidelines for Plot Development — 192

13 CHARACTER DEVELOPMENT — 195

The Importance of Characters — 197
Guidelines for Character Creation — 197

14 DEVELOPING THE SETTING — 209

The Importance of Setting — 211
Time — 211
Location — 215

15 WRITING FOR THE EAR — 223

The Golden Rule of Writing for Radio — 225
Guidelines for the Use of Dialogue — 225

Creating Word Pictures   230
Guidelines for the Use of Sound Effects   233
Guidelines for Using Music in Radio Serial Drama   235

16 SCENE DEVELOPMENT   241

Episode and Scene Division   243
Scene Guidelines   243
Timing and Optional Cuts   247

17 THE FINISHED SCRIPT AND THE WRITER'S CHECKLIST   249

Putting the Serial Episode Together   251
Writer's Checklist of Essential Features in a Well-constructed Episode   251
Message Presentation   253

18 SUCCESS OF RADIO ENTERTAINMENT–EDUCATION PROGRAMS   269

Entertainment–Education and Social Change   271

Credits   273

APPENDICES

Appendix A: Sample Design Document   275
Appendix B: For the Design Workshop   299
Appendix C: Design Workshop Question Guide   307
Appendix D: *Journey of Life* Episode Synopsis   323

References and Select Bibilography   326
About the Author   327

LIST OF BOXES

1.1	The meaning of entertainment and education	26
1.2	Characteristics of serial drama	28
1.3	Strengths and limitations of radio	30
2.1	Contents of the design document	37
2.2	SMART objectives	41
2.3	Sample program objectives	45
3.1	Main advantages of a team	55
3.2	Design team members	57
4.1	The 7Cs of message presentation	71
6.1	Reviewer guidelines	112
7.1	Preproduction tasks	125
8.1	Production house requirements	133
8.2	Production house personnel requirements	134
9.1	Golden rules for acting in serial drama	141
11.1	Structure of the episode for entertainment–education drama	175
12.1	The ten aims of plot development	183
12.2	Vital points of message information	187
12.3	Guidelines for creating original dramas	188
12.4	Steps in creating the full plot outline	190
12.5	Guidelines for plot development	192
13.1	Character creation	197
13.2	Range of characters for entertainment–education drama	201

14.1   Guidelines for creating drama locations   216

15.1   Guidelines for writing dialogue   226
15.2   Guidelines for the use of sound effects   234
15.3   Guidelines for the use of music in serial drama   236

DEFINITIONS

This list defines the words and phrases used in this book that have particular meaning in the context of radio drama for social change. Each definition is followed by the number of the chapter in which the word or phrase is first used or is described most fully.

ACTOR — A male or female person who portrays or acts the part of a character in a drama. (Chapter 9)

ADVOCATE — One who supports, speaks in favor of, or recommends to others a particular attitude, action, or practice. (Chapter 13)

ANNOUNCER — The speaker who introduces a radio program on behalf of the radio station. Sometimes referred to as station announcer, this person is not a character in the drama. (Chapter 11)

AUDIENCE PROFILE — Information about the audience's lifestyle, culture, economic status, and community that gives the writer a personal understanding of the listeners; included in the Writer's Brief. (Chapter 12)

CENTRAL UNITING CHARACTER — A character, such as a doctor, nurse, or health worker, who appears in and unites all the plots in a serial. (Chapter 10)

CHARACTER — A fictional person created for a story or drama; may also be an animal or a thing. (Chapters 1 and 13)

CHARACTER PROFILE — A list of all the details the writer should know about a character in order to portray him or her as a unique and believable person. (Chapter 12)

CLIFFHANGER   A suspenseful finale to a serial episode that leaves the audience eager to find out what will happen in the next episode. (Chapter 16)

CLIMAX   The point in a story where the conflict has come to a crisis and something must happen to resolve it. (Chapter 11)

CONFLICT   See DRAMATIC CONFLICT (Chapter 11)

COVER SHEET   The front page of a script that lists the serial title, program number, writer's name, purpose and objectives of the program, cast of characters, and music and sound effects needed for the episode. (Chapter 6)

CRISIS   The point in a story where the conflict has reached its height and must be resolved. (Chapter 11)

DESIGN DOCUMENT   An extensive document containing all information with regard to the design and content of the serial. (Chapter 1)

DESIGN TEAM   A group of specialists, including script writers, who work together to plan all the details of a radio serial message and who prepare the design documents. (Chapter 1)

DÉNOUEMENT   See RESOLUTION (Chapter 11)

DEVELOPMENT   The portion of the story following the introduction during which the dramatic conflict develops and intensifies. (Chapter 11)

DIALOGUE   The words that the characters utter in a drama. In radio dramas, the dialogue must provide listeners with an understanding of location, personality, and action as well as the message. Also referred to as SPEECH (Chapter 15)

DIRECTOR   The person who directs the actors and technicians in the studio recording of the serial. In some countries, the director is called the producer. (Chapter 2)

DISTRIBUTED LEARNING   The process of spreading learning throughout a radio serial, with particular attention to pace and repetition. (Chapter 1)

DRAMA   A story acted out on stage, radio, television, or film. (Chapter 1)

DRAMATIC CONFLICT The twists and turns and juxtapositions of life that are reflected in drama and provide its central interest as the audience becomes emotionally involved in why things happen and how they will turn out. (Chapter 11)

ENTERTAINMENT– EDUCATION A format that blends entertainment and education to disseminate social messages. The use of this term originated with Johns Hopkins University Population Communication Services. (Chapter 1)

EPISODE Individual programs into which a serialized radio or television drama is divided, usually broadcast once a week. Also known as an installment, an episode of a radio drama is similar to a chapter in a book. (Chapter 1)

FLASHBACK A scene from a past time that interrupts the present action of a drama. (Chapter 14)

FORMAT The form or design of a radio or television program; includes interview, talk, drama, and news shows. (Chapter 1)

FX An abbreviation for "sound effects" commonly used in a script to indicate where sounds should be included. Sometimes written as SFX. (Chapter 6)

HEADER Standard information listed on the top of every page of a script, including the program number, date of writing, writer's name, and page number. Also known as script header. (Chapter 6)

HERO The principal "good" male in a literary work or dramatic presentation. (Chapter 13)

HEROINE The principal "good" female in a literary work or dramatic presentation. (Chapter 13)

HOOK Exciting opening dialogue or action that commands the immediate attention of the audience with an element of surprise or shock and keeps them listening. (Chapters 1 and 16)

INDEPENDENT DRAMA A drama that starts and completes a story within a single program, usually no more than 60 minutes long. (Chapter 11)

INSTALLMENT	See EPISODE (Chapter 1).
LOCATION MAP	Map of the village or town where a plot's main scenes are set, drawn by the writer to ensure consistency in description of distances, travel time, etc. (Chapter 14)
MESSAGE	The information to be given to listeners in order to motivate and enable them to make changes that will improve the quality of their lives and that will alter social norms. (Chapter 11)
MEASURABLE OBJECTIVES	The outcomes that project planners hope the audience will demonstrate as a result of listening to the radio serial. These outcomes generally fall into three categories: what the audience will know; what attitude they will have to the topic, and what behavior they will practice. (Chapter 2)
MODELING	See ROLE MODELS (Chapter 2)
MOOD MUSIC	Music that is designed to inspire a particular mood in listeners and should be avoided or used very sparingly in radio drama. (Chapter 15)
MUSIC	Music should be used carefully in radio programs so that it does not interfere with or contradict the dialogue. (Chapter 15)
NARRATOR	A person who tells a story; frequently used at the beginning of a radio serial to remind the listeners of what happened in the previous episode and at the end to encourage listeners to tune in again next time. (Chapter 11)
OPTIONAL CUT (o/c)	A part of the script marked by the writer to show that it can be removed if the script is too long. (Chapter 11)
PILOT PROGRAMS	Programs created before regular scripting begins in order to test format, characters, and message presentation on a sample of the audience. (Chapter 10)
PLOT	The chain of events and web of personal relationships that make up a story or drama. (Chapter 1)
PRODUCER	The person who manages and oversees all aspects of a media project, including finances, staff hiring, office procedures, and time lines. Also known as the program manager (see PROGRAM MANAGER). May be used interchangeably with DIRECTOR in some countries. (Chapter 5)

PROGRAM MANAGER	The person in overall charge of a radio series; sometimes called the Executive Producer or Program Director (see PRODUCER) (Chapter 1)
PURPOSE	The approach the writing will take to encourage the audience to adopt new behavior. (Chapter 2)
REAL TIME	The idea that the action within a scene should occupy the same length of time that the scenes takes to broadcast. (Chapter 14)
RESOLUTION	The part of a story following the crisis which shows how the crisis is overcome. Also called denouement. (Chapter 1)
ROLE MODEL	Real person or fictional character on whom others choose to model their behavior. (Chapter 2)
SCENE	A subdivision of a dramatic episode that is set in a specific place and time; one episode of a drama may contain several scenes. (Chapter 11)
SCRIPT	Written transcript of the words, music, and sound effects that will be used in a radio program; also indicates actions and dialogue for a television program. (Chapter 1)
SCRIPT HEADER	See HEADER. (Chapter 6)
SCRIPT REVIEW PANEL	The small team of people who review every script of a serial for production quality, technical content, and/or dramatic quality. (Chapter 2)
SCRIPT SUPPORT TEAM	The people selected by the design team to provide the writer with necessary information and support during the script writing process. (Chapter 2)
SERIAL	A multi-episode drama in which the story continues from one episode to the next. (Chapters 1 and 11)
SERIES	A collection of short dramas which share several of the same characters; each episode contains a complete story. (Chapters 1 and 11)
SETTING	The time and place where the action of a drama is set. (Chapter 11)
SEVEN CS OF MESSAGE PRESENTATION	Seven words that guide accurate presentation of serial drama messages. (Chapter 17)

SIGNATURE TUNE   Music played at the beginning and end of every episode in a serial which the audience grows to recognize; may be abbreviated as "Sig. Tune," also known as theme music. (Chapter 8)

SITUATION COMEDY   A type of drama series that is exaggeratedly humorous. (Chapter 11)

SOAP OPERA   Common name for a serial characterized by melodrama, stereotyped characters and situation, exaggerated emotions, and maudlin sentimentality; in contrast to an Entertainment–Education serial which is closer to real life. The term was coined in the United States of America in the early days of radio drama when big American soap manufacturing companies (such as Lever Brothers) sponsored sensational serials that were likened to classical opera. (Chapter 1)

SOUND EFFECTS   Sounds, either recorded or made live in the studio, that are used to add a sense of reality to the drama and help listeners "see" the action and the setting. (Chapter 6)

SPEECH   Lines spoken by the actor in a radio or television drama. Also referred to as DIALOGUE. (Chapter 6)

STEPS TO BEHAVIOR CHANGE   The five stages that people commonly go through when moving from one type of behavior to a new and markedly different behavior; these consist of knowledge, approval, intention, practice, and advocacy. (Chapter 2)

STORY   An event or series of events that can be either true or fictional; may be presented in a narrative, a drama, a poem, or a song. (Chapter 1)

SUB PLOT   A lesser storyline woven into the main story or plot of a serial drama in order to enrich it and to help convey the message to the widest possible audience. (Chapter 5)

SYNOPSIS   Narrative outline of all the plots (main plot and subplots) of a radio serial that is written before scripting of individual programs begins. (Chapter 6)

THEME   The emotional focus on a drama, which reflects a universal moral value or emotion that is understandable to all people at all times, such as truth, courage, love, fear, greed, or envy. (Chapter 2)

THEME MUSIC   See SIGNATURE MUSIC. (Chapter 7)

TREATMENT   An alternative word for SYNOPSIS.

UNITY OF PLACE   Assigning each plot in the drama an established location or setting in which the action of that plot most often occurs. (Chapter 12)

UNITY OF TIME   Careful adherence to a predetermined and limited amount of time between the beginning and end of the serial's story. (Chapter 12)

WORD PICTURES   Carefully chosen words (such as verbs, adjectives, or adverbs) and figures of speech (such as similes and metaphors) that assist the listener to "see" what is taking place in the drama. (Chapter 1)

WRITER'S BRIEF   Specific information given to the writer about the objectives, purpose, and message content of the series; par to the full design document. (Chapter 2)

PART 1

Introduction
to
Entertainment–Education
Radio Drama

1

Radio Drama for Behavior Change

Radio drama entertains and informs the audience.

Topics

- *Radio for Social Development*
- *Entertainment–Education Serial Drama*
- *"Soap Opera" or "Serial Drama"*
- *Using Serial Drama for Social Development and Behavior Change Communication*
- *Characteristics of Serial Drama*
- *Characteristics of Entertainment–Education Serial Drama*
- *Characteristics of Radio*
- *Strengths and Limitations of Radio*
- *Creating the Radio Serial Drama for Social Development*

RADIO FOR SOCIAL DEVELOPMENT

Radio is a universal and versatile medium of communication that can be used for the benefit of society. Throughout the years, radio has been used to encourage positive individual behavior change and constructive social change through formal lessons or didactic lectures delivered by renowned scholars and authorities. Radio can be used more effectively, however, to bring exciting, entertaining dramas into the homes and lives of millions of listeners—dramas that engage listeners' emotions while informing them of new ideas and modeling for them new behaviors that can improve their lives and their communities.

ENTERTAINMENT–EDUCATION SERIAL DRAMA

One of the most effective uses of radio for social change is "Entertainment–Education" serial drama. The term "Entertainment–Education" describes any communication presentation that blends a social development educational message into an entertainment format. "Entertainment–Education" is similar in meaning to the terms "info-tainment" and "edu-tainment" that are common in some countries. The term "Entertainment–Education," however, has special merit because it puts emphasis on the vital primary ingredient that will attract and hold the attention of the audience—entertainment.

Box 1.1

THE MEANING OF
ENTERTAINMENT AND EDUCATION

Education and entertainment have never been mutually exclusive. An examination of the meaning of the two words shows how easily they can fit together.

The English word "entertainment" comes from the Latin, "*intertenere*." The prefix "*inter*" means "among" and the verb "*tenere*" means "to hold." The whole word has the meaning "to hold or command attention."

"Education" also has its origins in Latin. The prefix "*e*" meaning "out of" and the verb "*ducere*" meaning "to lead." Originally, the verb "*educere*" meant "to assist at the birth of a child." It now means "to rear or to raise," or in other words, "to lead a person forward," or "to encourage a person's growth and development."

Entertainment–Education, therefore, can be defined as "commanding the attention of the audience while encouraging their growth and development," and Entertainment–Education serial drama can be understood as a powerful method of motivating positive social change and personal development.

"Entertainment" does not necessarily mean "amusement." A wide range of emotions and situations can attract and hold attention—including education itself.

The idea of combining entertainment and education is not new; examples can be found throughout human history. **Myths** have served important functions in societies around the world. **Parables** have been used by prophets and preachers to illustrate religious tenets. **Fables**, often with animals as the central characters, have been used to demonstrate the validity of moral teachings. The rhythms of poetry and song are constantly employed to help people remember information. *For example*, alphabet songs for small children and musical jingles in commercial advertising.

The use of radio drama for social development purposes is undergoing a rebirth. In the early days of radio it was not uncommon, especially in young countries such as Australia, Canada, and South Africa, for helpful messages on such topics as agriculture and wild fire control to be incorporated into serial dramas. In England, *The Archers*, a serial about a farm family, played an important role in agricultural development and held national attention for decades. With the advent of television, however, interest shifted to visual soap operas featuring highly exaggerated characters and emotions, and radio drama went into decline.

In the mid-1970s Miguel Sabido, in Mexico, expressed his belief that television serials could "do more than reinforce attitudes toward specific events and characters; they could also stimulate behavior," (Nariman 1993). Sabido recognized that, while conventional soap operas presented values unconsciously and, therefore, sometimes incoherently, it would be possible to create value-coherent serials that encouraged positive behavior such as adult literacy or family planning without being boring, pedantic, or moralistic.

What Sabido demonstrated on Latin American television with "telenovellas" for social change has proved just as effective in radio serial drama. Radio serial writers can create dramas that have a positive effect on individual behavior and on social norms (Nariman 1993).

"Soap Opera" or "Serial Drama"

The term "soap opera" originally referred to dramas that were melodramatic, highly exaggerated and therefore, in many ways, unreal. Classical drama, "real" drama is not melodramatic; it pulls out and concentrates on specific human behaviors and invites the audience to think about them and reconsider their own lives with regard to these behaviors. The great Greek dramas by writers like Aeschylus are certainly dramatic, but not melodramatic. Dramas that are being used to motivate important changes in the lives of a society should not be looked upon as melodramatic or unreal; they should reflect reality in the strongest possible way so that the audience will believe in them and be motivated by them. The term "serial drama," therefore, is considered to be more appropriate than "soap opera" for Entertainment–Education work.

Using Serial Drama for Social Development and Behavior Change Communication

Throughout the world, radio and television are popular media for disseminating social development messages. Spots, jingles, and commercials have proved effective in delivering information to a large audience, particularly on radio, which has an almost universal reach in most countries. These formats, however, are not always as effective as desired in actually motivating behavior change, because they tend to be didactic rather than persuasive. The messages are generally too short and offer limited knowledge too quickly to allow for a demonstration or modeling of how behavior change actually occurs. More successful is an ongoing format that blends the educational message into an entertaining format: the serial drama. This popular entertainment medium can be employed successfully for development purposes, however, only if it is very carefully designed. In order to adapt serial drama to development needs, it is necessary for all involved to understand something of the characteristics that contribute to its universal appeal.

Characteristics of Serial Drama

Serial drama is a story, in dramatized form, that continues over weeks, months, or years. Serial drama can be likened to a novel in which the story is revealed chapter by chapter over many pages rather than being completed in a few paragraphs or pages like an essay or a short story. Similarly, serial drama divides the dramatized story into episodes that are broadcast regularly, sometimes at the rate of one a day, but more commonly at the rate of one a week, over an extended period of time. Most often this is a 12-month period, but some serial dramas run much longer. In Australia, the rural department of the Australian Broadcasting Corporation commissioned a drama serial in 1942 to encourage farmers to adopt new agricultural methods. This serial, *Blue Hills*, ran five days a week for 21 years. In Nepal, the radio serial drama, *Cut Your Coat According to Your Cloth*, has been on the air for more than six years, and is still attracting listeners.

Box 1.2

Characteristics of Serial Drama

Serial drama gives the audience:

- An ongoing story.
- Intimate involvement in the lives of others.
- A rich diversity of characters.
- A collection of different plots.
- Vicarious emotional outlets.
- The opportunity to develop strong feelings (positive or negative) about the characters.

Serial drama is popular because it reflects the simple saying, "people like people." Serial drama's ongoing story allows the audience to become intimately engaged in the lives of people other than themselves. It involves a rich diversity of characters (many of whom closely resemble real people known to the audience) in a collection of different plots. Serial drama highlights emotions and thereby provides a vicarious emotional outlet for the audience. Perhaps this is the strongest attraction of serial drama, that the ongoing nature of the story allows the audience to develop deep feelings about the individual characters and what happens to them. Audience members find themselves loving some characters dearly, despising others, wanting to help those in need, and to be like those they admire. Serial drama can have a powerful effect on individual behavior and on social norms.

Characteristics of Entertainment–Education Serial Drama

It is not surprising, therefore, that serial drama is being used increasingly, not only for entertainment, but also—in the form of Entertainment–Education drama—as a major component of multifaceted behavior-change projects. Every Entertainment–Education product consists of two equally important parts: the format (entertainment) and the message (education).

The purpose of **entertainment** is to attract and hold the attention of the audience by engaging their emotions. The purpose of **education** is to enhance the relevant knowledge and skills of the learners so that they can make better use of their personal abilities to enrich and improve their own lives.

Entertainment does not have to be amusing or funny. Tragedies, mysteries, love stories, and even the events of everyday life can be entertaining if they engage the emotions of their audiences. Education does not have to consist of boring, didactic, teacher-directed lessons. The real purpose of education is to provide those who are being educated with the best chance of realizing their full potential and talent. The education that is most appreciated and most sought after is that which is clearly relevant to and usable by the learners. The aim of Entertainment–Education serial drama is to blend harmoniously these two equally important elements, emotional involvement and relevant knowledge, so that the audience can learn about and realize—through the role model characters and the subtly presented messages—the advantages of the new behavior to their own lives.

CHARACTERISTICS OF RADIO

All those involved with a project that plans to use radio serial drama as part of its behavior change plan should have a clear understanding of the characteristics, and the strengths and limitations of radio (see Box 1.3).

Radio, like every other communication medium, has its own characteristics, strengths, and limitations. While it is true that listeners can become completely absorbed by a drama, it is equally true that many people listen to radio while doing other things. This means that sometimes listeners can miss important points—even inadvertently. Similarly, it is sometimes difficult for listeners to recall details of important messages they have heard only once on radio. For this reason, the creators of every social development radio serial should ensure that there are supplementary materials available—print, posters, jingles, etc., that reinforce the most important messages. It is advisable to recognize that one medium alone is never enough to ensure appropriate behavior change.

CREATING THE RADIO SERIAL DRAMA FOR SOCIAL DEVELOPMENT

Serial dramas that are to be used for behavior change or social development purposes require rigorous preparation and design. This design can begin only after the start-up

Box 1.3

STRENGTHS OF RADIO

• Radio is based on oral tradition. Every culture has traditions of story telling, and the fascination of listening to a good tale well told has never been lost. Even today, when television is so widespread, people in many cultures experience much of their entertainment through *listening*. A successful radio serial writer knows how to use this tradition to create an intriguing story that attracts and holds a listening audience.

• Radio appeals to and relies upon the imagination of the listeners. The radio writer is not limited by what the audience can *see*, so there is ample opportunity to invite listeners to *imagine* a wide range of people, places, and events. A good radio writer knows how to tap into the imaginations of the listeners by using strong word pictures, engaging characters, and action-filled events.

• Radio can cross time and space without limit. The radio writer can move through time freely and create environments without restriction, as long as they are appropriate to the audience. For example, listeners in a remote rural village can "visit" and understand the inside of a large city airport if word pictures and sound effects are used effectively.

• Radio can go places and evoke images that are impossible in real life, on stage, or even on television (except with animation). For example, a radio writer can transport listeners to the inside of a whale, to the surface of the moon, or to the world of a microbe.

• Radio is a personal medium. Although it can reach millions of listeners at the same time, radio nevertheless has the power to speak to each listener individually. The good radio writer recognizes that radio's message can be heard by people en masse and, at the same time, can be interpreted personally by each individual listener.

LIMITATIONS OF RADIO

• The total experience of radio is received by the ear alone. This is in contrast to the multi-sensory perception of everyday life. The writer therefore must remember to fill in details that, in real life, would be provided by the listeners' other senses, such as vision or smell. The writer must create scripts that allow listeners to *visualize* what they are hearing.

• Listeners are accustomed to using radio as a background to their lives, without paying full attention to what is being broadcast. When radio is used to motivate positive social change, the writer must be sure to attract and hold the listeners' *full* attention, and to encourage listening literacy.

• Radio offers great opportunities for the use of sound effects and music. The good radio writer, however, uses these aids judiciously, recognizing that overuse of sound can be more destructive than constructive on radio. Successful radio drama depends more on powerful dialogue and strong emotional attraction than on added noise.

• Radio can be used to teach many things, but there are some areas where it falls short. For example, it would be difficult for a doctor to learn how to remove an appendix just by listening to a radio program. To overcome such difficulties, the writer should recommend support materials in other media (such as visuals or print) if the subject cannot be dealt with adequately through radio alone.

• A radio story or message is heard only once. The radio cannot be rewound like an audio cassette or turned back like the pages of a book. The radio writer, therefore, must ensure clarity, simplicity, and repetition in the delivery of important messages or educational information.

phase, involving considerable research and analysis, has been completed. Details of the Start-up Phase, which are handled by the program manager, are given in Chapter 5, in the section on the Role of the Program Manager. Once all details of the Start-Up Phase have been completed, the actual design of the serial can begin. The Design Stage, which is described in detail in subsequent chapters, involves all those who will be engaged in any aspect of the message design, the story creation and the production.

The Design Stage

The Design Stage is integral to the success of an Entertainment–Education serial drama. It comprises three elements: the **design team**, the **design workshop**, and the **design document**.

- The **design team** is the group of advisors—audience representatives, content advisors, researchers, producers, writers, and any others who might be necessary—who come together in the design workshop to determine the scope, sequence, and details of the messages to be included in the drama.
- The **design workshop** is a designated period of time (usually five working days) in which this team meets and works together to compile the design document.
- The **design document** is the **reliable reference** that presents, in written form, all the details required by everyone involved in the writing, reviewing, production, and evaluation of the serial drama. The special task of the design document is the detailed notation of every aspect of the message to be delivered to the audience in each episode of the drama. It is essential that the specification of this information should not be left to the writer, but should be determined and agreed upon by all members of the design team working together.

Details of the design document are discussed in the next chapter.

2

The Design Approach: The Design Document

The writer relies on the design document to provide accurate messages within the drama.

Topics

- *Design of Serial Drama for Social Development and Behavior Change*
- *The Role of the Writer*
- *The Design Document*
- *Contents of the Design Document*
- *Advantages of the Design Document*
- *Design Document Contents*
- *The Writer's Brief*

DESIGN OF SERIAL DRAMA FOR SOCIAL DEVELOPMENT AND BEHAVIOR CHANGE

Entertainment–Education (E–E) serial dramas have special design requirements that differ from those required by other communication interventions. A rigorous and thoroughly orchestrated design is essential to ensure the harmonious blending of story and message throughout a number of plots and characters and a continuum of episodes that span several months, if not one or two years. Creating successful E–E serial drama calls for a complex mix of specialists (content advisors, writers, reviewers, researchers, directors, actors, support and promotional material producers, evaluators, etc.) as well as technical staff (typists, media technicians, monitors, and quite frequently, translators, etc.) over an extended period of time. The success of Entertainment–Education serial drama is greatly enhanced by encouraging all involved to employ and adhere strictly to the Design Approach that has proved successful in many countries around the world.

THE ROLE OF THE WRITER

One major difference between writing serial drama for entertainment purposes alone and writing serial drama for Entertainment–Education projects is the role of the writer. Those who write for entertainment purposes are accustomed to having considerable creative leeway with regard to the story and the characters in it. Writers for Entertainment–Education serial drama face the much more daunting challenge of having to blend specific details of an educational message into their personal, imaginative story and the lives of their fictional characters. This difference means that where the entertainment writer can work alone, the Entertainment–Education writer cannot. He or she needs to be provided with complete and specific details of the educational messages to be woven into the story. The writer cannot be left to determine alone the sequence of the messages and the precise words in which the message will be delivered. It is essential that the writer is given every detail of message scope and sequence and the precise words in which important aspects of the message are to be delivered to the chosen audience. It is the design document that provides this information for the writer.

THE DESIGN DOCUMENT

Often more than a hundred pages in length, the design document is put together by a team of people who have interest in and knowledge of the project. Individually, team members are "specialists" in such matters as the audience, what the message should say, the medium to be used, and the qualities of good drama. The design team members pool their knowledge to determine exactly what educational messages should be included in the serial drama, the sequence in which these messages should be included, and even the precise words that drama characters should use to express certain parts of the messages. All of the design team's determinations are contained in the design document, which becomes the reliable reference for all those involved with the serial.

Contents of the Design Document

The exact content of each design document will vary and depend in part on whether the Entertainment–Education serial drama is to be designed for a general audience or for professional distance learning purposes. Similarly, other variables, such as the number and length of the episodes and the frequency of broadcasts, can affect the document contents. As a rule, however, the design team will make determinations on all matters given in the Design Document Content list (see Box 2.1). The final details of Part 3 (Implementation) of the document might not be completed within the week of the design workshop, but preliminary discussions and determinations on them should be made at that time.

Box 2.1

CONTENTS OF THE DESIGN DOCUMENT

Part 1
Background and overall description

1. Justification for the desired behavior change the project wishes to encourage
2. Audience profile
3. Justification of the chosen medium and format
4. The overall measurable objectives of the serial
5. The overall purposes of the serial drama
6. The overall message and emotional focus
7. The number of episodes in the serial
8. The duration of each episode
9. The topic scope and sequence
10. The number of episodes to be devoted to each topic

Part 2
Individual episodes or groups of episodes: Specific message content

11. The measurable objectives of each individual episode
12. The purpose of each individual episode
13. The precise message content of each episode
14. A glossary of topic-specific words and terms, together with the definitions (and translations) to be used in the scripts. An acronym list should also be included.

Part 3
Implementation

15. The script review panel and the script support team
16. Listing and description of proposed support materials
17. Promotion plans
18. The monitoring and evaluation plan
19. The time lines for:

    - all phases of script writing, reviewing, recording, editing, and broadcasting
    - all phases of support and promotional material writing and dissemination
    - all phases of evaluation
    - pilot testing of scripts, support materials, and promotional materials
    - ongoing monitoring
    - summative evaluation

20. Story outline and sample episode

The finished design document might also include a responsibility list (or job description) for each person on the design team. This helps to avoid confusion over chain of command and individual responsibilities. It also may include the names of all those who contributed to the successful completion of the document. (A full explanation of each component of the design document follows.)

The Three Major Sections of the Design Document

Part 1: The background and overall outline of the serial drama project.
Part 2: Details related to individual episodes.
Part 3: Details related to the production, presentation, evaluation, and other needs of the series.

Part 1: Background and Overall Description

1. Justification for the desired behavior change the project wishes to encourage: This section outlines the justifications for undertaking this particular social development project. For instance, the analysis phase (see Chapter 5) may have found that the prevalence of contraceptive use in a given area is low, while the desire for smaller families is increasing. Subsequently, the desired behavior change would be to increase couples' knowledge of and willingness to use contraceptive methods, and where such contraceptives can be obtained. The justification for wanting to motivate this change is based on what has been learned from baseline research, not just on the whims of the project directors. All those working on the serial drama need to be clear about the justification for and benefits of the desired behavior change in order to focus the drama correctly.

2. Audience profile: Clearly defining the audience(s) for the serial drama is essential for the writer to determine the type of story and characters that will be needed. It is necessary also to know where the audience stands with regard to the desired behavior change, so that the message presentation in the story can follow a reliable behavior change model. The audience position can be examined initially by seeing where they stand on the Steps of Behavior Change (see Figure 2.1). These five steps are knowledge, approval, intention, practice, and advocacy.

(a) Knowledge is the obvious first step in any behavior change. Without knowledge of how to carry out a specific behavior, and of the advantages of such behavior, people cannot move forward in a new direction.

(b) Approval: Knowing about something does not necessarily mean that the behavior is acceptable. People learning about a new behavior, even something like learning to use a computer, need to be sure that they like the idea and that the new behavior is relevant to them. When an audience is being asked to make a significant change in their normal

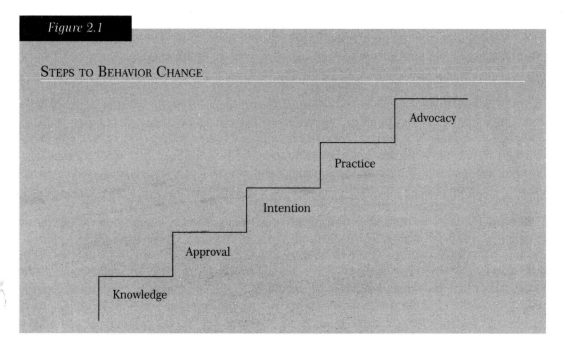

Figure 2.1

STEPS TO BEHAVIOR CHANGE

behavior (such as always using a condom when engaging in casual sex), they will make no move in the direction of the change if they do not like the idea.

(c) Intention: Once having approved the new behavior, the usual next step is for people to plan to or "intend" to adopt it. Sometimes, that is as far as people go. Perhaps they just don't get started on the new behavior, because it is not sufficiently attractive to them, or perhaps because the resources needed for the change are not available to them. Every social development project must ensure that it is actually possible for the intended audiences to make the change when they intend to. Similarly, it might be that the recommended behavior change is not appropriate at this stage of their lives. For example, everyone learns about immunization, but for people who do not yet have children, intention is as far as they can go.

(d) Practice: This is the stage at which people have determined that the new behavior is appropriate to them at this stage of their lives, and that it is possible for them, and that it does have benefits for them. Obviously this is a good step forward; the challenge is to ensure that audience members **maintain** the change. Some changes—such as always sleeping under insecticide-treated nets as protection against malaria—start out as attractive, but become less inviting when such things as regular retreatment of the nets are required. Motivating the audience to maintain the change until it becomes a normal part of behavior is an important essential of behavior change communication.

(e) Advocacy: If a recommended change is to become a social norm, it is essential that those who adopt the change encourage others to do the same. Role modeling in entertainment–education dramas is an excellent way of encouraging advocacy.

Using the Steps to Behavior Change: The types of events and characters that the writer includes in the various plots of the drama will vary depending on what is known about where the audience members are situated on the Steps to Behavior Change. For an audience that already has considerable knowledge about the topic, say the dangers of drugs, it might not be necessary to provide detailed information. It might be necessary, however, to include characters who are in the process of moving from intention to practice. These characters can demonstrate to the audience the wisdom of moving to the "practice" step and model ways in which this can be done.

Similarly, it is important to determine if only one audience requires the message or whether it will be necessary to reach more than one audience. For example, in projects dealing with adolescent behavior, it is almost always essential to include parents as a secondary audience. This, in turn, raises the question of whether all audiences can be reached through the same programs or whether it will be necessary to devise separate programs for the different audience segments. An advantage of the serial drama is that with its several plots it has a good chance of meeting the needs of several audiences at once, because individual plots can be specifically designed to attract a particular audience.

Initial understanding of the audience and where they are on the Steps to Behavior Change can be gained from reviewing research reports that have been prepared in the analysis phase. It is always necessary, however, for design team members to understand exactly why the members of their audience or audiences are behaving the way they are with regard to the desired practice. While it may seem on the surface that lack of knowledge dictates the continuation of existing behavior, this is not always the case. For instance, it has been found in some countries that the low prevalence of condom use is more due to belief in unfounded rumors about the effects of condoms on male potency than to a lack of knowledge about condom effectiveness. A serial drama might redress some of these fears by including, perhaps, a character who uses well-known proverbs to point out the foolishness of listening to rumors rather than seeking facts.

Intention–Practice Gap: It is always necessary for project leaders to examine the possible impediments between "intention" and "practice." For example, a family might have every intention of ensuring that their child is fully immunized in the first year of life, but find it impossible to carry out their intention because there is no health facility within reachable distance of their home. Similarly, a young girl might want to learn about changes in puberty, but cannot go to a health worker for guidance because her culture eyes with suspicion any unmarried woman who goes to a health worker. In preparing the audience profile, the project personnel need to be aware of impediments—such as these—to the desired behavior change.

3. Justification of the chosen medium and format: Because every communication medium has its strengths and weaknesses, the design team needs to be clear about its reasons for choosing a particular medium. *For example*, one major reason for choosing radio for Entertainment–Education projects is that it has the greatest reach in rural areas. It is also less expensive to produce radio dramas than television dramas and radio can reach an illiterate audience that could not take advantage of print materials. Alternatively, television might be chosen in city and peri-urban areas because it attracts greater attention than radio or print. The design team must believe in the validity of their final choice to make it work to their advantage. It is always advantageous to use several media to carry a message, even if the main medium is radio. Consequently, the design team should consider how other media can be used to support the serial drama. Radio also has the advantage of being the "medium of the imagination," that allows audience members to see themselves in the stories being told and the situations being described. Television, by showing the characters as the director perceives them, largely denies the audience this advantage. These strengths and limitations of radio have already been discussed in Chapter 1.

4. The overall measurable objectives of the serial: The statement of overall measurable objective refers to the audience and answers the question, "What changes does the drama hope to bring about in the audience's **knowledge, attitudes, and practices**?" These objectives should be measurable and stated as precisely as possible. It is helpful to check and ensure that the objectives are SMART (see Box 2.2).

The design team will use the overall measurable objective(s) of the serial drama to guide all their deliberations. The overall objective(s) will also be used as the basis for the final evaluation of the project's effectiveness. *For example*, a serial drama in India had the following overall objective: "As a result of this radio serial drama, there will be a measurable increase in the number of people who visit health clinics to inquire about antenatal services." This objective is measurable, because it is possible to take a count of people coming to the clinics before the serial broadcasts begin. A further count can be taken during and after the serial, and visitors to the clinic can be asked what inspired them to come. A response that they learned about the clinic or were motivated to come by listening to the drama suggests that the serial did affect their behavior. Other variables would have to be examined also, such as the influence of friends or family members, but it is possible for the overall objective to be measured. Usually, the objectives of a drama serial are not as specific in their precise measurements as they are in the

Box 2.2
SMART OBJECTIVES
Specific Measurable Appropriate Realistic Time-bound

overall project. Where the overall project might seek a 10 percent decline in maternal mortality over a five-year period, the radio drama is more inclined to claim that "there will be a measurable increase in the number of women who give birth at a health center." Clearly, a radio drama serial that is on the air for no more than six months cannot be held entirely and solely responsible for bringing about specifically measurable changes.

5. The overall purpose(s) of the serial drama: The overall purpose is an explanation of the approach the serial drama (the story and the characters) will use to bring about the desired changes. Measurable objectives indicate what is expected of the **audience**; the purposes explain the approach that **the drama** must take to make it possible for the audiences to attain the objectives.

    The purposes of the serial drama might be, singly or collectively, to teach, to persuade, to motivate the chosen audience, or, to model or demonstrate certain behaviors. In most cases, the serial drama will require two or more of these purposes. *For example*, the overall purpose of a serial drama might be *to demonstrate* the foolishness of believing rumors and *to encourage* listeners to seek the truth about condom use and effectiveness. These very specific statements of purpose help script writers structure a drama that has a real chance of bringing about changes in the personal lives of audience members. A serial drama that has the purpose of *educating* or giving instruction in new skills will require characters and events quite different from those needed in a serial drama that has the prime purpose of motivating behavior change by modeling. Education requires clear explanation and repetition of new facts. Motivation requires clear demonstration of the benefits of the behavior change and modeling of how these benefits can affect individual lives.

6. The overall message and emotional focus: In this section, the document records the clear, simple statement of the overall concept that the team has determined the drama should convey. This determination will be a general, overall statement, rather than the precise details that will be decided later. The overall message or concept might be, for example, something like this:

> The people of this nation, working individually, within family groups, and within the community, will have a good chance of improving the quality of their lives if they give equal status to men and women (placing genuine emphasis on the special needs of women during pregnancy and childbirth); space and limit their children appropriately; and take care of the environment and natural resources.

Throughout the serial episodes, the overall message will be delivered as smaller, specific messages to help guide the audience in the direction of larger change. It is helpful, however, for the design team and writer(s) to keep the overall message in mind at all times so that everything in the message, in modeling, and in the story will lead toward the same end.

Emotional Focus: Every Entertainment–Education serial drama requires a particular emotional focus or **universal theme** that flavors all the episodes. Every great entertainment drama is based on a universal theme. Shakespeare's *Othello*, for example, is based on the universal theme of jealousy. Similarly, every Entertainment–Education serial drama needs a universal theme or focus that reflects the feeling or attitude the serial would like to stimulate in the audience.

For example: A serial drama with a main message of the importance of the male role in family planning might focus on pride: the pride the man has in his healthy, educated family, the pride that his wife has in her caring husband, and the willingness with which she shows her pride to others in the community. A serial drama designed to increase the knowledge and ability of health workers might put the focus on confidence and express the spirit of professionalism throughout the episodes.

7. The number of episodes in the serial: The number of episodes is influenced by several factors: the amount and complexity of the message content, budget considerations, experience of the staff, and available media time. The more frequently the serial is heard, the more likely it is to influence the audience. Ideally, a radio or television serial should be broadcast at the rate of one episode a day, five or six days a week for a period of not less than 12 months. This is usually not a realistic expectation for inexperienced writers and production staff or limited budgets. It should be possible, however, to broadcast one episode a week over a 12-month period. A serial drama that runs for a shorter period (say, six months) might attract immediate attention but is not as likely to bring about permanent change. Broadcasting at the rate of one episode every two weeks is not recommended because listeners may lose the thread of the story, forget the message(s) and even forget the time of the broadcasts.

8. The duration of each episode: Decisions on the running time of each episode are influenced by the availability of "slots" (blocks of broadcasting time, also known as "air time") and production costs. Sometimes a project will be given only part of a radio station's previously allocated slot. *For example*, the project might be given only 10 minutes of a weekly 30-minute Ministry of Health magazine program. The program manager should determine, in advance of the design workshop, just what slots are available for this type of programming so that the team can design the serial drama to fit the time. Other considerations when determining program length include the amount of message information that can fit comfortably and naturally into each serial episode, and the period of uninterrupted time the audience usually devotes to listening to the drama. Usually, 15–30 minutes is the ideal length for an episode of a serial drama.

9. The topic scope and sequence: The **topic scope** can be likened to the table of contents in a text book. It outlines the major informational blocks or topics the serial drama will cover and gives the order in which they will be presented. It lists all the topics that must be covered between the first and the last episode of the serial. Careful topic planning will help to ensure that all the information the audience is likely to need is covered in the drama episodes.

The **topic sequence** shows the order in which the information will be presented. The sequence can be determined only when the team has a thorough understanding of the audience's current attitudes toward and knowledge of the desired behavior change, and of where the audience stands on the Steps to Behavior Change (see Figure 2.1). The writer must know and be guided by the scope and sequence in order to design the plots, actions, and characters of the story in a way that allows the message to blend into the drama naturally, gradually, and subtly. Examples of the scope and sequence listing can be found in the design document sample in Appendix A.

Distributed Learning: In determining topic scope and sequence, the design team should remember the importance of distributed learning. Distributed learning means distributing throughout the serial repeats of concepts that are new or difficult, or of behaviors that are the most important for the listening audience. The system of distributed learning ensures that new concepts, once introduced, are repeated or at least referred to several times throughout the drama.

10. The number of episodes to be devoted to each topic: The number of episodes required for each topic is usually determined at the same time as the sequence. Again, a thorough knowledge of the audience and the subject matter is necessary for the team to determine which parts of each topic can be covered lightly and which will require a slower, more thorough, repetitive approach. It is also important to determine at this time if a certain number of episodes should be set aside for Summary Programs or for Listeners' Question and Answer programs. In a serial that has 52 episodes or more, it is often helpful to set aside every 10th episode for audience response programs of this nature.

Part 2: Individual Episodes or Groups of Episodes
Specific Message Content

Part 2 of the design document deals with individual episodes. As with the series as a whole, so with each episode, the team must designate stated measurable objectives and specific purpose(s). At the same time, the team must spell out in detail the precise message content to be included in each episode. Without this information, it is virtually impossible for writers to create serial dramas that will both appeal to and influence the behavior of the audience. The design team must never assume that the writer can look up or find out certain facts as the scripts are written; **all information must be provided in the design document**.

11. The measurable objectives of each individual episode: The objectives must be SMART and, particularly, must be realistic. Major changes in audience behavior are not

always likely as the result of listening to just one episode of a serial. *For example*, the measurable objectives for an episode of a drama emphasizing home treatment of malaria might be expressed as shown in Box 2.3.

Box 2.3

SAMPLE PROGRAM OBJECTIVES

After this program, the audience will:

KNOW

- What malaria is and what causes it.
- How to manage malaria treatment at home correctly.
- Benefits of prepackaged antimalarial drugs.

DO

They will:

- Begin to correctly manage malaria in children under five, in their homes.
- Plan to give prepackaged antimalarial drugs to their children when needed.
- Share correct information about home treatment of malaria with others.

HAVE AN ATTITUDE OF

- Confidence in their ability to manage malaria in children at home.
- Desire to use prepackaged antimalarial drugs.

Some people prefer to list the **attitude** objective before the **do** objective. Others find it more logical to plan what they hope to have the audience **know** and **do** before determining what **attitude** must be encouraged in the audience to make the "know" and "do" objectives reachable. The arrangement of objectives can be a matter of choice, as long as all three objectives are included and all are realistic.

It is also important to take into account what has become known as the KAP (knowledge/attitudes and [related] practices) gap. In other words, there can be a big gap (or difference) between the audience's knowledge of and even their attitude towards the topic and an actual change in their behavior. The placement of the **attitude** objective after the **do** objective can help program designers to recognize and stress the need for a truly action-motivating attitude to be demonstrated in the drama.

12. **The purpose of each individual episode:** The purpose defines **the approach** the episode will adopt in order to encourage appropriate changes in audience behavior. The approach can be, perhaps, to:

- educate
- model
- demonstrate
- motivate
- reinforce
- encourage, etc.

Not infrequently, one episode might have two purposes. For example, in the malaria program above, the **purposes** were:

- **To teach** the audience exactly what malaria is and how it is caused.
- **To explain** to the audience what prepackaged antimalarial drugs are, where they are obtained, and how they should be used.
- **To motivate** audience members to act promptly and correctly to provide home-based malarial treatment for their children.

13. The precise message content of each episode: The design document provides the precise information and, where necessary, the specific words and explanations the writer must use in presenting the message. The wording and content of the message are not the responsibility of the writer. It is up to the design team to provide the writer—in the design document—with the exact wording and order of the messages. *For example*, if a program is presenting information about Acute Respiratory Infection, the design document should provide the writer with a simple definition of how this technical term should be interpreted for the chosen audience. Many countries today are replacing the term Acute Respiratory Infection with the much more easily understood expression, "cough and cold," because that definition is more easily understood by the average person in the community. The design team can help ensure the power of the messages by adhering to the 7Cs of Message presentation (see Box 4.1), and by asking themselves the following question:

> How can we word this particular message concept so that it will be expressed correctly by a writer who has no prior knowledge of the subject, and so that it will be understood by audience members who have either little knowledge of or little interest in the subject?

The design team will need to spend considerable time together (usually working in small groups) to determine exactly how the message must be expressed in each episode and to ensure that every message used more than once is expressed consistently. The following sample shows the care taken by the design team to explain to families why food items sold by street sellers (vendors) in Ghana are not always appropriate for young children.

Measurable Objectives

After this episode the audience will

KNOW

That vendor food is not always the best for children.

That vendor food should be examined carefully before purchase and use to ensure cleanliness and freshness.

DO

They will:

Avoid buying food from an unclean environment.

Check vendor food for freshness and cleanliness before serving to children.

HAVE AN ATTITUDE OF

Concern that vendor food might not always be the best for children, and determination to check the quality and cleanliness of such foods before serving them to children.

Purpose

The purposes of this episode are:

- To inform caregivers about the possible dangers of giving vendor food to children.
- To encourage caregivers to examine vendor food carefully and, where necessary make vendor food more nutritious before serving it to children.

Message Content of this Episode

- To grow properly, children need a variety of good food. Such food should provide the child with what is necessary for good growth, and must always be clean and safe for the child.
- Food bought from street sellers or vendors is not always safe for children because it may not have been prepared in truly hygienic conditions, or it may have been prepared for adult taste.
- Vendor-prepared soups and stews made for adults are too spicy or peppery for children.
- Vendor-prepared porridges are often watery and do not provide enough energy to meet the needs of a growing child. If vendor-prepared porridge is to be given to a child, it should first be enriched with groundnut paste, vegetable or palm oil, or milk. For older children, the porridge can be enriched by serving with bofrot, koose or bread.
- If vendor foods are to be served to children, it is important to check that they have been prepared and sold in hygienic conditions.
- If you have to use vendor foods for children, it is best to go with your own clean bowl and spoon to get the food.
- Whenever possible, reheat bought food before serving it to children.
- The best food for a baby or child is the food that is prepared at home and caregivers should try to ensure that this is the food their children receive in order to ensure good health and growth.

14. Glossary: The glossary acknowledges the importance of consistency in message presentation. Information is easier to retain and use if it is expressed in the same words each time it is presented. The glossary provides the writer with the precise definitions and explanations to use for words and terminology that might be unfamiliar to the audience. Definitions should be simple and appropriate to the audience.

For example, "Permanent contraceptive methods" can be defined as "those contraceptive methods that are used only when a husband and wife decide together that they are perfectly sure that they will want no more children at any time in the future."

Whenever the phrase "permanent contraceptive methods" is used in the design document it is followed by an asterisk (*) so that the scriptwriter knows to look in the glossary for the definition or for words that must be used in discussing this aspect of the topic.

The glossary has special significance in cases where the scripts will be prepared in more than one language, or where the document is being prepared in English, but the scripts will be written in a local language. In those cases, the glossary should give the local language words that must be used.

An **abbreviation list** can follow the glossary, if necessary. This list spells out in full (and in translation where required) all abbreviations used in the document.

Part 3: Implementation

This section of the design document contains information that the design team compiles on important aspects of the project, other than message content. Some segments of Part 3 of the design document may not be completed within the time limit of the design workshop, but it is valuable to have design team members discuss these points together and make initial decisions about them.

15. The script review panel and script support team: All publishers of books employ proofreaders to check manuscripts for inadvertent errors and inconsistencies before they are printed. Even the most famous authors acknowledge the need for and value of proofreading. In the same way, every episode of every Entertainment–Education serial drama written to motivate positive social development should be reviewed for consistency and accuracy. For this purpose, the design team will nominate a **script review panel** that comprises a few members of the design team who will review each script for its adherence to the design document and to the spirit and intentions of the series. Ideally, this group is made up of no more than five people:

- the program manager
- the media director

- a content specialist
- an Entertainment–Education drama script specialist
- a representative of the relevant ministry (where necessary)

It is usually unnecessary to have every script reviewed by a member of the audience. As long as there are audience representatives in the Design Workshop, and sample scripts have been pilot tested (see Chapter 10), script review can be handled by the team suggested earlier.

Sometimes, it is necessary to have a language specialist on the panel in those countries that require all broadcasts to be given in the official national language, or where programs are being written in several languages. If it is necessary to ensure that the programs are acceptable to the broadcast station, the panel can also include a representative of the station, unless the media director is employed by the radio station and knows policies.

The completed design document should also list a **script support team**: the names of a few members of the design team who can provide advice during the scriptwriting process. Although scriptwriters are present throughout the design workshop and have the design document as a detailed guide, sometimes questions arise during writing that only an expert can answer. The **support team**, therefore, is made up of the following members of the design team:

- program manager
- content specialist
- media director
- evaluator
- researcher
- representatives of both the audience and the relevant ministry or government

Not all of these people will be needed by the writer at the same time, and some of them may not be called upon by the writer at any time. It is important, however, that the writer knows the people to call when help is needed, and that these people will be available when needed.

16. Listing and description of proposed support materials: A communication campaign is always more effective when more than one medium is involved. While the goal of a radio serial drama is to convey the message clearly on its own, the design team should consider what other materials might be included in the project. The nature of support materials can be determined during the design workshop and may include items such as Listener Group Guides, brochures, flyers, and the addresses of places where listeners can obtain further information on the recommended behavior change.

(Guidelines on the preparation of support materials can be found in Chapter 6.)

17. Promotion plans: The promotion plans determine how the radio or television series will be publicized, and they should be created as far in advance as possible. Promotional spots that highlight a few exciting lines from the serial's episodes are often effective. If they have been planned in advance, these spots can be recorded easily at the same time as the episodes.

Promotion plans may include prizes or other incentives that also need to be considered as early as possible, so that the scriptwriter can include references to any competitions and prizes in the announcer's remarks at the end of the episode. (Guidelines on the preparation of promotional materials can be found in Chapter 6.)

18. The monitoring and evaluation plan: The evaluation plan is included in the design document so that all those involved in the serial drama can understand what has to be done to assess the project's success. To gain a full understanding of the program, evaluators participate in at least the first stages of the design workshop. Their participation allows them to understand how the drama is designed and what it is intended to do. Working with this information, they can complete the pilot testing, monitoring and evaluation plan outside the design workshop and submit it at a later date for inclusion in the design document.

19. The time lines: The time lines set out in detail the dates by which each activity of the drama creation and production must be completed. The time lines can be grouped under three main headings:

- The scriptwriting, reviewing, production, and broadcast time line
- The support and promotional materials time line
- The testing, monitoring, and evaluation time line

The time lines might not be completed within the design workshop, but when finished, they should be recorded in the finalized design document, so that all those involved in the project know what is expected of them. A sample script time line for the 10 weeks from the start of scripting to audio production is included on pages 100–1.

20. Story outline and sample episode: The program manager requests a full story outline(see page 173-174 for sample) from scriptwriters immediately after the design workshop. This outline sketches the various plots and major characters to be included, shows how the message will be incorporated, and presents one complete sample script.

Advantages of the Design Document

The compilation and use of a detailed design document provides the following assistance and assurances to the behavior change communication project:

- **Helps prevent inaccuracies and possibly critical mistakes.**
  Even a writer with the best of intentions creating an Entertainment–Education drama without detailed message instructions might include, however inadvertently, information that is either misleading or in fact harmful to the audience. The precise and detailed message information in the design document significantly lowers the chances of this happening.
- **Strengthens the possibility of appropriate audience response.**
  The design document provides an organized scope and sequence for message presentation, consistency of language and terminology, and a clear delineation of the most appropriate ways in which the message can be made relevant to the chosen audience. These factors greatly enhance the possibility of positive audience response to the desired behavior change.
- **Enhances accurate and timely script review.**
  The design document provides script reviewers a clear reference against which to measure each scripted episode. Reviewers will know exactly what the objectives, purposes, and message content of each script should be, and the way in which the message content should be expressed. The story outline in the design document also allows reviewers to determine quickly whether or not the story (the entertainment side of the drama) is on track.
- **Saves time and money.**
  Reviewers, writers, evaluators, and the program manager save a great deal of time, and therefore money, by having the detailed, agreed-upon design document as their guide and reliable reference through every step of the development and evaluation stages. Writers and reviewers need less time to do their job. Therefore, there is less expenditure on rewriting, typing, translation, copying, and materials when scripts do not have to be rewritten many times. Production costs are also saved, because working from the design document virtually eliminates the chances of a bad or inaccurate episode having to be rerecorded when its weaknesses are realized too late.
- **Encourages a sense of confidence and professionalism.**
  Because design team members are asked to commit their beliefs and decisions about the project in writing, they are more likely to ensure the accuracy and appropriateness of their comments and messages than they do when their ideas are not recorded.
- **Enhances project sustainability.**
  The existence of a document containing all elements of the project design makes it much easier for the project to be continued or replicated as needed. It also provides a reliable and accurate reference for anyone wanting to check exactly what message will be or has been disseminated by the project.
- **Increases the accuracy and usefulness of evaluation.**
  By using the design document as their guide, evaluators know exactly what the project is trying to achieve and they can create test instruments that will accurately assess the strengths and weaknesses of the project.

THE WRITER'S BRIEF

Ideally, scriptwriters should receive a copy of the complete design document before they begin to write. Completion of the entire design document can take some time, however, so a writer's brief can be prepared immediately at the close of the design workshop that will allow writers to begin their work as soon as possible. The writer's brief is a short version of the design document and must contain the specific information listed in segments 1–15, 19, and 20 of the design document (see Box 2.1).

DESIGN DOCUMENT: POSSIBLE TABLE OF CONTENTS

- Signatories* (optional)
- Preamble or Foreword
- Design Team Member List
- Job Descriptions** (optional)
- Justification for the project
- Overall Measurable Objectives
- Overall Message and Emotional Focus
- Episode Topics and Sequence
- Special Instructions to the Writer(s)
- Individual Episode Listing
- Measurable objectives and purpose(s)
- Detailed Message Content
- Glossary and Acronym List
- Script Review Panel and Script Support Team
- Story treatment and sample script
- Support Materials Description
- Promotional Plans Outline
- Time Lines
- Evaluation Plans

The contents of the completed design document can be arranged as required by those working on the project, but a completed table of contents for a radio serial drama design document typically will contain the list given above.

---

* Signatories: Important stakeholders can be invited to sign off on the design document as a way of ensuring to all who use it that its messages and methods have been approved.

** Job Descriptions: If the project is working with a production company or in cases where office staff are not familiar with the preparation of radio programs for social development, it is useful to list in the design document the specific tasks that everyone will be expected to fulfill.

3

The Design Approach: The Design Team

The design team works together to create the messages.

Topics

- *The Need for the Design Team*
- *Advantages of the Design Team*
- *Design Team Members and Their Roles*

THE NEED FOR THE DESIGN TEAM

Drama that is intended purely for entertainment can be created by one writer working alone. Entertainment–Education drama, as explained in the previous chapter, is quite different from pure entertainment drama. A team, rather than a writer alone, is needed to design and guide the messages in the serial drama intended for behavior change purposes. Having a design team whose members work closely together offers many advantages to the project.

ADVANTAGES OF THE DESIGN TEAM

- The team can provide a more thorough consideration of all aspects of the proposed serial drama. Various team members bring differing perspectives and aspects of information to the project. All of these perspectives need to be considered and reconciled in order to present consistent and correct information to the chosen audience in the most appropriate manner.
- Continuous formative evaluation is ensured from the outset by the involvement of a team of resource people such as the content specialists and the audience representatives.
- Settlement of differences of opinion about such important matters as government policy, production standards, and cultural appropriateness

---

Box 3.1

MAIN ADVANTAGES OF A TEAM*

Together
Everyone
Achieves
More

*This is how the Johns Hopkins University defines a "team".

can be effected harmoniously by consultation among team members. This prevents the occurrence of major stumbling blocks during writing and production, or the demand that the serial be pulled from the air because it is considered inappropriate or offensive by someone who was not consulted in the early stages.

- Gaps in knowledge can be identified and redressed in a timely fashion. It may be found during the design workshop that certain information about such matters as audience practices is insufficiently understood. Steps can be undertaken at this stage to have design team members fill in the knowledge gaps so that when scripts are written they do not mislead, insult, or confuse the audience.

- A team approach can shorten and sharpen the scriptwriting process. The writers understand from their involvement in the design team exactly what the serial drama is intended to achieve, and how best to express the ideas to the chosen audience. They do not have to spend time looking for information to include in the drama. The writing process is sharpened because the writers will have a clear understanding of the need for the communication intervention and a full realization of factors that have made it difficult for the audience to adopt the proposed behavior in the past. Writers also have ongoing access to a support team (chosen from the design team) who are familiar with and in agreement with the design document.

- Fast and reliable script review is achieved as a result of the work of the design team. All those on the review panel are members of the design team and have first-hand understanding of the project's intention. In creating the design document together, team members help establish the guidelines based on which all scripts and support materials should be reviewed.

- Evaluation accuracy is enhanced because evaluators have been contributing members of the design team from the outset and know what to measure.

DESIGN TEAM MEMBERS AND THEIR ROLES

The design team is made up of the people needed to make essential decisions related to the content and presentation of the radio serial drama. Design team members should:

- Have a belief in and sincere dedication to the aims of the project.
- Be available—barring unforeseen circumstances—throughout the duration of the design and development stages of the project.

- Be committed to their responsibilities as team members, and have the backing and support of their supervisors throughout their involvement with the project.

The program manager should ensure that all those who have a stake in the project are represented on the team. At the same time, it is wise to limit the number of people attending the design workshop to no more than 35.

The make-up of the team and the number of its members will differ depending on the local culture, the nature of the project, and the organizations to be involved with it. Typically, a design team includes the people listed in Box 3.2, all of whom can make valuable contributions to the design workshop and document.

Box 3.2

DESIGN TEAM MEMBERS

Program Manager
Funding Agency Representative
Content Specialists
Audience Representatives
Ministry Representatives
Broadcast Outlet Representatives
NGO and Donor Agency
　Representatives
Scriptwriter(s)
Resource Representatives
Media Director
Researcher/Evaluator
Support Materials Writer
Promotions Manager

Program Manager

The program manager heads the team, manages the design workshop, is responsible for organization of all aspects of the serial drama creation and production, and keeps the project on track.

An important aspect of the program manager's work is the setting up and running of the design workshop, and includes ensuring that

- Decisions made by the team are acceptable and practical under the terms of the overall project.
- Every item in the design document is fully and thoroughly explored by the team.
- Team members reach an agreement on the details.

Contribution to the team: Information about project intentions and aims; project duration and limitations; available resources and staff; work done to date (overview of analysis phase).

Funding Agency Representative

Someone in a position of authority with the funding agency—perhaps the Project Director or Country Representative—who can make decisions on behalf of the funding agency with regard to policy and commitment of resources. Sometimes this role will be filled by the program manager. This team member has the responsibility of ensuring that all decisions made by the design team are within the scope and intention of the project.

Contribution to the team: Budget allowances and restrictions; time lines and expectations and limitations for project development.

Content Specialists

Generally, it is advisable to have at least two content specialists on the team for every topic to be covered in the serial. These content specialists should be people who are local, recognized authorities in their subject area. A child health project, for example, should have as content specialists people who are currently working locally in the area of child health (training, policy making, managing a child health project, etc.). In almost every content area, whether it is child health, HIV and AIDS prevention, family planning, environmental protection, Adolescent Reproductive Health, etc., there are differences of opinion on what actions should be taken in certain circumstances or on how particular ideas should be expressed. The presence of at least two content specialists for each major topic helps to ensure that these differences are discovered and that acceptable compromises are reached. Occasionally, it may be necessary to bring one or two extra content advisors into the workshop temporarily as special needs arise. The content specialists will be responsible for ensuring the absolute accuracy and appropriateness of all message content to be included in the serial drama.

Contribution to the team: All printed technical knowledge (particularly local materials) relevant to the topic of the project.

For example, content specialists for an HIV and AIDS campaign should bring with them the latest accurate information on such things as where Voluntary Counseling and Testing (VCT) can be obtained. Print materials and demonstration kits currently used by health workers in the field or in the clinic are also useful to help ensure that information to be included in the programs can be made consistent with what is already in print. All information brought to the design workshop must be up-to-date, and must reflect relevant and current government and/or donor policies.

Audience Representatives

These should be people who are actual members of or who work closely with the chosen audience in the subject area(s) that the broadcasts will address. *For example*, in a serial drama that aims to encourage adolescents to understand the mental and physical changes they are undergoing and to know how to deal with them, there could be two types of audience representatives: adolescents, and adolescent guidance counselors.

The audience representatives should have an understanding of local traditional beliefs and know what current misunderstandings and personal fears might be standing between the audience members and the acceptance of the new behaviors.

Audience representatives can also give advice and guidance about the language and terminology that is most likely to be understood by and acceptable to the chosen audience. They will be responsible for ensuring that the serial drama and its message contents have the best possible chance of appealing to and appropriately influencing the chosen audience.

Contribution to the team: As much knowledge as possible about current audience attitudes and practices related to the project topic; information about common language and terminology that is used by the audience with regard to the topic; information about current misunderstandings, rumors, and beliefs; information about audience preferences in entertainment.

Ministry Representatives

Many, if not most, development communication projects involve at least one host country ministry (the Ministry of Health in the case of health-related projects). It is essential that every ministry that is involved in or will be affected by the project be represented on the design team. These representatives should be people well acquainted with the policies of their ministries and have the authority to speak on behalf of the ministries on matters of policy.

For example, in some countries, it is the policy of the Ministry of Health to recommend that a woman should not marry until she is 20 years of age. The messages in the serial drama, therefore, should reflect this policy and promote the same recommendations. It is the responsibility of the ministry representatives on the team to ensure that nothing is included in the message content that could be criticized at a later date as contravening ministry policies.

Contribution to the team: Must bring up-to-date information about ministry policies (preferably from printed sources) related to the topic of the project.

Broadcast Outlet Representative

The team should include a representative of the broadcast station that will air the serial drama—someone who knows broadcast station policy and can speak on behalf of station management. The team needs to know, for example, whether there are any broadcast restrictions on the discussion of matters related to sex and adolescent development. The broadcast outlet representative should have knowledge of audience likes and dislikes with regard to radio programming, and must take responsibility for ensuring that the serial drama will not be pulled from the air because it contravenes broadcast policy in any way.

Contribution to the team: Must be able to inform the team (preferably from printed sources) of any policies relating to the topic.

For example, some broadcast outlets have very strict guidelines for words that can be used during the discussion of anything related to sex.

NGO and Donor Agency Representatives

NGOs and donor agencies working in the same field, or one similar to the project, should be represented on the design team. Their involvement can cut down on competition or animosity among organizations. It is also possible that another agency will be able to assist the project in some way—perhaps through the distribution of resources or materials. It is always valuable to enhance cooperation with other organizations and NGOs carrying out projects in a related field.

Contribution to the team: Information about projects in which they are currently engaged which might complement or be complemented by the radio serial drama; information about the precise message being delivered by these agencies so that contradictions can be avoided by the new project and consistency can be enhanced.

Scriptwriter(s)

As mentioned earlier, the involvement of the scriptwriter(s) from the very outset of the design process is extraordinarily beneficial, fostering a much deeper understanding and appreciation of the message to be disseminated. Their presence on the design team allows the writers to ask questions about technical matters they do not understand which the audience, similarly, might not understand. It also allows the writer to become personally acquainted with the members of the script review panel and the script support team, which encourages a much closer working relationship. The scriptwriter has the enormous responsibility of blending all the message content needs into a story that will capture and hold the attention of the audience. If this responsibility is to be fulfilled, then it is clear that all other team members must uphold their responsibilities faithfully.

Contribution to the team: An awareness of the type of drama currently appreciated by the chosen audience; an open mind and a willingness to learn about the topic. Writers might also like to bring with them examples of other scripts they have written.

Resource Representative

Some behavior change projects—such as those promoting Vitamin A supplementation—rely for their success on the availability of needed resources as much as they rely on the effective communication of a message. It can be useful, therefore, to invite a resource representative to attend at least part of the design workshop, as a visitor if not as a team member. The resource representative might be a government supplier, or a private entrepreneur who is interested in supporting the broadcast drama by ensuring resource supplies at the appropriate time. Where a resource representative is included in the team, he or she must take responsibility for ensuring that the listening audience is not prevented from reaching the desired project objectives because the resources needed are not available.

Contribution to the team: Up-to-date information on current and future availability of the resources needed by the audience to meet the project objectives.

Media Director

The person who will be in charge of directing the performance and recording of the drama should be a member of the design team, so as to contribute invaluable guidance about the capabilities and limitations of the chosen medium, about the type of programming that currently attracts the chosen audience, and about the availability of local talent. Such a person's presence on the design team will help the director to understand that Entertainment–Education production is a team effort and that the director cannot make changes to the script or to its interpretation without reference to the program manager. The media director will take both artistic and logistical responsibility for the recording and broadcast activities of the project.

Contribution to the team: Information about availability and costs of actors, recording studios, equipment, and technicians; estimation of possible training needs for actors or technical staff.

Researcher/Evaluator

It is valuable for the team to have the input of one of the researchers who worked with the analysis phase of the project. While printed reports on the findings of the research team can be made available, these are never as valuable as personal comments and anecdotes from someone who took part in the initial audience research. The evaluator can also assist in the framing of the measurable objectives of the project, and in the determination of which theory of behavior change might be most appropriate to the given topic and audience. The researcher/evaluator takes on the responsibilities of ensuring that the project objectives are realistic; of recommending ways in which both the message and the story can enhance audience potential for reaching these objectives; and of assisting in determining the most effective monitoring and summative evaluation tools.

Contribution to the team: Information (preferably in Powerpoint or overhead presentation form, as well as print) giving evidence of current attitudes and practices of audience, together with some personal anecdotes from the field during the research phase.

Support Materials Writer

If it is known at the outset that new support materials will have to be created, then the person overseeing their creation must be part of the design team and be present when design decisions are being made. It is essential that message information contained in the support materials be consistent with that in the drama episodes. It can happen, too, that ideas from the support materials writer can be incorporated advantageously into the program scripts. The support materials writer is responsible for ensuring the compatibility of the radio serial drama and the support materials, and for ensuring that support materials are produced on time and up to standards.

Contribution to the team: Information about existing support materials in the topic area; information about ideas for and possible costs of various types of new support materials.

Promotions Manager

In some large communication projects, there is one person designated to handle promotions for all activities. In such a case, this person should be included as a member of the design team and should participate in the design workshop. This is particularly important in cases where the radio drama is part of a larger campaign for which such things as logo, slogan and general branding have already been determined. The Entertainment–Education serial drama is likely to attract more attention if all aspects of it—the script, the support materials, and the promotional materials—express the same ideas and have the same approach. As with support material design, there is always the possibility that a promotional idea that comes up during the design team discussions can be incorporated to enhance the scripts. The promotions manager has the responsibility of finding ways to attract and hold the attention of the audience, both with regard to the radio serial drama and to the overall aims and objectives of the project. In many projects, two or more of the design team roles might be filled by one person. For example, the support materials writer might also fill the role of promotions manager.

Contribution to the team: Promotional ideas, suggestions, and possible costs.

The role of the design team members should be recognized, both in the permanent record of the design document, and in press releases and other promotional materials. In order to encourage team member dedication to the project, the program manager can hold a short preworkshop meeting with team members to advise them of the national importance of the project and to explain to them what will be expected of them as team members. During this advance meeting, the program manager can provide team members with suggestions about the types of materials and information it would be helpful for them to bring with them to the design workshop. Sometimes it is not appropriate or possible to get all invited participants together at an advance meeting. In that case, a letter should be sent to each of them, explaining the purpose of the design workshop and requesting that they bring the necessary materials with them as has just been discussed. (A sample invitation letter can be found in Appendix B.)

4

The Design Approach:
The Design Workshop

Design team members work together in the design workshop.

Topics

- *The Design Workshop*
- *The Design Workshop in Progress*
- *Major Considerations in Design Workshop Activity*
- *Small-group Working Guidelines*
- *Message Preparation Guidelines*
- *The Value of Change Agents*
- *Changing Traditional Behavior and Encouraging Prevention Behavior*
- *After the Design Workshop: Completing the Design Document*

THE DESIGN WORKSHOP

The design workshop is the crucial element of the design approach because it is the meeting at which all decisions related to the shape and substance of the Entertainment–Education serial drama must be made. Consensus must be reached on all details of the educational side (the messages), and all logistical details such as the writing and production time lines. The success of the design workshop determines the success of the serial drama project. The outcome of the design workshop will be the draft version of the design document, the reliable reference on which all future activities of the project will be based, and without which the writer cannot begin to work.

For a serial of 26–52 episodes, the design workshop will usually occupy a full week. It is always preferable for the team to meet for one continuous week rather than in a series of separated meetings. It is imperative that the design workshop run smoothly and that all participants have the opportunity to contribute fully. For the design workshop to be as successful as possible, there are a number of tasks the program manager must complete in advance. All activities of the analysis phase must be completed and documented, as must the list of start-up activities that relate particularly to the initiation of radio serial drama. The results of all these investigations should be compiled in a manner that can be shared readily with design team members at the beginning of the design workshop. Then there are several tasks to be undertaken that relate to the workshop itself. (Guidelines on steps the program manager must take to prepare for the design workshop are given in Chapter 5.)

THE DESIGN WORKSHOP IN PROGRESS

Once the design workshop is underway, it is up to all participants to help ensure that it runs smoothly and that all necessary work is completed within the given time frame. The slogan for a well-run design workshop might well be, "Leave no stone unturned." The design workshop is a demanding experience as technical advisors, audience representatives, creative artists and project managers work together to determine the messages that are most likely to inspire appropriate change in the chosen audience(s).

Major Considerations in Design Workshop Activity

A great deal of the work in the design workshop will be undertaken in small groups. The following guidelines can help ensure that small groups work harmoniously and have the best possible chance of meeting their goals:

Small-group Working Guidelines

Restrict each group to no more than three or four people. Wherever possible, these groups should comprise a mix of professional expertise (content specialist, audience representative, media representative, etc.).

Ensure that each group understands clearly the task before them. Usually, each group will work on a specific topic and its subtopics. Group members will be required to determine the objectives, the purpose(s), and content of episodes related to one of the subtopics of the overall message. One group, for example, might work on all programs relating to contraceptive methods, a second group might work on counseling methods, a third on safe motherhood guidelines, etc.

Explain the need for precise message content definition. Many people find it difficult to understand just how specifically the message content must be spelled out in the design document. *For example*, it is not sufficient for the content to state "This episode will give an explanation of nutrition and the importance of a balanced diet." The content must state exactly how the writer should explain "nutrition" in the script and exactly what a "balanced diet" is and why it is important. For instance, the content portion of the message might state:

- "Nutrition" means the right amount of the right types of food to maintain a healthy body and a healthy mind.
- A "balanced diet" means having the following foods in the right amount every day (the content would then list locally available foods that are normally included in a balanced diet).

It cannot be overemphasized that it is not the writer's job to determine the message or to select the words in which precise message content must be given. It is the writer's job to create an exciting and attention-grabbing story, and then to weave into that story the exact message content that has been worked out by the design team.

Ensure that content specialists are available. During small-group work it is essential to have content specialists (those who are knowledgeable and up-to-date with local information relevant to the topic) available for each group. If it is not possible to have one with each group, then those who are available should move from group to group to assist all groups so as to ensure content accuracy.

Ensure that audience representatives are available to each group. Audience representatives are the best ones to help determine whether certain words or messages will be fully understood by listeners. Again, if there are not enough audience members to have one in each group, make sure that they circulate and that every message is "tried" on them before it is included in the design document.

Ensure that all groups have access to vital information. At the commencement of group work, make sure that each group has access to all research and reference materials that they will need to help them make determinations in their given topic. Group participants should be reminded frequently of such matters as the overall message and emotional focus agreed upon as they prepare the objectives, purpose, and content for individual episodes. In fact, it is a good idea to have these important points written on flip chart paper and displayed on the wall.

Ensure that all groups adhere to the elements of a well-constructed message. Groups should be reminded to check that every message they prepare is in accordance with the 7Cs of message presentation (see Box 4.1).

Ensure that all groups complete glossary and acronym definitions. In the episode content they prepare, groups should mark with an asterisk (*) all words or phrases that will be defined or translated in the glossary and all acronyms that are spelled out in the acronym list. This ensures that the writer(s) will know which words and terms require exact definition. It is helpful to have several flip chart sheets hanging up, where groups can enter their glossary and acronym suggestions as they come across them.

Message Preparation Guidelines

All members of the design team should be encouraged to help guarantee that the following points are understood and observed during message preparation:

Ensuring that objectives are attainable: The average Entertainment–Education radio (or even TV) drama serial runs for 26 episodes. That is once a week for six months, and the average episode is 15–20 minutes long. While it certainly is possible to bring about significant behavior change in that time, it should be remembered that significant and lasting changes in social norms usually take longer than that to achieve. The workshop leader must encourage the design team to ensure that the objectives of the serial as a whole and of the individual episodes are realistic.

For example, it is unlikely that after listening to one 20-minute episode a drug addict will "give up drugs permanently." More realistically, the objective could be that the addict will "consider seeking help for overcoming the addiction."

Recognizing the difference between program objectives and program purposes:

Objective = Audience

Purpose = Program

The Objectives describe the desired changes the project wants to achieve in the audience.These changes are usually expressed as changes in knowledge, in attitude and in behavior, or, as is more commonly expressed, Knowledge, Attitude, and Practice (KAP).

The Purpose refers to the approach(es) the program must take to enable the audience to reach those objectives. How must the program be designed, written, and presented in order to assist the audience to reach the desired objectives? The purpose guides the writers in the approach the program must take to help ensure that the audience can achieve the program's objectives.

Avoiding negative reinforcement: All too often a program that tries to dissuade negative or inappropriate behavior ends up reinforcing the negative behavior. People tend to hear what they want to hear.

For example, men who believe that vasectomy results in impotence are likely to be reinforced in their belief if they hear a character in a drama attempting to contradict this belief. For this reason, it is always better for a behavior change message to stress the positive than try to contradict the negative. The message on vasectomy would be more forceful if the character were to make no attempt to contradict the incorrect belief, but instead say something like, "The great thing about vasectomy is that it *increases* a man's virility because it removes his fear of unwanted pregnancy. Vasectomy has a really positive effect on virility."

Ensuring that the messages adhere to the 7Cs of message presentation: In order to be effective, educational messages in Entertainment–Education programming must be Correct, Clear (and logical), Concise, Complete, Consistent, Culturally appropriate, and Compelling.

Ensuring that the message is CORRECT: Ensuring the correctness of the message is the task of the content advisors. They must be sure to come to the design workshop equipped with the very latest up-to-the minute knowledge on the topics to be included. Researchers also play a major part in ensuring the correctness of the message. The baseline research that must be completed ahead of the design workshop will help participants understand how much correct or incorrect knowledge the audience members already have. Research information can also help with decisions relating to what "change agents" are most likely to encourage audience members to adjust or change their behavior.

> **Box 4.1**
>
> THE 7CS OF
> MESSAGE PRESENTATION
>
> Messages in Entertainment–
> Education dramas must be:
>
> Correct
> Clear and Logical
> Concise
> Complete
> Consistent
> Culturally appropriate
> Compelling

Keeping the message CLEAR and LOGICAL: The aim of the workshop is to ensure that the "educational messages" blended into the drama by the scriptwriters(s) will be accurate and appropriate to the chosen audience. Writers can play an important role during the workshop in questioning any parts of the message that are not clear to them. It is sometimes difficult for content advisors to remember that average citizens do not always understand technical language and terminology.

For example, many radio listeners do not know what ARH means or what a "placebo" is. Research has shown that many adolescents throughout the wold believe that "abstinence" means "abstaining from alcohol" and that "faithfulness" means going to church regularly. To many people "positive" means good and "negative" means bad, so all too often the mistaken belief is that a person who is found to be "HIV Positive" is in good physical condition—namely, free from the disease. Design team members must ensure that the language they use for the messages is simple, clear and completely unambiguous to the audience. It is also important to consider the **logic** of each message being delivered to the audience. Is it logical to recommend that people keep their windows closed at night to ward off mosquitoes, when the houses of most members of the audience have no glass in their windows? Some people in countries around the world have questioned the logic of saying that "there should be no stigma against people who are HIV positive," while at the same time assuring listeners that they will not be required to give their names when they go for testing.

Keeping the message content CONCISE: The general rule is that an audience cannot absorb and remember more than 3 **new** points in a 20-minute radio program. The tendency for many content specialists is to try to give the audience ALL the information they possess. The secret of success is to give the audience **the least amount of knowledge**

required to encourage a change in behavior or to facilitate the recognition of a need for change in behavior.

For example, almost all programs on immunization list all the immunizations a baby must have in the first year of life together with the ages the baby must be for each immunization and the diseases against which a baby will be protected. It is virtually impossible for a listener—or even a viewer—to absorb and remember all this detail from one program, or even several programs. The vital pieces of information the audience needs are:

- The number of immunizations the baby must have in the first year of life.
- That these immunizations will help protect the child from serious and often deadly diseases.
- That the midwife or birth attendant will tell the mother when to bring the newborn baby for the next immunization.
- That advice and information about where and when to get future immunizations can be obtained from the nearest health facility or health worker.
- That it is the responsibility of parents to ensure that their children receive ALL the necessary immunizations in the first year of life.

It is equally important, when discussing this topic, to avoid confusing the audience by referring to "immunizations" and "vaccinations" in the same program. Any message that is complex or ambiguous is highly likely to be disregarded by the audience.

Keeping the message CONSISTENT: Successful advertisers are well aware of the importance of consistency. It is for the sake of consistency that they create slogans and repeat these slogans many, many times, until the audience learns—and usually believes—them. Entertainment–Education message designers can learn from this approach. One of the big advantages of using the drama format is that writers can ensure that all characters express the main points of the message in the same way. One serious disadvantage of the magazine or panel discussion format is that producers usually have little or no control over the way the guest speakers will deliver the message, and therefore no way of ensuring that the messages will always be consistent.

Making the message COMPLETE: Design team members often see a contradiction in the need to keep the message concise and yet make the message complete. There is a tendency to want to inform the audience that "we will give you more details about this topic next week." There are two problems with this approach:

(a) It might not be possible for all audience members to tune in next week.
(b) The listeners might not be able to wait until next week for the information they need.

A classic example is the radio program that told listeners about a simple remedy for childhood diarrhea, for which "all you need is sugar and salt and water, and next week we'll tell you the proportions and how to mix it." What the program designers did not take into account was that many children were suffering from diarrhea even as the first program was being aired. With the parents being told to wait until next week to learn how to mix the appropriate oral rehydration solution, several of those children could have died.

If a particular topic requires more information than can comfortably fit into one program, the best approach is to tell listeners where they can go for more information if they need immediate help with a problem, e.g., the local clinic.

Making the message CULTURALLY APPROPRIATE: It is extremely important that all members of the design team have an intimate knowledge of the culture in which they are working, and of what is and is not culturally appropriate. In some Muslim countries, for example, the common phrase "ARH," or "Adolescent Reproductive Health" is very offensive. This must be respected and a new term, such as Adolescent Physical and Mental Health (APMH), used instead. The writers must have a sincere understanding and appreciation of the cultural norms of the chosen audience in order to create dramas that will, without offending, appeal to the audience. It is for this reason that writers are advised to spend some time in the environment of the audience before commencing final scriptwriting.

Making the message COMPELLING: This is where it is important for all design team members to remember that "knowledge alone does not always lead to change." Virtually everyone knows that one out of every two people who currently smoke, will die as a result of the habit. Yet millions of people around the world, equipped with this knowledge, still smoke. Knowledge is an essential first step, but it is extremely important for the design team to consider how the chosen audience will be moved from knowledge, up the other steps of behavior change (see Figure 2.1).

THE VALUE OF CHANGE AGENTS

Behavior change communication programs often put too much emphasis on giving the audience knowledge and too little on providing them with motivation. This is why it is important for all design team members to consider what "change agents" are likely to motivate the audience(s). Change agents are the motivators. They can be people, such as religious or community leaders; benefits, such as increased earning or greater personal respect; improved health; role models, such as people who are famous (for any number of reasons) in the community and who lead a life that others would like to follow. Finding the most powerful change agent(s) for a particular audience is a vital step in creating a compelling message and bringing about behavior change.

CHANGING TRADITIONAL BEHAVIOR AND ENCOURAGING PREVENTION BEHAVIOR

Perhaps the two most difficult behaviors to change are traditional behavior and prevention behavior. Attempting to change **traditional behavior** requires both knowledge and sensitivity from the design team and the writers. It is important to understand whether traditional behaviors are based on religious tradition or on cultural behavior that has gradually been adopted and accepted over generations as being religion based. Sometimes, behaviors that are considered untouchable because of their religious roots are found, upon examination, to have no basis in religious texts or teaching. An example is female genital cutting (or mutilation). In several countries that have always claimed a religious basis for this behavior, there is now clear evidence that no such religious basis exists. In cases like this, religious teachers can be helpful in explaining the misunderstanding and helping to motivate the desired change. Where the traditional behavior does have a religious foundation, it is obviously essential to work with the religious leaders to consider if, when, and how acceptable change might be introduced.

Prevention behavior is perhaps even more challenging. Everyone, the world over, disregards certain prevention behaviors, either regularly or occasionally. People ignore the use of seat belts, even while being fully informed of the dangers of traveling without them. Some people insist on eating foods that they know will cause them to be obese and put them in danger of heart problems. Universally, people ignore the teaching on preventing sexual infections and simply refuse to use condoms. Most people will adjust their behavior once they have suffered, personally, but the universal attitude "it won't happen to me," makes teaching prevention behavior extremely challenging.

Design team members—content specialists and writers alike—must work together to determine the best ways of making their messages so **compelling** that audience members will be inspired to follow them. Consistently **modeling** the preventative behavior, without necessarily referring to it, has been found to be helpful in this situation.

For example, if the characters in a drama **always** wash their hands before touching food (even without mentioning what they are doing), it is not uncommon for the audience to find themselves—almost subconsciously—doing the same thing.

AFTER THE DESIGN WORKSHOP: COMPLETING THE DESIGN DOCUMENT

At the end of the design workshop, the design document will be in first draft form. There will still be considerable polishing or finalizing work to be done on it. Details of how this is done are in the next chapter.

PART 2

For the Program Manager

5

Starting up the Radio Serial Drama Project

The program manager leads the team in all aspects of the project.

Topics

- *The Role of the Program Manager*
- *Starting up the Radio Serial Drama Project*
- *The Development Phases*
- *Preparing for the Design Workshop*
- *Running the Design Workshop*
- *Guiding Workshop Discussion*
- *Reviewing the Design Document*
- *After the Workshop: Design Document Finalization*

THE ROLE OF THE PROGRAM MANAGER

The program manager is the person who has full charge of all aspects of the design and production of the serial drama. In different countries, the program manager has various titles: executive producer, media producer, program director, etc. Whatever the title, the duties are the same. The program manager has a senior position in the project office, and will be answerable to the project director in charge of the Social Development or Behavior Change Communication (BCC) project as a whole. The program manager should be a person with strong managerial skills, a commitment to the project, and, where possible, previous experience with the organization of a project making use of the media for behavior change or social development purposes. It is the program manager who, first and foremost, must have a thorough understanding of all the steps necessary to design, create, and produce a successful social development serial drama.

STARTING UP THE RADIO SERIAL DRAMA PROJECT

For the creation of radio serial drama, as for the creation of any other product such as a building or an automobile, the stages of development are much the same: from conception to production to testing to refinement and then possible redesign in response to experience, evaluation, and changing needs.

The Development Phases

There are six main phases of any communication project: (*a*) analysis, (*b*) strategic design, (*c*) specific program design and development, (*d*) pilot testing and production, (*e*) ongoing management, implementation, and monitoring, and (*f*) impact evaluation. The first three are essential steps in the start-up of the project. The other steps will be discussed in later chapters.

Analysis Phase Activities

The following activities are undertaken in the analysis phase of the project:*

Understanding the problem: Review thoroughly the existing health and demographic data, survey results, study findings, and any other available relevant data to ensure complete understanding of the basic health, social, or economic problem to be addressed by the project.

Knowing the audience: Study the geographic, demographic, economic, and social factors that shape the behavior of the chosen audience. These factors include differences in knowledge, attitude, practices, and advocacy; in age, literacy, income, fertility, personality, lifestyle, values; or in other individual and community variables and mass media exposure. Knowing the audience also involves identifying distinct audience segments that are most likely to respond to differing appeals from the serial drama. The importance of constantly listening to and learning from the audience cannot be overemphasized.

Reviewing existing programs and policies: Review existing health programs and policies to see what is legal and where and what supplies and services are available to assist the audience in reaching project objectives. Identify strengths and weaknesses in service delivery so that communication programs can accentuate the positive, help correct or redirect the negative, and maximize access and quality. Interviewing policy makers is essential at this stage.

Identifying leading organizations: Pinpoint organizations that can support the project with advocacy if not with financial support. Identify public or private organizations that have the competence, commitment, influence, coverage, and continuity to carry out or support a communication program. Identify leaders, interested cooperating agencies, and potential corporate and commercial sponsors who can provide continuing support.

Assessing community capacity: Assess the availability, reach, and cost of the media that will be needed for the project: broadcast, print, and community activities.

---

*The various steps that make up the analysis phase have been delineated by the Johns Hopkins University.

Identify the communication habits and media access of both primary and secondary audiences.

Once all this information has been collected and collated in the analysis phase and the project leaders are satisfied that they have the information and facilities necessary to establish a social development project, the design of the components and activities can begin.

Strategic Design of Entertainment–Education Serial Drama

The strategic design phase involves making overall determinations about what changes can actually be encouraged based on resources, culture, audience receptivity, etc. Frequently these decisions are made at a strategic design workshop involving all interested parties and audience representatives. When the overall strategy is designed to include a radio serial drama, then the next steps will begin.

Specific Program Design and Development: Preliminary Tasks

Radio program design is carried out by the design team at the design workshop, as explained in the first part of this book. Prior to the design workshop, however, there are a number of important tasks for the program manager to undertake.

The program manager should check on the following:

Availability of a broadcast station (government or privately owned): Locate a station willing to carry the serial drama.

Availability of a broadcast time-slot that is suited to the intended audience: Airing a serial drama at a time when most people are working is likely to result in a less than favorable degree of behavior change. Evenings or weekends are a more appropriate broadcast time.

Availability of a broadcast time-slot covering a sufficient number of weeks or months: Some preliminary determination should be made with regard to the number of weeks or months during which the serial will be heard. A radio serial should run for no fewer than six months (at the rate of one episode a week) and a run of 12 months is preferable if it is to have a positive effect on social development. Most radio stations operate on a quarterly schedule, meaning that they prefer any new programs to start airing at the beginning of January, April, July or October. Knowing the broadcast station policy in advance allows the program manager to determine the time line for all aspects of design and writing.

Production house and recording facilities: Either with the government radio station or with an independent production house.
(Guidelines for choosing a production house can be found in Chapter 8.)

Writing talent: (Guidelines for selecting writers can be found in Chapter 6.)

Acting talent: Radio acting is different in many ways from stage acting and from acting for TV. If radio drama has not been commonly used previously, it is likely that actors will need some specific training in how to perform in front of the microphone.

Resources required by the audience: For example, a project promoting voluntary counseling and testing for HIV should be sure that such services are widely available before advocating their use through a serial drama.

Non-governmental organizations (NGOs), as well as other organizations that might be willing to support or promote the serial drama. At the same time, it is wise to determine if these NGOs or other organizations are currently engaged in projects that might replicate, complement, or contradict the proposed radio project. There is little value in duplicating an existing program. Where complimentary programs exist, it is wise to work together on message consistency. If programs are found that appear to be giving contradictory information, it will be necessary to try to effect some type of compromise before going into production.

On-air date determination: The start-up date should be not less than six months after the inauguration of the project, and in most cases a more realistic goal is 12 months from project commencement to first on-air presentation. It is important for the program manager to have, prior to the design workshop, a start-up date in mind, so that appropriate time lines can be devised.

Program duration: The running time (duration) of each episode may be determined by broadcast slots that the radio station has available. The program manager should be aware of available slots before the design workshop because the time available to run the program can affect the amount of information that can be put in each broadcast.

Availability of existing support materials: The use of several media together is always more powerful than using one medium alone. The program manager should check to see if there are print or other materials already available that could be used to support the intended radio serial drama. If such materials do exist, the program manager should make copies of them to share with design workshop participants to ensure message consistency.

Promotion and publicity: Any new radio program will need to be well promoted both before it goes on the air and during its broadcast life. It is generally best to employ an experienced agency to handle promotion, but it is also possible to work with the production house to prepare radio spots that should be broadcast several times a day for at least three weeks before the programming begins.

Evaluation: Arrangements should be made for regular evaluation of the drama once it is on the air. While it is obviously important to test the programs before they are regularly aired, it is equally important to provide some type of ongoing evaluation or feedback throughout the life of the program.
(Guidelines on pilot testing and evaluation can be found in Chapter 10.)

Keeping archives and records: A copy of every finalized script should be filed (either on CD/diskette or as a paper copy, or both) and a history of the project should be maintained as it develops. This history can be an excellent guideline for helping future projects to avoid mistakes or follow successful examples.

PREPARING FOR THE DESIGN WORKSHOP

The following tasks need to be accomplished prior to the design workshop:

1. Appoint the workshop facilitator.   Usually, the program manager will head the workshop personally. If this is not possible or appropriate, then a leader, perhaps an experienced consultant, must be invited in good time, and provided with adequate background information about the project and its objectives. The program manager can assist the facilitator with workshop organization and management. Some guidelines for managing the discussion that occurs during the workshop are given later in this chapter.

2. Determine the dates and duration of the workshop.   It is helpful to plan the dates several months in advance so that participants, when chosen, can be given advance notice. Follow-up reminders should be sent one month prior to the date, and then again a week or so before the opening day of the workshop.

3. Locate and reserve the venue.   The design workshop venue should be a comfortable meeting place with facilities for both plenary sessions and small-group work. Using an out-of-town location can be an advantage because it dissuades team members from having to absent themselves to attend to their regular office business. It is advisable to visit the selected site in advance of the workshop to ensure its suitability.

4. Invite the chosen team members.   The invitation should be made through the department head of the appropriate ministry or organization rather than on a personal

basis, although it is advantageous to be able to recommend a particular person by name. The invitation should be given in writing and be accompanied by a brief explanation of the project to be undertaken, the goals to be achieved, and the importance of the design team and the design workshop. (See sample invitation letter in Appendix B.)

5. Organize workshop resources.   The materials and equipment needed for the workshop include materials for presenters, for computer users and for participants. A list of the most commonly needed materials includes:

For participants

- Writing paper and a pen
  (Some participants might prefer to bring and use their own laptop computers for taking notes.)
- Background notes on the project
- Copy of the daily agenda
- A daily sign-in sheet to ensure that all participants are present

For the workshop

- Two flipchart stands
- A plentiful supply of flipchart paper, flipchart pens, and something with which to attach sheets to the wall
- Overhead projector, transparencies and transparency pens (participant groups will use these to share the messages they have written with other group members)
- Powerpoint apparatus might also be needed for the presentation of project goals and research details.
- Computer
- Printer
- Copier
- Paper for printer and copier
- A trash bin or wastepaper basket
- Microphone—only if the room is extremely large. The handing of a microphone to any participant who wants to speak in a plenary session is awkward and time consuming. It is better, where possible, to have a room small enough to allow everyone to be heard.

In spite of modern inventions like overhead projectors and Powerpoint, flipcharts still have an invaluable role to play. As decisions are made on the various aspects of the design document, they can be written down and displayed where they can be seen all the time by the team members, and revised quickly and easily as changes are made.

Flipchart paper is more adaptable to this progressive process than are overhead transparencies because several flipchart sheets can be displayed side by side for information comparison, whereas overhead transparencies can be shown only one at a time. A chalkboard is altogether too limited because of its size, and because information must be erased before more can be written up.

6. **Prepare reference materials:** A clearly marked table or shelf should be set aside where copies of all necessary reference materials available, including those brought by participants, can be stored for easy use. It might also be necessary to make advance copies of various books, manuals, audio tapes, and videos that will be need to be shared during the workshop. Be sure that reference materials are up-to-date and are approved by the participating ministries and content specialists. If materials—such as promotion or support materials—have already been created for other parts of the overall project, copies of these also must be available for the team.

7. **Prepare design document samples:** At least one design document sample such as that provided at the end of this book, should be available to share with participants who are new to the design experience.

8. **Prepare message content pages:** Design team members will be working in small groups to complete the message content for individual programs. They will need copies of a message content page (see Appendix B) on which they can write down the precise information to be included in the design document. As these sheets are completed by the groups, they can be given to the secretary for entry into the design document draft, or if the program manager so chooses, they can be reviewed by the program manager or another facilitator before being entered into the computer.

9. **Prepare the design document template:** A great deal of time can be saved during the design workshop if a template is prepared in advance, listing—on a diskette—the main headings of the design document. The typist can then fill in the template as the design workshop progresses.

10. **Prepare a project overview:** This overview will be presented at the outset of the design workshop and will give a brief outline of information relating to:

- the funding agency,
- the research work that has already been accomplished to ensure the appropriateness of and justification for the project (including a brief overview of baseline research),
- the overall aim of the project and the intended audience(s),
- the work to be accomplished by the design team, i.e., the design document content list.

This overview can be presented orally, with the use of a Powerpoint display or with an overhead projector in the opening session of the design workshop.

11. **Determine workshop agenda:** Because the design workshop requires a considerable amount of hard work for all those involved, it is often necessary to be flexible with the agenda as the week goes by. Nevertheless, it is advisable to begin with a clearly defined agenda so that participants can have a clear sense of what has to be accomplished. A suggested design workshop agenda can be found Appendix B.

12. **Arrange secretarial assistance:** A secretary or scribe is needed to take notes on decisions made by the design team during the design workshop. The quickest approach is to enter all final decisions into a computer as they are made. Where a computer is not available, notes can be taken on a typewriter or even with a pencil and paper, to be transferred later to a computer.

13. **Invite the necessary participants** in plenty of time, and remind them of their commitment as the workshop dates draws near. The sample letters of invitation that can be used as guidelines when inviting participants to the design workshop can be found in Appendix B.

RUNNING THE DESIGN WORKSHOP

Getting Acquainted

As indicated in the agenda mentioned earlier, it is beneficial—but not essential—to have an opening dinner on the day prior to the commencement of workshop activities. This dinner not only gives participants a chance to get to know one another, it also helps ensure that everyone is present when the real work begins.

If the participants meet for the first time on Day 1 of the agenda, they should be given an introductory exercise of some type to encourage them to get to know one another. The program manager should point out to participants the necessity for all participants to attend all sessions of the workshop to ensure total team agreement on all points in the design document.

Small-group Work

In preparing for small-group work, it is helpful for the program manager and one or two others to determine in advance who should be in each group. This will help ensure that content specialists, audience representatives, writers and other media representatives are evenly distributed among the groups. Each group will work on a particular subtopic of the main message.

For example, if the overall topic is child health, there could be small groups working on subtopics such as breastfeeding; weaning foods; vitamins and other supplements; correct feeding habits, etc.

Sample Program

It is helpful to share an example of an Entertainment–Education radio drama with the participants if they are not accustomed to the format. If there are local examples available on audio tape, one of these can be shared with the group. If the use of radio drama for social development is new to the group, the episode of *Life in Hopeful Village* given on page—of this book can be read aloud by some of the participants. It is obviously more successful if the chosen participants have time to prepare for the reading before they present it.

Justification

Design team members need to understand the reasons for undertaking this behavior change project. An overview of the research on which the project is based should be provided early in the workshop. This overview should be given by someone who has been closely involved in, or has sound knowledge of the baseline research. This presentation can be given on Powerpoint (if it is available) or with the use of an overhead projector. Copies of the main points of the presentation should be made available for groups to refer to as they create their messages.

Explaining the Design Approach

For participants who have not previously been part of a design workshop, it is helpful to explain the process to them briefly. This can be done with a brief Powerpoint or overhead presentation, or by providing participants with a copy of this book or relevant pages from it.

Topic Scope and Sequence

In determining the main topic for each program in the series or each episode in the serial, it is useful to break the participants into small groups. Each group will decide how many programs they need to cover their topic, and which part of the topic will be covered in each program. They should then write their topics on cards.

For example:

Environmental Hygiene: *Clean Water*	Environmental Hygiene: *Latrine Building*	Environmental Hygiene: *Rubbish Removal*

When all groups are ready, the cards can be attached to a large board with pins or sticky tape. In a plenary session, the participants decide on the final order of the topics and the cards are rearranged accordingly.

Individual Program Messages

Each group is given copies of the message content page to fill in for each of the programs in its particular topic. These pages should be handed to the program manager or to someone assigned by the program manager to be briefly reviewed and checked off as completed before being handed to an assistant to enter into the computer.

Glossary

A flipchart sheet should be hung on the wall, and group members should be encouraged to write on the sheet each word that they believe needs to be specifically defined, together with their proposed definition. On Day 4, these definitions can be examined and, where necessary, refined by the plenary group. The glossary should also list all acronyms that are used in the programs, together with their correct complete wording.

Writers' Presentation

Writers who have been invited to the design workshop should work closely with the groups on the message creation to ensure that they fully understand every word and every intention of each message. While they are participating in group work, the writers should also be thinking about the type of story and characters that would appeal to their audience, and about how they can weave the messages into their story naturally, subtly, and gradually. Some time during the workshop (usually the afternoon of Day 4) the writers can absent themselves from the workshop and prepare a brief outline of their story (main plot and subplots) and some brief character sketches. Their outlines will also show how the messages will be incorporated. On the last day of the workshop each writer gives an oral presentation. The participants are given an evaluation form to complete. These evaluations help the project management team to determine which writer to choose (if writers are being auditioned) or if the selected writer is capable of completing the job. It is generally better to invite participants to give a written evaluation only and not to engage in lengthy discussion of the presentations, which can only result in confusion.

A sample of the type of evaluation form participants can be asked to complete can be found in Appendix B.

Guiding Workshop Discussion

The main aim of design workshop discussion is to examine all questions and all aspects of the program design and arrive at mutually agreed-upon answers. While there will be many, many questions to explore in the course of the workshop, there are three underlying questions that should be kept in mind at all times:

1. What do we know as **fact** about this aspect of the message or the project, and by what evidence do we know it is fact?
2. What do we **not** know that we **should** know?
3. Where, or how, or from whom can we find out what we do not know?

The overarching question with which to assess everything that the team decides is:

> What could be misunderstood by our chosen audience, or what could possibly go wrong for them, if we present this information in this manner?

These questions should be kept in mind at all times during the workshop, even while numerous other questions are being explored for each part of the design document. It is the workshop leader's task to keep probing until all doubts are removed and the design team reaches full agreement on every aspect of the project.

Obviously, questions will stimulate discussion and a few simple techniques can help keep the discussion on target and make it more productive:

Establish at the Outset the Aim of the Workshop

The aim of the workshop is to reach agreement on all aspects of the serial drama design and to complete a working draft of the design document. Participants can be reminded that it is not as important for them to champion their own causes as it is for them to contribute their expertise to establish a solid foundation for a serial drama that has a good chance of stimulating desired behavior change.

Set a Time Limit for Discussion of Each Point

When the time limit is up, one member of the group should be invited to outline briefly the position as it now appears. If there is still any confusion, the workshop leader should frame some specific questions to redirect the team to towards finalizing discussion of the point. (See design workshop question guide in Appendix C.)

Set Limits on Problem Rehashing

Remind participants that the point of the workshop is to find answers, not to expound on problems that are already well known to all participants.

Record Decisions as They are Finalized

Invite one team member to record the decisions being reached by the participants. It is easiest for participants to understand what decisions have already been made or where the discussion has gone off track if the points are written on a flipchart where they can be seen by all participants at all times. While it might be useful for someone to be collating these questions on a computer as a permanent record, it is also valuable to have the points written on a flipchart where everyone in the group can see and, where necessary, adjust them right away.

REVIEWING THE DESIGN DOCUMENT

As soon as possible after the design workshop, the program manager should arrange a review workshop. The quickest and most reliable way to ensure that the design document is thoroughly reviewed is to arrange a short review workshop of two to three days depending on the number of program outlines to be reviewed.

The review team should be made up of people who were present at the design workshop and should include the program manager, several content specialists (one for each of the major topics included), one or two audience representatives and (where possible) the selected writer(s). Design team members can be asked to volunteer for this review team or the program manager can invite them.

The program manager can lead the review workshop and should begin by reminding the review team of the main goals and objectives of the project, the primary audience (and any secondary audiences), and the nature of the radio program to be presented. The review team's task is to ensure that all design document content is:

- Accurate
- Complete
- Appropriately expressed for the chosen audience(s)
- Appropriate to the amount of time allowed for each broadcast

Once all review team members have agreed that all changes and completions are correct, the program manager can go ahead with the finalization steps.

AFTER THE WORKSHOP:
DESIGN DOCUMENT FINALIZATION

- Have the completed document draft entered accurately into the computer.
- Have the document translated (where necessary). If the document was prepared in English and the writers will be working in the local language, it will be necessary to have the translation carefully examined to ensure its accuracy. This is where it is extremely helpful for the design team to have included in the glossary local language definitions of vital words and concepts.
- Have review team members sign the finished document to indicate that it has been officially approved by knowledgeable people.
- Make and distribute copies of the signed, approved document to all those who will need them, especially the writer(s), script review panel, funding agency home office, appropriate ministry heads, project director, design team members, media director, evaluator or evaluation team, and support and promotional material writers.
- Arrange for an official document-signing ceremony if desired. It can be useful to arrange a special ceremony at which ministerial representatives and other important authority figures meet to sign the completed document together. This event can be the occasion for press coverage and perhaps some oral statements of commitment to the project from those whose input and influence can be beneficial in ensuring project continuation and success. (A sample of a "signatory page" from a design document can be found in Appendix B.)

The completed design document, besides being the reliable reference for all aspects of the drama, should also be something of which all design team members are proud. It is the published and archival record of their knowledge and intentions. Frequently, program managers about to start up a new project request copies of previous design documents that they can use as templates or guidelines. All members of the design team should feel confident that their document presents a secure and safe foundation on which to build a social development project.

6

The Program Manager and the Writing Process

The program manager ensures that all scripts adhere to the design document.

Topics

- *Script Preparation*
- *Selecting and Contracting with the Writers*
- *Writing the Script*
- *Sample Script-tracking System*
- *Script Presentation*
- *Guidelines for Team Writing*
- *Script Review*
- *Briefing the Script Review Panel*
- *Guidelines for Reviewers*
- *Review Steps for Radio Serial Dramas*
- *Support Materials*
- *Guidelines for Preparing Printed Support Materials*
- *Other Support Materials*
- *Promotional Materials*
- *Guidelines for Preparing Promotional Materials*
- *Promotion Suggestions*

SCRIPT PREPARATION

When the design document has been completed and approved, it is time for writing to begin on a continuous basis. If several writers have been invited to audition for the job, these audition packages must now be examined and the final choice made. The selection of a competent and appropriate writer can be a difficult task.

SELECTING AND CONTRACTING WITH THE WRITERS

Selecting a writer for an Entertainment–Education serial drama is often a challenge. The temptation is to look for a well-known playwright or novelist, but this can be a mistake. Creative writers often find it extremely difficult and at times impossible to adjust to the discipline of writing an Entertainment–Education serial drama. The suggestion that a famous writer will attract a large audience has a certain validity, but it may be better to turn a new writer into a celebrity through a successful Entertainment–Education drama than to have a famous writer fail to incorporate the messages appropriately.

It can be equally fruitless to ask experts in the content area, such as health workers or doctors, to write drama scripts. While they may have expertise in the message area, they usually lack the necessary creative skills to write good drama. Success most often lies in finding a competent writer who is willing to learn the new skill of Entertainment–Education writing. As mentioned in Part 1, the selected writer(s) must attend the design workshop.

Determining the number of writers: For a serial that is to be broadcast once a week for 6–12 months, it is generally preferable to have one writer only. If the serial is to be broadcast five or more days per week over an extended period of time, it might be necessary to use more than one writer—especially if their writing is a part-time occupation. (Guidelines on team writing can be found at the end of this chapter.)

Contracting with writers: Writers for Entertainment–Education serials should be given written contracts spelling out exactly what their duties are with regard to:

- The number and length of episodes to be written
- The frequency with which episodes must be handed in to the program manager
- The quality of writing expected
- The limit on the number of characters permitted in any one episode
  (This is sometimes made necessary by budgetary limitations or a shortage of competent actors.)
- The need to revise scripts in accordance with comments from the review panel and in accordance with a designated time line
- The need to adhere to both the time line and to the design document
- The program manager's position as final authority on all script decisions

Incentives and penalties

Some program managers also like to include incentives and penalties in the writer's contract: a financial penalty for every script that comes in late (barring unavoidable circumstances), and a financial bonus every time 10 scripts have come in on time. If such a clause is included in the contract it is wise to include a rider about "unavoidable circumstances" causing lateness of scripts. The unavoidable circumstances should be spelled out as accurately as possible. *For example*, documented illness of, or accident involving the writer, accidents of nature (weather-related), etc. A similar penalty and incentive system can be offered to other essential personnel, such as the director and the actors. (See sample contract in Appendix B.)

The contract can be made directly with the appointed writer or writers, or it can be part of an overall contract made with the production house. A writer's contract that is part of the production house contract should include a clause stating that the program manager has the right to see and approve samples of the writer's work before the final contract is signed.

It is advisable to give contracted writers some written guidelines to ensure a clear understanding of the writing obligations.

WRITING THE SCRIPT

Training: Few writers have had previous experience of the Entertainment–Education format, which blends a message with a story, and they will require some training in this method. Training should be given by a recognized and experienced consultant who may be local or international. The training is usually either a one week concentrated workshop or a series of one-on-one sessions over a period of one or two weeks as the writers prepare scripts for the serial drama.

Visiting the audience: Unless writers have personally lived for some time among the audience for whom the serial is designed, it is essential that they visit a representative group. A week-long visit is beneficial if writers spend the time wisely: listening, observing, and making notes. They are likely to obtain a more realistic understanding of the audience if they are in the community purely as visitors and do not share the real purpose of their visit with the people. The firsthand knowledge gained from this time in the community will contribute significantly to the quality and relevance of the scripts. The program manager should plan with the writer(s) where and when this visit will take place and make the necessary arrangements for transport, accommodation, and per diem.

Regular script meetings: Even where the serial is being created by one writer alone, regular script meetings should be held with the writer, program manager, content specialist(s), and perhaps an audience representative. At these meetings, the writer can discuss any difficulties, and ask for help or suggestions as needed. These meetings should be seen not so much as opportunities for criticism, as occasions for sharing, reviewing, and strengthening. Writers often find it helpful to have inputs from others when their own ideas are flagging, and it is always encouraging to know there are people who are sincerely interested in how the story is developing.

The script-tracking system: Scripts change hands many times during development: from writer to program manager to review team, back to the program manager, to typists and translators, and then to the director, technicians, and actors. The program manager needs to have a recording or tracking system that allows anyone involved in the project to know, easily and quickly, where a particular script is at a given time. The tracking system

SAMPLE SCRIPT-TRACKING SYSTEM

PROGRAM #1	PROGRAM #2	PROGRAM #3	PROGRAM #4	PROGRAM #5	PROGRAM #6
Script to P.M. Due: Jan 1 (Fri) Rec'd:	Script to P.M. Due: Jan 8 Rec'd:	Script to P.M. Due: Jan 15 Rec'd:	Script to P.M. Due: Jan 22 Rec'd:	Script to P.M. Due: Jan 29 Rec'd:	Script to P.M. Due: Feb 5 Rec'd:
Translated. Due: Jan 6 (Wed) Rec'd:	Translated. Due: Jan 13 Rec'd:	Translated. Due: Jan 20 Rec'd:	Translated. Due: Jan 27 Rec'd:	Translated. Due: Feb 3 Rec'd:	Translated. Due: Feb 10 Rec'd:
In computer. Date: Jan 7 (Thu)	In computer. Date: Jan 14	In computer. Date: Jan 21	In computer. Date: Jan 28	In computer. Date: Feb 4	In computer. Date: Feb 11
To reviewer. Due: Jan 8 (Fri) Sent:	To reviewer. Due: Jan 15 Sent:	To reviewer. Due: Jan 22 Sent:	To reviewer. Due: Jan 29 Sent:	To reviewer. Due: Feb 5 Sent:	To reviewer. Due: Feb 12 Sent:
From reviewers. Due: Jan 14 (Thu) Rec'd: 1: 2: 3: 4:	From reviewers. Due: Jan 21 Rec'd: 1: 2: 3: 4:	From reviewers. Due: Jan 28 Rec'd: 1: 2: 3: 4:	From reviewers. Due: Feb 4 Rec'd: 1: 2: 3: 4:	From reviewers. Due: Feb 11 Rec'd: 1: 2: 3: 4:	From reviewers. Due: Feb 19 Rec'd: 1: 2: 3: 4:
To writer (Revise) Due: Jan 15 (Fri) Rec'd:	To writer (Revise) Due: Jan 22 Rec'd:	To writer (Revise) Due: Jan 29 Rec'd:	To writer (Revise) Due: Feb 5 Rec'd:	To writer (Revise) Due: Feb 12 Rec'd:	To writer (Revise) Due: Feb 19 Rec'd:
To P.M. Due: Jan 20 (Wed) Rec'd:	To P.M. Due: Jan 27 Rec'd:	To P.M. Due: Feb 3 Rec'd:	To P.M. Due: Feb 10 Rec'd:	To P.M. Due: Feb 17 Rec'd:	To P.M. Due: Feb 24 Rec'd:

	Item 1	Item 2	Item 3	Item 4	Item 5	Item 6
To translator.	Due: Jan 21 (Thu) Sent:	Due: Jan 28 Sent:	Due: Feb 4 Sent:	Due: Feb 11 Sent:	Due: Feb 18 Sent:	Due: Feb 25 Sent:
From translator.	Due: Jan 22 (Fri) Rec'd:	Due: Jan 28 Rec'd:	Due: Feb 5 Rec'd:	Due: Feb12 Rec'd:	Due: Feb 19 Rec'd:	Due: Feb 26 Rec'd:
In computer.	Due: Jan 25 (Mon)	Due: Feb 1	Due: Feb 8	Due: Feb 15	Due: Feb 22	Due: Mar 1
To media director.	Due: Jan 26 (Tue) Rec'd:	Due: Feb 1 Rec'd:	Due: Feb 9 Rec'd:	Due: Feb 16 Rec'd:	Due: Feb 23 Rec'd:	Due: Mar 2 Rec'd:
Recorded, edited, copied.	Due: Feb 19 (Fri) Complete:	Due: Feb 19 Complete:	Due: Feb 19 Complete:	Due: Mar 12 Complete:	Due: Mar 12 Complete:	Due: Mar 12 Complete:
Archive script filed:	Date: Feb 22 (Mon) Master tape filed: Feb 22	Date: Feb 22 Master tape filed: Feb 22	Date: Feb 22 Master tape filed: Feb 22	Date: Feb 22 Master tape filed: Mar 15	Date: Feb 22 Master tape filed: Mar 15	Date: Feb 22 Master tape filed: Mar 15
Broadcast.	Planned date: May 5 Actual date:	Planned date: May 12 Actual date:	Planned date: May 19 Actual date:	Planned date: May 26 Actual date:	Planned date: June 2 Actual date:	Planned date: June 9 Actual date:

Note: P.M. is Program Manager.

can be as simple as an exercise book where the location and progress of the script is recorded. A better approach, however, is the use of a "big board" set up on the wall in the project office. The board lists each episode by number and shows the date by which each script should arrive at each step in the scripting and production process. Each step is checked off and dated as it is completed. This allows for a quick and easy check on script progress and also allows the program manager to see where delays are occurring (see sample on pages 100–1).

The program manager may want to enter the tracking information personally in order to stay acquainted with the status of each script. Alternatively, individuals—such as writer, reviewer, and director—can be responsible for filling in the big board as they complete their individual task and the script is passed to the next person.

The script-tracking system sample on the previous page is based on a continuous system with scripts being written, reviewed, revised, and recorded on an ongoing basis. Episodes are recorded three at a time once a month.

Script Presentation

Script cover sheets, script headers, and script review sheets can be prepared in advance of need and given to the writer to use in script preparation.
The script cover sheet (on the following page) shows:

- The serial title and the episode number
- The date of writing, and whether the script is a draft or a final version
- The writer's name
- The page number in the design document where the episode content is listed (so that reviewers can check content details if necessary)
- The measurable objectives and purpose of the episode
- The list of characters in the script
- A list of the music and sound effects needed for the episode

Listing the measurable objectives and purpose of the episode on the front cover sheet of the script ensures quick and accurate reviewing, and assists the director and the actors to understand the educational intent of the episode. The writer's listing of characters, sound effects, and music assists in the quick and accurate production of the episode.

Script pages: Each page in the script should be set out as demonstrated on the sample script pages (page 107). In some projects, scripts will be written in one language and then translated to another (English, for example) so that they can be reviewed at the home office of the funding agency. Where translation is necessary, it is important that all page and line numbers are the same in both languages, so that comments in one language version will apply accurately in the other language.

SAMPLE SCRIPT COVER SHEET

HE HA HO—SERIES 2
EPISODE # 17
Writer: Celestine Nudanu

FINAL: March 26
20 mins. 12 pages

TOPIC: SAFE MOTHERHOOD: DANGER SIGNS DURING LABOUR AND DELIVERY

DESIGN DOCUMENT PAGE: 40

OBJECTIVES: After this episode the audience will:

KNOW: The problems that can arise during labour and delivery.

What to do when any of these problems arises.

DO: Recognise the danger signs during labour and delivery.

Take a woman who is having problems during labour or delivery to a hospital or well-equipped health center immediately for proper care.

ATTITUDE: Willingness to ensure that every woman is properly cared for during labour and delivery and be prepared to send the woman to a hospital or well-equipped health center if any danger signs occur.

PURPOSES: To educate the audience about the danger signs that can occur during labour and delivery.

To motivate women, partners, family members and community members to act promptly when danger signs occur.

CAST OF CHARACTERS	MUSIC & FX
NARRATOR	
TAKYIWA	Pg. 4 L 60 FX: Sound of door being opened & banged
MAMA DRUG STORE	
ESAABA	Pg. 7 L 109 FX: Sound of a vehicle revving up
MOKOA	Pg. 8 L 128 FX: Sound of heaving
KWESI PAPA	Pg. 8 L 131 FX: Sound of door being opened and banged shut, and general pandemonium
	Pg. 8 L 133 FX: Sound of taxi door being opened and banged and then taxi speeding off

Script Presentation Guidelines

The program manager should ensure that scriptwriters are given these guidelines and that they abide by them in every script. Having uniform script presentation makes the use of the scripts easier for everyone: writer, reviewer, director, actor.

Page header: Each page of the script will have a header that indicates series title, program number, writer's name, writing date, and page number. Notice that the page number is given as 1 of 10. Giving the number of the last script page as well as of the current page allows those using the script (actors, reviewers, director) to be sure they have all the pages of the script. If a computer is used for scriptwriting, this header can be entered and saved for regular use.

Speech numbering: The group of lines spoken by one actor is referred to as a "speech." Each new speech on the page is numbered. Each new sound effect or musical cue is also numbered. This numbering allows the director to cue an actor or technician quickly to a particular line in the script. Perhaps the director wants to stop the recording, go back, and rerecord from a particular spot. The director can easily and quickly give the direction to the actor or the technician, "Go back and pick up from the beginning of line 27."

Some writers recommence speech numbering on each page with the number 1. Others prefer to continue the numbers sequentially throughout the entire script. The disadvantage of this second method is that if, during editing or rewriting, a line is added or omitted early in the script, it mandates the renumbering of every line from there till the end of the script. This is, of course, no problem if the writer is working on a computer that automatically renumbers the lines if one line is changed.

Character names: The name of the character who is speaking is written in upper case. The name is followed by a colon (:) and a reasonable space is left on the same line before the speech begins. The lines in each speech are single-spaced. A double space is left between the end of one character's speech and the beginning of the next character's speech so that it is perfectly clear where one actor's lines end, and those of the next begin.

Actor instructions: Instructions to the actor about how to deliver the line, or about directions to move toward or away from the microphone are given in upper case letters in parentheses at the beginning of the actor's line.
For example:

DOCTOR: (COMING INTO THE ROOM) Now, Mrs. Garda, let's see what we can do to help you today.

In cases where the actor must change tone or make a move in the middle of a speech, the instructions are included in parentheses at the appropriate place. *For example*:

MOTHER: I just don't know what to do with these children .... (CALLING OFF) ... Come here at once all of you. (ON MICROPHONE, SADLY) I suppose I'm just not a good mother.

Speech pause or break: An ellipsis (a series of full stops) is used to indicate a pause or a natural break in a character's speech. *For example*:

NARRATOR: And once again it is time for us to hear the beautiful music of Harold's flute ... I'm sure you remember Harold .... Well, it is time for us to hear him once more.

Technician's directions: All directions for the technician—MUSIC and FX directions—are given in upper case print and underlined, so that the technician can identify quickly those areas of the script which are his responsibility. The first word in a musical direction is **MUSIC**. The first word in a sound effect direction is **SFX**, or simply **FX**. This clear identification helps the technician prepare music and sound effects that can be fed in as the recording takes place. *For example*:

1. MUSIC. THEME MUSIC UP :05. CROSS FADE TO
2. JOSEPH: Oh well, back to work. Every day it's the same old thing ... chop the wood; milk the cows.
3. FX: SOUND OF WOOD BEING CHOPPED. MIXED WITH
4. FX. CATTLE MOOING IN DISTANCE

End of page: A speech must never be broken at the end of the page. If all the lines in a speech will not fit at the end of the page, then the whole speech should be transferred to the top of the next page. This is for the actor's sake. Actors must turn their heads briefly away from the microphone as they move the script from one page to the next; it is difficult to read lines while doing this. In the sample script (page 106), line 14, which is an incomplete speech, should have been moved to the next page.

Remarks column: The remarks column is optional and is essential only in scripts where the writer needs to include comments or suggestions for the support materials writer or for monitors or evaluators (see sample on page 107). *For example*, the writer might include in the script a list of special conditions that a health worker should check for before advising a client to use a specific contraceptive.

The writer wants to be sure that this list is included in the health worker's handbook, which is the support material being prepared for this particular series of programs. The writer, therefore, makes a comment to this effect in the appropriate place in the remarks column (see sample on next page). Similarly, the writer might be introducing a new activity or a new way of explaining a concept, and might want the program monitors to observe whether it works well with the audience.

Series Title: *Cut Your Coat According to Your Cloth*   Page 1 of 20
Episode #3   Draft #2
Writer: Kuber Gartaula   Date: June 23

1.	BIR BAHADUR:	(SLIGHTLY NERVOUS) What happened? Did you not ask the health worker?
2.	BELI:	(SARCASTIC) I should not ask the health worker such things? Rather I should do what the father-in-law told us to do. Do you know why your older sister-in-law had a miscarriage?
3.	BIR BAHADUR:	Why?
4.	BELI:	He said that after conception, Laxmi did not take enough nutritious food or enough rest.
5.	BIR BAHADUR:	Forget the past. Since you are home now, why don't you take care of her?
6.	BELI:	No, no ... something has happened to me like what happened to older sister-in-law. (VERY SHY) It is now two months ....
7.	BIR BAHADUR:	(VERY HAPPY) Is it so? Is it two months already? Have you told anybody else?
8.	BELI:	Yes. Other women always know women's business ... only you ....
9.	BIR BAHADUR:	And now, I know too. I am very happy.
10.	MUSIC. SCENE CHANGE MUSIC. BRIEF :05 FADE UNDER FX	
11.	FX. NOISE OF FRYING AND STIRRING VEGETABLE CURRY.	
12.	BELI:	(COMING IN) Why are you in the kitchen so early, older sister-in-law?
13.	LAXMI:	Today, I am preparing food early for the father-in-law ... only ....
14.	MAYADEVI:	Your father-in-law has to go to the fields early today, so you

SAMPLE SCRIPT PAGE WITH REMARKS COLUMN

5. H.W.:   I am glad you have come to ask my advice
               about the contraceptive pill. It may very
               well be an appropriate choice for you.
               First, however, we must be sure that you
               do not have any of the conditions that
               make it unwise for a woman to use the pill.
               May I ask you some questions?

6. SHANA: Yes, of course.

7. H.W.:   Are you taking any medication for TB or
              for epilepsy?

8. SHANA: Goodness, no. I am perfectly healthy.

9. H.W.:   Good. Then tell me, have you ever had any
              blood clots in your legs, your eyes, or
              your lungs?

10. SHANA: No.

11. H.W.:   What about bleeding? Have you had any
              bleeding from your private parts lately?

12. SHANA: No, again.

13. H.W.:   I have already checked your blood pressure,
              so I know you are not in the danger zone,
              which is anything higher than 140 over 90.
              So far things are looking good. And I have
              also checked your breasts and found nothing
              to suggest you might have breast cancer.

14. SHANA: Does that mean then that I can take the pill?

15. H.W.:   I think so. There is one more category of
              women who shouldn't take the pill, but you
              don't fit it.

16. SHANA: What is it?

**Support Writer
please note:**
Be sure to
include this list
of Conditions in
the Health Worker's
handbook

Overseeing Script Translation, Copying, and Distribution

The creative work of writing is only one part of script preparation for serial drama. Equally important and time-consuming activities are translation (where the script must be reviewed also in a language other than that in which it is written), typing, copying, and distribution to reviewers, director, actors, and others. Each of these tasks requires continual supervision from the program manager.

Maintenance of the Time Line

The program manager is responsible for ensuring that all those associated with the scriptwriting process stick as closely as possible to the time line. This begins with ensuring that writers have enough time to complete the script of each episode and revise previously written episodes—where necessary—at the same time. Scriptwriters might readily agree to a time line when the contracts are signed, but the demanding task of writing and reviewing one or more scripts per week can become overwhelming as work progresses.

Time must be allowed for the following steps with every script:

- Writing the first draft of the script
- Entering script into computer (if the writer does not work on a computer)
- Translating the first draft for review (where necessary)
- Reviewing the first draft (review panel)
- Determining which changes to include (program manager)
- Incorporating changes to finalize script (writer or program manager)
- Translating of final script back to original language (where necessary)
- Reviewing final script for typing errors
- Copying final approved script for distribution
- Distribution of script copies to director, actors, technicians, etc.

Activities beyond this point are included in the time line for preproduction and production. In determining the writing time line, it is necessary to consider the work habits of the writer(s). For a 52-episode serial, most writers are more comfortable writing consistently at the rate of two episodes a week for 26 weeks rather than writing 12 episodes at a time with two or three week breaks in between. Encouraging adherence to a consistent writing schedule helps assure the continuity and quality of the story and the accuracy of the message.

Supervised Writing

Some program managers require that scriptwriting be done in the project office. For many writers, simply having to sit down at a particular desk at the same time every day makes it easier to stay on track.

The importance of establishing and maintaining the time line cannot be overstressed. Even a time line that appears to have comfortable latitude should be strictly maintained. Unforeseen events occur in every project, and minor mishaps can throw the project irretrievably off schedule. Permitting the time line to slip once is tacit permission for it to happen again. The very first time scriptwriting falls behind deadline the program manager should discuss the problem with the writer and find a way of making up the deficit. Including penalty and incentive clauses in the contract can be helpful in ensuring maintenance of the time line.

Guidelines for Team Writing

Using a team of two or more writers is sometimes necessary when the serial drama is continuing for a long time, or when it is being broadcast more than once a week, or when the writing is being done as a part-time job. Team writing can be successful if certain guidelines are strictly followed:

Appoint a script editor: This can be one of the writers, and will be the person who keeps detailed records of the plots and characters and how they change as the story moves along. The script editor keeps the story on track and ensures that all characters remain true to their profiles. Scripts should also be reviewed by the script editor.

Ensure that a full synopsis for every plot has been completed: This is essential if more than one writer is working on the serial. The writers should work on the synopses together from the outset, so that all of them understand exactly how the story is going to move forward. (Notes on how to create the full synopsis of each plot and the detailed profile of all major characters are found in Chapter 12.)

Hold regular script planning meetings: During these meetings the script editor and the other writers will review everything that has happened in the stories so far, and make any necessary adjustments for forthcoming episodes.

Allocate the episodes to each writer: The usual arrangement is for each writer to create a number of successive episodes, perhaps 5 at a time. If one writer finds it really necessary to make any significant changes in character or plot, the other writers and the editor should be notified immediately of these changes.

Share the completed episodes: Each writer should be given a copy of all episodes written by the other writers as a means of helping to ensure that the stories stay on track and the characters adhere to their profiles.

SCRIPT REVIEW

Having all scripts reviewed by a small team of appropriate people is essential. Sometimes, however, those who are called upon to conduct the script review find it difficult to fit it into their schedules. Delay of script review can delay the entire production process. One answer is to have regular meetings of the review team where they sit down together to review a number of scripts. If this is not possible, time can be saved by asking each reviewer to restrict evaluation comments to his or her special area:

- The **director** checks the suitability of the script to the chosen medium.
- The **drama specialist** checks the dramatic structure and integrity of the plot, the portrayal and development of characters from episode to episode, and whether or not the dialogue sounds natural.
- The **content specialists** review, against the design document, the accuracy of the information, the suitability of language, and message presentation to the chosen audience.
- The **ministry representative** assures that everything in the script is in line with ministry policy.
- The **funding agency representative** ensures that nothing in the script contravenes agency policy. (This can also be done by the program manager.)
- The **program manager** reviews all comments and determines which will be included in the finished script and how they will be incorporated: will the program manager put them in or must the script go back to the writer for rewriting? Writers should be notified of any changes made by the program manager that affect the overall story or message. Every script given to reviewers should have the standard cover sheet and a review sheet for their use.

Briefing the Script Review Panel

The review panel is selected during the design workshop, but it will be necessary to determine a practical process that will allow for ongoing, accurate, and timely review of scripts. An initial meeting should be held with reviewers to discuss such matters as:

- how often reviewers will be given scripts,
- whether they prefer to receive electronic or paper copies of the scripts,
- how many scripts they will be given at one time,
- how much time they will have to review each script,
- how they should record their comments and suggestions,
- how scripts will be delivered to and collected from them,
- in what language each reviewer will need the script,

- how much time the program manager will need to reconcile suggested changes, and
- how much time scriptwriters will need to incorporate suggested changes into the scripts.

Script Review Cover Sheets

Despite the prevalence of computers in today's world, there are still many places where they are not available. Frequently reviewers will not be able to highlight and track their recommended changes on a computer. They will have to make handwritten notes. In such cases, their job and that of the program manager can be made easier if they indicate their suggested changes on a Review Cover Sheet such as the one given here. To save time, the program manager can indicate with a colored marker those parts of the script to which the reviewer should pay special attention.

SAMPLE REVIEW COVER SHEET

"HAPPY AND HEALTHY"
REVIEW TEAM COMMENT SHEET
(Office name, telephone number and e-mail address)

EPISODE #   DATE:

Page 4. Line 7:   *Change to "CHECK WITH HEALTH WORKER"*
Page 15. Line 2   *omit reference to local shops as places to put STD medicines.*

PLEASE RETURN THIS SCRIPT BY_____.
Note: Please list your comments on THIS PAGE (front and back if necessary) noting the page number, the line number and the change you want to suggest. Please comment ONLY on those parts of the script indicated by red marker.

Reviewer's Name   Organization

Date: Telephone number
                                         E-mail

Guidelines for Reviewers

It is helpful for those who have never undertaken script review previously to be given a copy of some guidelines, such as the following, to help them in their judgement of the script.

Entertainment–Education radio serial dramas are designed to encourage the general public to make beneficial changes in personal behavior and in social norms.

Box 6.1
REVIEWER GUIDELINES
In order to ensure accurate and timely review of treatments and scripts, the program manager can follow these guidelines:
1. Provide each reviewer with a finalized design document.
2. Explain the particular aspect of the script each team member should review.
3. Stress the importance of careful and on-time reviewing.
4. Give each reviewer a copy of the Script Time Line, showing when scripts will be sent to reviewers and when comments are expected back or review meetings will be held.
5. Explain to reviewers how to use the review sheet that will be at the front of each script they receive (where comments are not being input electronically).
6. Invite all reviewers to check with the program manager if they have any questions or difficulties.

The drama serial is created:

- to create a *strong main plot* that will attract and hold the attention of the audience by engaging their emotions. One of the main message topics will be woven into this plot.
- to create *3 or 4 subplots*; into each of which will be woven ONE of the message topics.
- to weave messages gradually, subtly, and naturally into the story.

Messages to be included in the drama serial are specified in the design document. It is essential that both writers and reviewers abide by the contents of the design document for every episode.

Reviewers must carefully study both the finalized design document and the approved story synopsis/treatment before they begin to review any episodes. The design document will acquaint them with the scope and sequence of messages to be included in the drama. The synopsis will summarize the action of the story and the characters (especially the role models) who will help motivate the audience to accept the behavior change.

The messages in the design document and in the episodes should adhere to the 7Cs of message presentation, which state that all messages should be:

Correct
Complete
Concise

Clear and logical
Consistent
Culturally appropriate
Compelling

It should be noted that being **complete** does NOT mean that every bit of information on the topic should be given. The message should be *restricted to the main points* that will arouse the interest of the audience. The completeness of the message means informing the audience (either in the drama or at the end of the program) where they can go for detailed information, guidance, and counseling on the topic. If the message is to be spread over two or more episodes, it must still be made **complete** in each episode by informing the listeners where they can go if they need more information right away.

Purpose of the Drama

Reviewers should keep in mind that it is **impossible** for a radio audience to take in and remember many message details in one drama episode. The main **purposes** of (or reasons for) the drama serial episodes are:

- to make the audience **aware** of the recommended behavior change and its advantages. Giving too much precise message in a drama serial episode tends to turn the audience away from, rather than attract them to the behavior change.
- to encourage the audience to **seek further information** (and, where necessary, counseling) from the most appropriate local source.
- **to motivate** the audience to want to make the behavior change or at least find out more about it.

The **purpose** is *not* to provide the audience with every detail of the topic.

If there are emergency situations to which the audience MUST respond for their own safety, it is more beneficial to present these messages as urgent **spots**. For example, if the local water supply has been found to contain poison, it would be unwise to try to make the community aware of this through a drama episode. It should be done through a clear, concise, attention-grabbing spot announcement and through the daily news.

Message Location in Episode

Each drama episode is made up of several **scenes**. Each scene usually continues the ongoing story of one plot (either the main plot or one of the subplots) although sometimes, there can be two or more scenes devoted to one plot.

This division of the episode into several scenes means that the message for this episode will appear in only one—or at the most—two scenes of any episode. The message should NOT appear in every scene if the drama is to be successful.

The message should NOT appear in the very first scene of a serial drama for the general public. Sometimes listeners do not turn on the radio at precisely the right time, or are not paying full attention right away, so the first scene should move the story forward without containing any specific message. It is generally most successful if the message appears in the **middle** of the episode.

Natural Message Presentation

As much as possible, the message should come into the story in a totally **natural** way. It should not be forced upon the audience like a lecture. There should be—**in every episode**—some mention of where the audience can obtain further information about the topic. This might be brought in quite naturally in the character's dialogue or it can be brought in by the narrator or the closing announcement at the end of the episode.

Message Summary

It is generally a good idea at the end of the episode for the narrator to remind the audience **briefly** of the message and the benefits of the recommended behavior change. A standard **Closing Announcement** can also be used to remind listeners where they can obtain further information on the topic. For example:

ANNOUNCER: You have been listening to *Knowledge is Power*. Don't forget to tune in again next week for the next exciting episode of our story. And also don't forget that if you would like further information about any of the important health messages in this drama, please ask your local health service provider.

Review Steps for Radio Serial Dramas

1. Know what the topic of the episode is; check with the design document.
2. Know the "learning style" of your audience. Again, check with the design document.
3. Check the story synopsis to know how far the action of the various plot should have advanced by this episode.
4. Opening narration should

    - be brief,
    - remind audience of recent action, and
    - introduce today's action and location with a sense of suspense or surprise.

5. Hook: Does something happen early in the script to grab the attention of the audiences?
6. Names: Do characters—especially in the early part of each scene—address each other by name or some other identifying word? (*For example*, in Nepal, husbands never address their wives by name.)

7. Location FX: If the scene is set in a location that is often used, is there a brief identifying FX, so the audience will know where the scene is taking place?
8. Are there too many FX or inappropriate use of them?
9. Does the first scene contain the message? (It should <u>not</u>.)
10. Do main characters have a "personality"? Is their personality identifiable through their speech, their actions and reactions, and through what others say about them?
11. Does each scene end on some type of question or suspense (even minimal)?
12. Do the scenes move logically from one to the next—in terms of time, action, message?
13. Are the appropriate **emotions** aroused with regard to the message? (See design document.)
14. Does the **message** come in naturally and logically?
15. Does the main part of the message come in towards the middle of the episode?
16. Is the message presented as a lecture or as a natural "conversation"?
17. Does the episode match the **purpose(s)** of the episode as well as presenting the message?
18. Are the main points of the message repeated, either in the same scene or in another scene?
19. Does the message abide by the **7Cs of message presentation?**
20. Does the episode end on some degree of suspense or question?
21. Does the closing narration make a brief, clear reference to the message as well as encourage listeners to tune in next week?
22. Does the story presentation suit the chosen audience(s)?
23. Is the script the right length and are all speeches (dialogues) of acceptable length?
24. Is any speech (dialogue) broken between one page and the next?
25. Are the pages presented and numbered correctly?

SUPPORT MATERIALS

Although the scripts for the serial drama constitute the number one writing task, the preparation of new support materials can be equally important. Frequently, the support materials for a media project are prepared by someone already employed by the project office. Sometimes, an outside consultant is hired on contract to do the job. In either case, the support materials creator should be prepared to work closely with the design document and with the program manager. The support materials creator(s) should be present during the design workshop and should prepare initial materials to be tested along with the pilot scripts.

It is important to ensure that the support materials suit the cultural and educational background of the chosen audience. Printed support materials, such as booklets, for example, might not be suited to low literacy audiences and for some projects they might be too expensive to produce and distribute. When new print materials are possible and appropriate, the program manager must make sure they are completed, tested and available for listeners before the serial goes on the air.

Guidelines for Preparing Printed Support Materials

Printed support materials that are designed to accompany an Entertainment–Education radio serial drama should follow these guidelines:

Use illustrations as much as possible. Since radio is an aural medium, the print materials should be used to illustrate what cannot be shown on radio. It is wise, however, to avoid using illustrations of characters in the drama. It is better to leave the appearance of the various characters to the imagination of the audience.

Use simple language and sentence structure. Even where listeners are fully literate, it is helpful for supplementary materials to be easy and quick to read and understand. Avoid complicated sentences and ambiguity.

Be consistent. Use the same terminology and definitions as are used in the broadcasts. Consistency is of paramount importance when print materials are designed to supplement a broadcast program.

Follow the broadcast sequence. For instance, Lesson #1, or Part 1, or Chapter 1 in the print materials should contain information that corresponds exactly with the message content of Episode #1 or perhaps episodes #1, #2, #3 in the drama serial, etc.

Check support materials carefully against every episode of the serial drama to ensure consistency. Generally, it is most efficient to have support material writing follow scriptwriting, because usually it is simpler and quicker to adjust the support material than the script.

Pilot test sample support materials with the pilot scripts to ensure that listeners understand how to use the materials and to ensure that the serial episodes are enhanced by, but not totally reliant upon the support materials.

Other Support Materials

There is a variety of support materials that can be used in conjunction with a social development radio drama. As noted earlier, they must be appropriate to the cultural and educational background of the audience.

Calendars

In many cultures, a wall calendar is a very welcome gift. Wall calendars can be prepared with a new page for each new month, or they can display all 12 months on one sheet. In either case, calendars can be designed to remind the audience of broadcast dates and to display reminders of special events such as National Women's Day. Where the audience is literate, a simple written message can be added to each page of the calendar.

Clinic Materials and Posters

Simple, inexpensive posters can be made to hang on the walls of clinics and health posts. These can carry brief supportive messages and pictures to encourage clinic visitors to do the main things being promoted by the drama: wash hands; have children immunized; use condoms; plan family size, etc. It is also possible to provide small leaflets and brochures for clinics in those areas where the clients are comfortable with reading.

Bright, illustrated leaflets on such matters as immunization and HIV counseling can also be placed in food shops (such as grocery stores and markets) which people visit frequently.

Youth-friendly Locations and Trained Volunteers

Support people are just as important as support materials. Indeed, a personal approach is often much more successful than print material.

For example, in Zambia, women in beauty salons and dressmaking shops were recruited to talk to their female clients about condom use. They were given wooden models of the male organ and taught how to teach their clients to put on a condom correctly. Many parents felt much more comfortable having their adolescent girls learn these things from a hairdresser than having to send them to a public place like a health clinic for the information.

There are many ideas that can be used to create support for a radio drama. The program manager and the design team should discuss various ideas and determine what would work best for their culture and their audience.

PROMOTIONAL MATERIALS

Promotional materials generally have two aims: to attract the audience to the broadcast programs, and to arouse in the audience an interest in the behavior change that the serial drama is recommending. Promotional materials do not have to be prepared at the time that drama scripting begins, but they must be ready for use at least one month before the serial drama goes on the air.

It is often best to use a professional advertising agency to create promotional materials, but where this is beyond the financial means of the project, the following guidelines can be helpful:

Guidelines for Preparing Promotional Materials

The main aim of all promotional material should be to remind listeners of the main behavioral objectives of the programs as well as the title and broadcast times. Standard promotional approaches include:

- radio spots, used several times a day, two to three weeks prior to the commencement of the serial broadcast, then once a day, and eventually once a week when the serial is on the air;
- television spots can be useful too, even for attracting a radio audience, but they are useful only when the chosen audience has access to television;
- newspapers can be used for paid advertising and for stories in the news and the editorial columns; and
- posters can be placed in health clinics, in general stores, and on the backs of buses, trucks, and other general transport.

All promotional advertising material should mention clearly the days and times of the broadcasts.

Promotion Suggestions

Create a Slogan

Express in a few words the main emotional focus of the serial drama. Sometimes, the slogan might be the title of the drama.

For example, a radio drama serial in Ghana had the title *He Ha Ho*, which suggested happiness and also stood for Healthy Happy Home.

Create a Jingle

A jingle is a very short song or musical rhyme (of 4–20 lines) that is catchy and easy to sing. The jingle can be used in promotional spots, and/or it can be something that one of the characters in the drama frequently sings.

Create a Logo

It's a good idea to usa a logo (or small picture) that can be quickly associated with the main objectives of the project.

For example, the *tota* and *maina* birds (seen above) were successfully used in India as part of a family planning drive, called *Aao Baatein Karein* (Come Let's Talk).

Work within the Local Culture

Be sure that both the logo and the slogan are understood and appreciated by the audience for whom the drama is created. Something that is exciting and meaningful in one culture might be totally inappropriate in another.

For example, an anti-diarrheal project in a West African country used posters in which the sugar-salt solution was mixed in a brightly colored, highly decorative bowl. The same poster was found to be quite inappropriate in some East African countries where such bowls are used only by very rich people.

Know the Entertainment Preferences of the Audience

If the chosen audience for the serial drama likes humor, use humor in the promotional material; if music is their choice, use music.

Use Characters from the Drama in Radio Promotional Material

Highly successful promotional spots can be designed around one or two of the most interesting characters in the drama. Pilot testing will help determine which characters are likely to have the greatest appeal to the audience. Remember that radio allows the listening audience to imagine the characters the way they would like them to look. It is perfectly all right, therefore, to use the **voices** of drama characters in promotional spots. **Pictures** of them should be avoided.

T-Shirts

T-shirts can be used to display the title of the drama and a particular slogan that the drama might be using. In some cultures, however, t-shirts are not appropriate for women. Head scarves displaying the name and logo of the drama have been used instead for women in some Muslim countries.

Grocery Bags

The manufacturers of plastic grocery bags are often willing to include, for a relatively small price, a few words about the radio drama, or even just the logo and a reminder about broadcast time.

Use Imagination

Using imagination in the preparation of promotional materials is very important. But always remember to test the promotional materials on a sample of the audience to ensure that they attract the right degree of attention and interest.

7

The Preproduction Phase

Script rehearsal is essential to maintain quality and accuracy.

- *Important Tasks to Complete before Production*
- *Training for Actors*

IMPORTANT TASKS TO COMPLETE BEFORE PRODUCTION

As soon as scriptwriting is in full swing, the project enters the preproduction and pilot stage. The program manager is responsible for ensuring that everything will be ready for the on-air date. The following tasks are part of this stage of the project:

Time Line Finalization

When the writers have determined their rate of writing and script revision to the satisfaction of the program manager, it is possible to finalize the time line for all other aspects of the serial drama project. Dates must be established for the following:

- Writing, recording, and testing of pilot scripts and support materials
- Review of pilot test results and specification of changes to be incorporated into future scripts
- Rehearsing, recording, editing and mixing of all episodes
- Creating promotional materials
- Organization of prize distribution
- Initiation of promotional activities
- Field monitoring
- Final evaluation

When the time lines have been completed, they must be distributed promptly to all who will be needing them.

Evaluation Contract Finalization

Finalize the contract with the agency that will carry out evaluation activities such as pilot testing, field monitoring, and final evaluation. Often, an outside agency is used for these activities, rather than having them done by project staff. The agency must be given a copy of the design document and be required to use it as the basis of all its evaluation tools.

Recording, and Testing of Pilot Episodes with the Sample Audience

Pilot episodes are part of the pretesting process. Once the pilot scripts have been reviewed and revised, they are recorded in a fully professional manner. The pilot recordings are then played to small sample groups of the chosen audience(s) who are asked to answer questions about the episodes. These questions are usually presented and discussed in focus groups, but, where appropriate, audience members can be asked to write their answers to the questions. (Questions that can be used to test pilot scripts are included in Chapter 10.)

Pilot Test Result Compilation

There must be as little delay as possible between the end of testing and the compilation of test results that can be shared with the program manager, the writers, and the content advisors. The writer continues with the rest of the scripts only once decisions have been reached, based on these test results, about changes that should be made in story or message presentation. These decisions should not be left to the writer alone, but should be made by the program manager in conference with the writer and other design team members.

Support Materials Testing

Support materials should be tested at the same time as the pilot scripts, and the results should be made available immediately to the support materials writers so that necessary changes can be incorporated. It is also necessary to test the logo and the slogan if this has not already been done by those who designed them.

Standard Announcement Preparation

Most radio serial dramas for social development are funded, sponsored, or supported by some organization or ministry, and these supporters should be acknowledged at the commencement of each broadcast. It is easiest to make this acknowledgment with a standard opeing announcement. (See examples in Chapter 11.)

These standard announcements can be prepared by the program manager and submitted to the appropriate government ministry for approval well in advance of regular recording sessions. Once approved, the announcements can be recorded on a master tape and copied onto the beginning and end of each episode without having to be rerecorded each time.

Air Time Confirmation

It is always wise to confirm that air time has been reserved as requested for the broadcast of the serial drama. Broadcast stations, especially those that are government-owned,

Box 7.1

PREPRODUCTION TASKS

- Time line finalization
- Evaluation contract finalization
- Preparation and testing of pilot episodes with sample audience(s)
- Pilot test result compilation and decisions made about changes needed, based on these results
- Support material (and logo/slogan) pilot testing and inclusion of recommended changes
- Standard announcements prepared
- Air time confirmation
- Promotional materials development and promotion times determined.
- Checking and replenishing essential supplies
- Actor (artist) confirmation and contracting
- Actor training
- Production team training
- Sound effects collection and collation
- Music composition or selection

are liable to change broadcast policies and times arbitrarily. It is wise, therefore, to reconfirm dates and times when production is about to begin.

Promotional Materials Development

This can begin once the scripts and support materials have been approved following the pilot tests. The precise time table for promotional activity development, testing, and use should be established at this time, together with determinations on the frequency of promotional activities. At the same time, agreements should be finalized with all outlets that will carry the promotional materials: newspapers, magazines, billboards, and electronic media, etc.

Essential Supply Checking

This should be done before program recording gets under way. There must be sufficient supplies of tapes or CDs for master copies and duplicates, storage boxes, editing equipment, sound effects storage tape, etc. The materials needed for production will depend largely on the type of production being done (digital, reel-to-reel, post-editing, etc.). The media director should check all requirements at this stage to ensure that there will be no delays once recording begins.

Actor Final Selection

This should begin well ahead of recording dates to avoid the disappointment of preferred actors not being available. The director is responsible for selecting the actors, but the program manager should ask for an audition performance (live or recorded) with actors chosen for leading roles to ensure their suitability for their designated roles. Once the pilot tests have been completed and the actors approved by the audience, the director should provide actors with a copy of the intended recording schedule. Actors who can comply with the schedule can be given written invitations or contracts to perform in the serial drama. In many countries, radio actors are not accustomed to being given contracts, but giving contracts can be a successful way of encouraging professionalism and reliability in actors. Inclusion of bonus and penalty clauses in the contract can also be advantageous. (See sample Actor Contract in Appendix B.)

Production Team Training

Digital recording is now widely used by radio stations and production houses. In many developing countries, however, recording studios are still using less sophisticated equipment. This should not be seen as a disadvantage, especially when it comes to the production of radio serial drama. A system using minimal equipment can work well for serial drama production. This "edit-free" system virtually eliminates expensive and time-consuming postproduction editing. Based on equipment and personnel available, the program manager will have to decide whether the edit-free approach is appropriate, and whether the production team will need training or guidance in this methodology. The guidelines given in Chapter 8 are usually sufficient to help a production team get started in the edit-free system. Technicians and directors new to this system will need to practice it several times (perhaps during pilot episode production) before going into full-scale production. Even where an up-to-the-minute recording studio is being used, it is wise for the production manager to ensure that the production team is experienced with drama recording or if they will need some training.

Sound Effects Collection and Collation

Once the story treatment has been approved and even before all scripts are finalized, the writer will be able to determine the need for local sound effects. Some radio stations and production houses have a supply of commercially produced sound effect tapes, but frequently these are not appropriate to local needs. Most commercial tapes are produced in Europe and America and do not include exotic sounds such as temple bells, local birds, and unusual animals. Such sounds should be recorded in the field and logged ready for recording needs. This task should be organized and completed by the director before regular production commences.

Music is Composed or Chosen

Music should be a distinguishing feature of every serial drama. Well-chosen music will attract the attention of listeners who will soon come to associate a particular melody with the serial drama. Existing tunes, especially traditional ones, are sometimes appropriate for the drama's theme music. In other instances, it might be more appropriate to have new music composed especially for the serial drama. Composition should be undertaken well in advance of recording time. If existing music is chosen, the program manager should ensure that the music is in the public domain (that is, it is not subject to royalty fees). Paying either royalty fees or a penalty for failing to obtain permission to use the music can add considerably to the budget. Copyright generally stays in force for a period of 50 years, so the use of modern music almost always requires copyright clearance or the payment of a fee. If there are any doubts about the rights to the music, the program manager should contact the recording company that produced the recorded version of the music. Failure to obtain the permission and pay the necessary fee can result in a very heavy fine in most countries. Music, whether it is chosen or composed for the serial, can be advantageous in promotional events. If original music is composed, it is advisable to test it with the chosen audience before settling on it.

Training for Actors

In some parts of the world, where radio is not widely used for drama presentations, there is a shortage of trained radio actors. Some directors like to think that they can use well-known stage or street theater actors in radio drama, but radio requires very different abilities and techniques than are needed for "live" theater. It is often necessary to provide some training for the actors who will take part in the drama serial. The training, which preferably should be conducted by someone experienced in radio acting, can take the form of a one-day workshop or can be spread over several shorter sessions. (Guidelines for the training of radio actors are included in Chapter 9.)

8

The Production Phase

A script monitor ensures production accurarcy.

Topics

- *Choosing the Audio Production House*
- *Requirements for the Audio Production House*
- *General Requirements*
- *Resource Requirements*
- *Personnel Requirements*

CHOOSING THE AUDIO PRODUCTION HOUSE

Of major importance to the success of a radio serial drama is the quality of the production house that will produce and record the episodes. For the recording of the serial drama to be carried out efficiently and successfully, the production outlet (whether it is a government radio station or an independent production house) must be able to provide adequate resources, trained personnel, and sufficient, regularly scheduled studio time.

Requirements for the Audio Production House

If the project is working with a local government radio station, it is sometimes difficult to ensure that certain resources and personnel are available regularly at desired times (government stations can be required to stop regular broadcasting at a moment's notice to allow for official announcements). This can result in delayed production or lack of quality. Where the project is working with an outside production house, it is easier to seek the fulfillment of certain requirements as a part of the contract.

General Requirements

Initially, the program manager will make inquiries about such matters as the previous reputation and production record of the production house with drama programs. Today, many audio recording companies specialize in music recording and making commercials. The requirements for serial drama recording differ from both of these. Wherever possible, a company or radio station with previous experience in drama production should be chosen. If no such facility can be found, it may be necessary to enter into a contract with an experienced radio expert (whether local or international) to provide the director and technicians with some initial training in the best methodology for recording serial drama.

Resource Requirements

The following resources are needed in an audio production house for the purposes of Entertainment–Education serial drama production:

Location: If possible, the production house should be located in reasonable proximity to the project office, so that the program manager can check on studio activities easily when needed.

Rehearsal space: The actors will hold an off-microphone rehearsal prior to recording, preferably in the same locality as the recording studio. It is possible to hold the off-microphone rehearsal in the recording studio, but this usually means paying for extra studio time and getting in the way of studio set up.

A studio that is soundproof and large enough: Many small audio production houses that specialize in music or commercials are not absolutely soundproof. For drama, the studio in which the actors work must have no sound leaks, and must have a door that can be locked from the inside so that accidental intruders can be kept out during recording. The sound quality can be checked by recording a short drama episode in the studio and then listening to the playback through headphones. Minor, but disruptive noises (such as a background hum from air conditioning or other equipment, or from street traffic outside the studio window) that may not be heard while standing in the studio will be audible on the recording tape. Such noises are exaggerated when broadcast. They detract from the quality of the finished product and are irritating to the audience. With digital recording, these noises can be "sweetened" in postediting, but it is always advisable to keep the sound as pure as possible during recording.

Each episode of the serial drama is likely to involve a minimum of five actors. There might also be an assistant director in the studio at all times, so it is necessary to have enough room for all these people to be in the studio simultaneously.

A sufficient number of microphones: It is possible to record with as many as six actors standing around one multidirectional microphone, but it is preferable to have no more than two actors sharing a microphone. The ideal situation is one microphone for each actor, so that each can be placed to accommodate the level of the particular actor's voice. This, however, is often an unrealistic expectation, but there must be a minimum of three microphones available for the actors in the studio. Also, it is helpful if each actor can have a headset so that the director can speak directly to him or her from the control room. Again, this is often not a practical request and can be overcome by having an assistant director in the studio receiving the director's comments through headphones and passing them on orally to the actors.

Some directors believe that they can record the various characters separately and then mix them together. This is certainly possible, but it is time consuming. It is also true that many actors find that they can be more convincing in their character portrayal when they are actually interacting with the other characters, as they would on stage.

Well-equipped technical control room: No matter what type of recording is being used, the control room should be next to the studio in which the actors will be working, and have a window between the control room and the studio so that the director can see and direct the actors. The control room should also be equipped with:

- an intercom system, so that the director can speak directly to those in the sound-proof studio.
- a headset for the director so that he or she can be listening to the sound quality as recording takes place.
- a small table or music stand on which the director can set the script, so that both hands are free for directing, and so that the script pages do not get lost when the director puts them down.

If the recording is being done digitally, it probably will not require more than two people in the control room. If, however, the studio still relies on reel-to-reel and cassette tapes, the control room must also be large enough to accommodate a minimum of four people. These four people are the technician working the board and handling the recording machine, an assistant technician who will handle the sound effects and music tapes, the script monitor (from the program office), and the director. In some places, the director likes to have three technical assistants in the control room—one on the board, one in charge of the recording machine, and the third inserting music and sound effects from a cassette tape machine.

In the case of non-digital recording, there is also need for:

- a reel-to-reel tape recorder (for recording the master tape of each episode and for the collection of local sound effects); one or two cassette recorders/players (for dubbing copies of the original); a turntable; and a mixing board. There must also be quality editing equipment. Even when the edit-free system is being used and

---

Box 8.1

PRODUCTION HOUSE REQUIREMENTS

- Location, near the project office if possible
- Rehearsal space
- Studio that is soundproof and sufficiently large
- A sufficient number of microphones
- A well-equipped control room
- Adequate supplies of CDs and tapes
- Adequate supplies of CD and tape storage boxes.

editing is kept to a minimum, there will be a need for a tape cutter, a splicer and editing tape to ensure quality editing.

Appropriate supplies of tapes or CDs: These are required for recording sound effects and other out-of-studio needs, and for making copies of the programs as needed.

Tape and CD storage cans or boxes: The CDs or tapes must be clearly labeled and properly packed immediately after recording to ensure that they are not mislaid or reused.

Personnel Requirements

The audio production house or radio station must be able to provide the following personnel:

Audio director with previous experience directing drama: If no one with previous drama experience is available, then some training must be provided for a director who has other types of audio experience (such as directing commercials). This training can be provided best by arranging for the director to spend some time with a practicing drama director, even if this means a short visit to another country. The director must be willing to work under the supervision of the program manager and to abide by the established time line. The director must appreciate that she or he does not have the right to make any changes to the scripts during production, unless there is a serious difficulty with a word that an actor cannot pronounce comfortably. Difficulties like this should be discovered during the off-microphone rehearsal and referred to the program manager for final decisions if necessary.

Box 8.2
PRODUCTION HOUSE PERSONNEL REQUIREMENTS
• Director
• Assistant director
• Trained technicians (at least 2)
• Actors
• Musicians

Entertainment–Education serial drama cannot allow ad-libbing (changing words or lines during performance) by the actors. Ad-libbing can cause information to be delivered inconsistently, confusingly, or even incorrectly. The director should be aware of this and should agree (perhaps in the contract) to stick to the script at all times or refer to the program manager if changes seem essential.

The program manager should meet personally with the audio director to explain the importance of his or her role and to discuss the working relationships that will exist among program manager, director, script monitor, actors, and scriptwriter.

Assistant director: In the production of a serial drama that will last over many months, it is advisable to have an assistant director, who—among other tasks—can stand in for the director in emergencies. The usual tasks of the assistant director are to assist with rehearsal, production, and final editing, and to ensure that both the studio and the control room are correctly set up in advance of recording.

Trained technicians: These people will operate in the control room and at the editing board, and must be fully trained and experienced so that they can work quickly, accurately, and efficiently, whether digital recording is being used or not. There must be a sufficient number of technical staff and trained backups available in case of emergency. Sometimes the assistant director will be a trained technician and can carry out technician duties in the event that one of the regular technicians is unavailable.

Actors: The production house should be able to provide a list of available actors (male and female), together with a notation of their previous acting experience. If it is found that few of them have previous experience in radio acting, it is wise to arrange a brief radio acting workshop to provide some guidance (see Chapter 9). An initial actors' meeting should always be held prior to the commencement of regular production, during which actors can be told about the aims and importance of the serial drama, and the value of the contribution they will be making.

Musicians: If new music is to be created for the signature tune* and musical bridges** of serial drama, it might be advantageous to request the selected production house to undertake the writing, performing, and recording of it. Musical work can be handled under a subcontract from the production house if necessary.

Other Considerations

- Number and types of previous clients and satisfaction experienced by these clients
- Philosophy, especially with regard to development programs
- Growth record
- Financial stability
- Willingness to consider, discuss and, where possible, accommodate realistic requests from the program manager with regard to production techniques
- Willingness to allow the program manager to attend recording sessions, and to allow a script monitor to sit in on all recording sessions
  (The director has so many things to do at once during drama production that it is helpful to have a script monitor sit in on all recordings, listening to the actors, and watching the script very closely to ensure that no important words are missed or mistaken.)

---

*The signature tune is the theme music that introduces and closes each episode of the serial.
**Musical bridges are the brief interludes of music that can be used to divide one scene of the drama from the next.

- Flexibility with regard to new approaches or ideas
- Willingness to accept that the script cannot be changed without permission of the program manager. Even changes that seem essential for acting purposes should have prior approval from the program manager.
- Ability to dedicate the necessary time, on a regular basis, for the recording of the drama. Many small production houses are eager to accept all the work they can get, even if this means interrupting a previously arranged schedule. In the creation of an Entertainment–Education serial drama, it is essential that the recording schedule be set and maintained (barring unforeseen inescapable difficulties). Agreement must be reached—and included in the contract—that the specified rehearsal, recording, and editing time will be held open for the project.

Provision of Resources

In some countries where there is a shortage of professional production houses, it can be difficult to find one that fulfills the necessary requirements. In such cases, it can be advantageous to arrange a contract between the production house and the funding body that allows for the latter to provide studio resources or equipment as part of payment for work done. If such a contract is to be organized, it should include a clause stating that the materials provided will remain the property of the project, until such time as the production house has completed its contract obligations to the satisfaction of the program manager.

9

Guidelines for Radio Actors

Radio acting requires special skills.

Topics

- *Introducing Radio Acting*
- *What is an Actor?*
- *Preparing for the Role*
- *Rules for Handling the Script*
- *Tips for Radio Acting*
- *The Radio Voice*
- *The Rewards of Entertainment–Education Acting*

1.

INTRODUCING RADIO ACTING

Radio acting is a specialized art, in many ways different from stage or television acting. The program manager should understand these differences, and arrange for radio acting training if the cast is inexperienced. The following guidelines can assist radio actors to understand their job and to give a professional performance.

What is an Actor?

An actor is a person who acts as, or pretends to be, another person (a character) in a dramatic performance. Actors perform in stage plays, in street drama, in films and television, and on radio. In some countries actors are referred to as artists. The term "actor" is more specific, however, because the word "artist" can refer to anyone who performs: musician, dancer, juggler, etc. "Actor" refers only to the people who enact the roles of characters in drama.

Why is the Job of being an Actor in Social Change Radio Serial Drama Important?

Serial drama can change people's attitudes and behavior, and allow them to improve the standard and the quality of their lives. The more convincing the actors are, the greater chance the audience has of believing what the characters are saying or modeling and of changing their lives for the better.

Does Entertainment–Education Serial Drama Require more than Normal Acting?

Yes. Entertainment–Education serial drama actors must be part actor and part teacher. They must be able to act very well so that listeners believe in the characters they are portraying. They must also understand how to present important information clearly and carefully so that the audience can hear it, understand it, and remember it.

PREPARING FOR THE ROLE

Entertainment–Education is a combination of two English words: "entertainment" and "education." Serial drama is a form of radio drama that continues over many months with one episode of the drama being broadcast each week. So, Entertainment–Education serial drama is a form of drama that both entertains and educates the audience over a period of months or years.

Serial drama **entertains** because it tells stories about believable people who have difficult problems in their lives and how they overcome their problems. It is entertaining because it engages the emotions of the listeners. It gives them the chance to love, to hate, to laugh, to be afraid, and to experience tragedy and triumph.

Serial drama **educates** when important behavior change messages are incorporated in the story, and when the characters provide role models for the audience—people they admire and would like to emulate.

Actors should be given the following guidelines to help them do a successful job as Entertainment–Education serial drama actors. They must understand the purpose and objectives of the Entertainment–Education series. The director should hold a meeting at which the program manager can explain the details of the serial drama series to the actors, so that everyone can fully understand what the programs are trying to achieve.

Actors should receive the script several days before the recording takes place and they should study the script carefully and thoroughly to ensure that they:

- Have ALL the pages. Every page is numbered on the top right hand corner with both the number of the particular page, and the total number of pages in the script: page 2 of 10; page 6 of 10; etc. The numbers are written this way so that it is easy for actors to ensure that they have all the pages in the script.
- Mark every speech that they will have to read. The actor can underline the character's name each time it appears; or use a highlighter pen to highlight the entire speech.
- Study the **objectives** of the program, which will be listed on the cover page of the script. This will provide an understanding of the **message** the program is trying to teach, and will help actors understand how to stress or focus the lines.

- Study the *whole* script thoroughly. It is important for each actor to understand the *whole* script, and not just his/her own speeches. Anything that is not understood should be discussed with the director during rehearsal.
- Read all allotted speeches ALOUD several times. Reading aloud allows the actors to find out if there are any lines or words that are difficult for them to pronounce or interpret. Diction marks should be inserted where necessary. More information about diction marks is given later in this chapter. Do not change any words in an Entertainment–Education serial drama. The information in this type of program has been very carefully prepared by experts in the field. Ad-libbing or altering the script in the studio could destroy the accuracy or consistency of the message content that the serial drama wants to bring to the audience. If actors have any question or concern about any of their speeches, they should discuss these with the director during rehearsal.
- Notice if there will be any sound effects heard during speeches. Consider the difference these sound effects might make to the lines that are being presented.
- Remember at all times that the director's decision is final. If actors disagree with the director's ideas they may, of course, discuss this with the director, but in the long run it is the director who makes the final decision.
- Believe in the character. Even if actors do not particularly **like** their assigned characters, they must make every effort to understand the characters and present them realistically.
- Eliminate paper noise. Stage actors have to learn all their lines. Radio actors do not. They can read from the script, but the script causes problems of its own, because the noise of the paper can be heard through the microphone. Actors must learn to handle the script pages very carefully.

Box 9.1

GOLDEN RULES FOR
ACTING IN SERIAL DRAMA

1. Understand the objectives and the importance of the serial drama to the lives of the listeners.
2. Rehearse the script thoroughly.
3. Be on time for all rehearsals and all recording sessions.
4. Do not have pages stapled together.
5. Do not ad-lib or alter any part of the script without the director's agreement.
6. Remember that the director is in charge. The director makes the ultimate decisions.

Rules for Handling the Script

- Never staple the pages together. Turning over stapled pages is very noisy. Do not clip the pages together in any way. If actors receive the scripts stapled or clipped together, they must be sure to release the pages before beginning to rehearse or record.

- At the microphone, separate the page being read from the rest of the pages. Hold the page being read in one hand. Hold all the other pages together in the other hand. To move to the next page, lower all the pages away from the microphone, slip the finished page behind the others. Separate the next page and hold it in one hand away from the other pages.
- Some actors prefer to drop the finished page onto the floor. That can work when there are just two or three people around the microphone, but it can be noisy if there are several actors moving around the microphone. Also, pages dropped to the floor can get lost and confused unless actors write their names on every page of the script before recording begins.
- Keep the script at microphone level while reading from it. Looking down to read the script lowers the chin towards the throat and can hamper the clarity of the voice. At the same time, the script should not be put between the actor's face and the microphone. It should be a little bit to one side of the microphone so that the voice can reach the microphone directly.
- Keep the script from bumping into the microphone or the microphone stand. The slightest bump of script on microphone can create an interruptive noise.

TIPS FOR RADIO ACTING

Speak into the Microphone at all Times

Even though engaging in conversation with one another, actors should not turn their faces towards each other as they speak, as they would on the stage. Turning away from the microphone immediately alters the level and pitch of the voice. However, if the script gives directions such as "turning away" or "leaving the room," the actor can turn away or walk away from the microphone while speaking.

Stand up while Acting

In general, it is better to stand up while recording Entertainment–Education programs. Actors feel more lively and energetic while standing, and it gives more of the feeling of stage acting.

Making a Mistake while Recording

If an actor makes a mistake during recording, he or she should not stop, but keep going until the director calls for a stop. Sometimes what seems like a major mistake to the actor can sound quite natural in the recording. If the recording is stopped, the director will then cue the actor as to where to pick up and start rerecording. Actors are much less likely to make mistakes if they have marked their scripts correctly and rehearsed them thoroughly.

The Radio Voice

Radio acting is very different from stage acting. Stage actors perform before an audience that can *see* them as well as hear them. Stage actors use the whole body to convey the message. Stage actors use a *big* voice—a voice that carries and can be heard from all directions. Stage acting is big acting. Radio acting is small acting. The audience cannot see the actors. They must understand everything through the actor's voice. Radio actors, therefore should imagine that they are speaking to one person only, as if having a one-on-one conversation. The actor's voice must be clear, and all words must be pronounced carefully, but without shouting or making the voice too loud.

Possible Voice Problems

The microphone is very sensitive and picks up sounds that human ears do not normally hear. Actors should listen to their own recorded voices and find out if they have any words or sounds that do not come through clearly on the microphone. Listed here are some common problems that occur while speaking through a microphone:

"S" sound: The sound of the letter "s" can be a problem for some actors. The slight hissing sound of this letter is not really heard in everyday speech. It certainly CAN be heard on the microphone. With some people any word containing an "s" comes through the microphone as a distinct hiss.

This problem of the hissing 's' sound can be overcome by speaking slightly sideways, across the microphone. The problem can also be overcome by pronouncing the "s" sound more quietly than other sounds. This requires practice.

Plosive letters: Certain letters are called "plosives" because they sound like small explosions. In the English language these letters are "p," "b," "d," "t" and they can cause real problems. Through the microphone, they can come out with a loud popping sound. There is a difficulty with some plosive sounds in every language. The radio director and actors should determine which sounds are likely to cause these problems in their own language.

The plosive problem can be overcome by putting more emphasis on the second half of the word and less on the first: petrol becomes petról. In severe cases, the popping sound can be further reduced by speaking across the microphone, rather than directly at it.

Losing the ends of words: As people converse in everyday life, they see each other's faces. People understand what others are saying not only because they hear them with their ears, but also because they see their faces and their mouths as they speak. People **see** what others say as much as they hear what is said.

Listeners cannot see the face of the radio actor. They can only hear the voice. So the actor's voice must be a little bit clearer than in everyday speech. It is important that every word is completed. Words should not be carelessly run together as they often are in everyday speech.

Losing the ends of sentences: In normal speech, many people lower their voices toward the ends of sentences. This is hardly noticed in everyday conversation, but on the radio, it is a problem. A voice that loses strength or fades out suggests that the speaker is moving away from the microphone. For normal radio speaking, actors should keep the voice on the same level right to the end of each sentence.

Speaking too quickly: When acting in an educational radio program, actors should speak a little more clearly than normal. Listeners need a little extra time to take in the new ideas the program is teaching. It is not a matter of speaking more slowly or artificially, so much as saying important words with a little more emphasis than usual.

Using Different Voices

It is very helpful for every radio actor to be able to create two or three different voices. Perhaps, one like a very old person, one like a child, and one like someone from another part of the country or another part of the world. Actors should practice these different voices until they become easy to produce.

Emphasis

In Entertainment–Education radio drama, it is sometimes necessary to give special emphasis to words or sentences. On the stage, emphasis can be given by saying the words loudly, or by accompanying them with clear gestures. Using gestures on radio is obviously not helpful. Using a louder than usual voice also is not very successful on radio, because the microphone distorts loud sounds. Emphasis can be given by leaving a little space on each side of the word or phrase that has to be emphasized.

For example, "There are … FOUR … facts I want you to remember."

Sometimes, the scriptwriter will show where the emphasis is needed by putting dots before and after the word, as in the example above.

Diction Marks (Speaking Marks)

These are also marks that actors can put into their speeches to help them remember when to divide a word so it is easier to understand or easier to pronounce. Actors can also use these marks to indicate when to emphasize one particular word in the sentence. The marks are like this: //. These are called diction marks and can be put into the script during rehearsal.

For example: (Breaking up a long or difficult word) "It is dis//ad//van//tage//ous to have too many students in one class."

For example: (Emphasis) "I would rather//**die**//than go through//**that experience**//again."

Diction marks can also be used to break up a very long speech. *For example*, the actor would have to break up the following speech in order for the listening audience to understand it.

> On this day, which was, after all, one of the most important days of the year, being as it was the President's birthday, the school children had already gathered in the town square for an early morning parade.

Diction marks could be added to this speech in the following way to assist the actor to read the speech clearly:

> On this day,// which was,// after all,// one of the most important days of the year,// being as it was the President's birthday,// the school children had already gathered// in the town square// for an early morning parade.

THE REWARDS OF ENTERTAINMENT–EDUCATION SERIAL DRAMA ACTING

1. Actors get to know their characters well. As they act the part of the same character in many programs, they get to know that character well, and acting the part becomes easier and easier. Actors also get to know all the other characters in the story, and as they work together, they find that the acting job becomes easier and more interesting.

2. Actors know that their acting is helping a great many people to gain a better understanding of life and how to improve it.

3. Actors get paid!

10

Pilot Testing the Scripts

Programs are tested with a sample audience.

Topics

- *The Importance of Pilot Testing*
- *The Purpose of the Pilot Scripts*
- *Five Areas to be Tested*

THE IMPORTANCE OF PILOT TESTING

Pilot scripts guide the success of future programs in the same way that the coastal pilot vessel guides the big ships safely into port. The purpose of the pilot scripts is to ensure that the story ideas and message presentation (in words and by modeling) are appropriate and likely to be successful with the chosen audiences. During pilot testing—which takes place before full time scripting and production begins—focus groups of the sample audiences listen to programs especially created for the pilot testing process. They then respond to a written or spoken questionnaire or participate in discussions related to the programs.

Even before formal pilot script testing is done, some writers like to try out their ideas on representatives of the chosen audience. This preliminary testing can be done without recording the programs. The trial scripts are simply read aloud to the audience representatives, either by the writers themselves or by actors.

The program manager and the evaluation team decide when, where, and how to test the pilot scripts. The writers can be present during the testing, as long as the test respondents do not know who they are. Being aware of the writers' presence can seriously affect the response of the listeners.

Normally, it is necessary to test no more than two or three scripts, as long as the writer has fulfilled these three essential obligations while writing:

- Has become well acquainted with the audience for whom the behavior changes are intended.
- Has consistently been guided by the design document for message development and appropriate language.
- Has structured the plots, setting and characters of the serial correctly.

Pilot scripts need not necessarily be the first few episodes of the drama. If a wide variety of topics is to be introduced in the serial and if more than one audience is to be reached, it is better for the writer to prepare pilot scripts from different parts of the story, and highlight various topics.

If the serial has been well designed and well written, the pilot tests are unlikely to result in a need for major rethinking or rewriting. Rather, the episodes tested will result in minor improvements that will enhance the ability of the serial to hold the attention of the audience and bring about the desired behavior changes.

THE PURPOSE OF THE PILOT SCRIPTS

Pilot scripts should be carefully written to

- introduce the major characters of the drama, including the central uniting character, in order to ensure that they are acceptable and recognizable to the chosen audience;
- convey and model one or two aspects of the message in different ways (or through different characters) to ensure that the audience can understand and appreciate the message; and
- demonstrate the type of emotional involvement and dramatic suspense that listeners can expect in forthcoming episodes.

QUESTIONS THAT CAN BE ASKED DURING PILOT-TESTING

The evaluation team will probably prepare the questionnaire or discussion guide for the testing of the pilot scripts. Their focus usually is on whether or not the audience has absorbed and understood the message. To compile detailed information on these vital aspects of the radio serial drama, pilot-tests (whether they take the form of written questionnaires or focus group discussions) can include some or all of the following questions. The program manager, however, should ensure that the following five questions are answered:

Does the audience accept the programs?

- Does it believe that the program was designed and is appropriate for people like themselves?
  - Do you think this program is about people who live in a community like yours, or is it about total strangers?
  - Do you think it is more suitable for men or for women? Or both?
  - What age people do you think would enjoy this serial? People of your age or people of a different age? What age would that be? Or people of all ages?

- Do any of the characters in the story remind you of anyone you know? Which character(s)?
- Did any of the characters in the story say or do anything that you think would offend or upset any of your friends and relatives?

Does the Audience Understand the Story and the Message?

- Do the listeners understand the program, including the progress of the story, the meaning and importance of the message, and the language used—including message-relevant terminology?

  - What are the names of some of the characters and what are they like?
  - What major events do you think are happening in the story?
  - What do you think is likely to happen next in the story?
  - What do you think might happen eventually?
  - Talk about any part of the story that seemed foolish or unbelievable to you or anything that you did not understand.
  - In one episode of this story, the people of the community will be faced with an AIDS epidemic. How do you think each of the following two characters will react to that news? (Name two characters.)
  - What words or phrases used by any of the characters did you not understand?
  - Were you uncomfortable with the words or language used by any of the characters? If so, what?
  - What information did you hear in the drama that might be useful for you or your friends?
  - What main points of the information do you recall? (This question will help determine if the pace of the teaching is correct.)
  - Was the amount of information given too little, too much, or just right?

Does the Audience Trust the Programs?

- Do they believe that the characters in the drama can be accepted as reliable authorities on the subject being discussed?

  - Who were the people in the story that you felt you could trust if you knew them personally?
  - Who were the people you would *not* trust?
  - Was there anything discussed in the story that you do not believe? If so, what was it?
  - Do you think that characters in the story can be relied upon to give good advice? Why or why not?

- Do you trust the source of information in the story?
- Is there someone else you would rather turn to for advice? Who?

Is the Audience Attracted to the Story?

- Do they genuinely want to hear more of it?
    - Which of the following words would you use to describe this story?

boring	emotional	other words
exciting	interesting	
funny	suspenseful	
ordinary	gripping	
realistic	offensive	

    - Describe any of the characters that particularly attracted your attention. Tell me why this person attracted your attention.
    - If you had the choice of listening once a week at the same time to this program, or to a music program, or a magazine program, which would you choose? Why?
    - Do you believe that this story could happen in real life? Why or why not?

Does the Audience Appreciate the Programs?

- Do they appreciate both the story and the message?
    - Do you think people would be likely to listen to this program on a regular basis? Why? or why not?
    - Tell me why you think this drama is or is not an interesting way to learn some valuable lessons in life.
    - Would you prefer to learn important matters through a drama like this or by listening to an expert give a talk?
    - Why would you recommend or not recommend the drama to your friends and family?

PART 3

For the Writer

11

Writing
Entertainment–Education Drama

An exciting story is an essential ingredient.

Topics

- Entertainment–Education Drama
- Challenges of Learning through Listening
- Fundamentals of Learning
- The Meaning of Drama
- Dramatic Conflict
- Components of a Drama
- The Structure of a Drama
- Types of Radio Drama
- The Multiplot Nature of a Serial
- Advantages of Multiple Plots in an Entertainment–Education Serial
- The Structure of a Radio Serial Episode

ENTERTAINMENT–EDUCATION DRAMA

All radio drama is a form of communication. Drama for social change is special, because its aim is not only to entertain but also to model and motivate positive behavior change in the audience. Creating radio drama for social change offers both an opportunity and a challenge to the writer. There is no doubt that the Entertainment–Education approach can create an appealing and attractive radio serial, but writing such material is very different from writing either pure entertainment or pure instructional messages. The secret of creating an effective Entertainment–Education serial drama lies in blending the entertainment format with the educational message. To create this blend, the writer needs to understand:

- The challenges of learning through listening.
- The intended audience.
- The message(s) and modeling that the drama is to impart and the best way that these can be expressed to the intended audience.
- The structure of successful drama.
- The multiplot structure of a radio serial.
- The advantages of this multiplot structure for introducing and repeating social messages naturally and subtly.
- The function of believable role-model characters as a means of conveying the message and modeling, motivating and sustaining change in the audience.

- The importance of emotion in the drama for attracting and holding the listeners' attention and for inspiring new behavior.
- The power of radio as a medium for entertainment and education.

CHALLENGES OF LEARNING THROUGH LISTENING

In many developing countries, listening skills are better developed than in so-called technological countries where, with the spread of print materials, television, and computers, learning has become less oral and more visual. Nevertheless, learning through radio presents certain difficulties to both instructor and learners, even in developing countries. Most radio audiences are not "listening literate." That is, they are not necessarily accustomed to absorbing new knowledge from radio programs. The radio writer faces the following obstacles in delivering new knowledge by radio:

The use of radio as "background": Much of the time listeners do not truly concentrate on what is being broadcast on the radio. Writers need to motivate the audience to listen with full attention. While the entertaining serial format helps to attract and hold listeners' attention, it is equally important to ensure that listeners appreciate the relevance of the message and its potential for improving their lives.

Informational messages on the radio usually take the form of spot announcements or talks by important people.   Most listeners mentally tune out these messages if they have no immediate relevance to their own lives, and they tune in again when music, news, or something of personal interest comes on the air. They listen in a fragmentary manner, picking and choosing—often quite arbitrarily and unconsciously—which information to absorb and which to ignore. For this reason, the writer must introduce social messages subtly and naturally.

Radio is a one-way medium. Audio directors, actors, and program designers cannot receive immediate feedback from listeners during a broadcast, unlike classroom teachers or participants in a conversation. They cannot respond immediately to listeners' questions or behavior by changing the pace or direction of the message, nor can they stop to inquire if the information is understood fully. It is difficult, therefore, to ensure that learning is taking place and that listeners have the chance to clarify what they have misunderstood.

The **serial drama** format is an excellent medium for overcoming many of these difficulties of learning by radio because it includes:

- a strong and relevant story,
- exciting, believable characters,
- a wide range of emotional stimulation, and
- a variety of ongoing plots.

In order to create successful Entertainment–Education serial dramas, writers should begin with a clear understanding of the fundamentals of learning and of serial drama and its components.

FUNDAMENTALS OF LEARNING

Writing a radio serial drama for social development does not require experience as a classroom teacher. It does require, however, an understanding of three fundamental principles of learning, especially adult learning, since most social change dramas are created for adult audiences. The three fundamental principles are:

Relevance

People learn best when they see that the knowledge being offered to them is relevant to their own lives. A social change drama must show clearly how people can use the recommended behavior changes to benefit their personal lives. This means that not only must the characters and the setting of the drama be appropriate to the audience, but the language (including dialect, proverbs, sayings, etc.) as well. The drama must clearly **demonstrate** how people can put the new behaviors into practice and how they will benefit from them.

Pacing and Incremental Learning

Instruction is most effective when it is delivered at a pace appropriate to the learners. Determining that correct pacing, and at what speed to increase the amount of knowledge given, requires a close understanding of the "students" who are being instructed. The writers must be able to rely on the fact that those creating the design document have a sufficient understanding of the audience to ensure that new knowledge is introduced at an appropriate pace. However, writers must also visit the intended audience(s) and learn—from personal interaction—how quickly and clearly this particular audience can absorb new information.

Distributed Learning

Different people learn in different ways. Some learn from direct instruction, while others are more apt to learn by observing and copying the behavior of their peers. Some **absorb** knowledge after being exposed to it only once, while others need to be exposed to it several times before fully accepting it. "Distributed Learning" (de Fossard et al. 1993) is the term used by educators to describe the process of presenting the same information in several different ways over time. Allowing for distributed learning involves determining how much time (how much of how many episodes of the drama) will be spent on the most important aspect of the desired behavior change. This determination must be made by the design team. The writer needs to be aware of which parts of the message are being deliberately repeated and stressed and be sure to allow for this in the story line.

The Meaning of Drama

The English word "drama" derives from the Greek word "*dran*" meaning "to do." Thus, a drama is a **story** performed or "done" by actors on stage, radio, film, television, in an open field, or even on the street. A drama, like a story, recounts a chain of events and describes a web of relationships involving a person or persons. A drama can be true, but is more often fictional. The major difference between a serial and other types of drama is duration. While a typical drama lasts one or two hours, a serial continues for weeks, months, or years. The story is presented in short episodes on a regular basis, usually once a week or once a day. The typical drama focuses on one major character and the chain of events and relationships in which he or she is involved. In contrast, a serial follows the lives and fortunes of several characters, showing how they relate to and affect one another. A writer must understand the classic structure and components of a typical drama to be able to weave the multiple stories of a serial together harmoniously.

Dramatic Conflict

Dramatic conflict is a vital feature of any drama, whether performed on stage, television, or radio, because it attracts and holds the attention of the audience. Dramatic conflict refers to the unusual, often unexpected, turns that occur in all human activities and that create uncertainty, tension, suspense, questions, or surprise in the audience. Every event, every circumstance, every relationship in life is subject to uncertainty. The most careful preparations can result, inadvertently, in disastrous errors or unanticipated benefits. Even well-intentioned people can make unwitting mistakes with amusing, tragic, or sometimes unimportant consequences. Individual people react differently—sometimes in unexpected ways—to the very same event. These twists and turns and uncertainties constitute the dramatic conflict that creates much of a drama's appeal. Listeners stay tuned to a radio drama to find out how the tensions, the suspense, and the unanswered questions will be resolved. A story without dramatic conflict is static, boring, and unattractive.

For example: Compare the following brief story outlines. Each focuses on the same character and tells a similar story. Version A, however, lacks dramatic conflict, while Version B uses dramatic conflict to increase the interest level and appeal of the story. Version B is far more likely than Version A to attract the interest and sustain the emotional involvement of the audience.

VERSION A	VERSION B
Outline of Story without Dramatic Conflict	**Outline of Story with Dramatic Conflict**
Marta is a midwife who lives in a rural village. She leads a very busy life. Much of her time is spent encouraging young couples to delay the births of their first children and to space later children appropriately.	Marta is a midwife who lives in a rural village. She leads a very busy life. Much of her work involves encouraging young couples to delay the births of their first children and to space later children appropriately.
Marta is an inspiration to all who know her, and she does a great deal of good for the community she serves.	In her private life, she is busy caring for a desperately ill husband and two teenage sons. At the same time, she is plagued by an old traditional healer who lives in the village and believes that the ways of modern medicine are evil.
The story follows Marta through several typical days as she advises and counsels various clients	There are times when it seems that Marta will have to give up her work in spite of the pleas of the community members who need her and love her.
	The story follows Marta through her joys and heartbreaks: the death of her husband, the eventual cooperation of the traditional healer, and the support she enjoys from her sons and her community.

Dramatic conflict follows one of three patterns:

1. A person (or persons) against "fate" or the unseen forces of life. This type of dramatic conflict is not suitable for Entertainment–Education drama, which must assure audience members that they can take control of and improve their lives.
Example A: A famous athlete is planning to take part in the Olympic Games and try for a gold medal. He practices hard and takes good care of himself in preparation for the contest. A month before the Games begin, he is riding home on the bus. A tire bursts, and the bus skids, crashes into a light pole, and overturns. The athlete's leg and hip are injured and he is taken to the hospital. It is clear that he will not be able to compete in the Olympics. He is depressed and angry at his bad luck but is determined to run again, declaring that he will not be defeated by a problem that was not of his own making.

2. One person (or group of people) against another:
Example B: A young woman has a burning ambition to become a doctor. Her father can afford to send her to medical school, but he refuses to pay for her education. He believes that women should not pursue a profession but should devote their lives to the care of their husbands and children. The young woman must either obey her father's orders, find a way to persuade her father to change his mind, or run away from home and find a way to support herself.

3. A person against himself or herself: Many of the most difficult decisions that people make in life are those they must make alone on their own behalf. Choosing between two equally valid options can create a difficult dilemma, although it need not be tragic or earth-shattering.
Example C: A young mother, Glenda, has to decide whether to name her baby daughter Jessie, as she would like to do, or to name her Magda after her paternal grandmother. Glenda realizes that it is important to both her husband and her mother-in-law that the little girl be named for her grandmother. At the same time, Glenda—who was herself named after her mother's sister—knows how much she would have preferred to have a name that no one else in the family had. She would like her daughter to have a name of her own.

The more emotionally charged the choice to be made by an individual, the more likely it is to attract and hold an audience. The dilemma described above, therefore, would not make good drama unless the mother faces dire consequences if she makes the wrong decision about naming her daughter.

Dramatic conflict can cause the audience to be horrified, amused, or emotionally affected in some more moderate way. Indeed, the very same conflict can give rise to different reactions in the audience, depending on how it is handled in the drama. Consider the following storyline, in which people confront a situation over which they have no control (people against fate).

Example D: A man and his wife plan a wonderful wedding anniversary party and invite all their friends. They are extremely anxious that everything will go well, so they spare no expense and they go over every detail a hundred times to make sure nothing will go wrong. Ten minutes before the guests are due to arrive, there is an sudden electricity blackout.

The response to this unexpected turn of events might be:

Tragic, if, in the sudden darkness, the wife falls down the stairs and is killed.

Humorous, if the husband, who has to finish dressing in the dark, puts on mismatched shoes and rubs toothpaste into his hair instead of hair oil.

Emotionally affecting, if the party has to be canceled as a result of the sudden and prolonged blackout. The audience shares in the disappointment of the couple, who see their party ruined after their weeks of preparation and anticipation.

Dramatic conflict is influenced or even caused by the personalities of the characters involved. In Example A, the athlete's personality determined his response to the unfortunate accident, that is, whether or not he would continue to pursue his Olympic dream. In Example B, the father's personality led to his laying down the law for his daughter. Her personality, in turn, will determine how she responds to his treatment and will shape the outcome of the conflict between them. In Example C, the personalities of the mother, father, and grandmother may influence the decision made about the little girl's name. In Example D, the personalities of the husband and wife will influence their behavior during the electricity blackout.

COMPONENTS OF A DRAMA

Every story and every drama—whether it is a one-hour performance or a serial continuing for 10 years—contains the same four components:

Characters

The people about whom the drama is created. (Sometimes, characters are animals or things, as in children's stories, folk tales, and fables.) Most stories revolve around one major character whose strongest personality trait—which may be positive, negative or both—is responsible for or contributes to the dramatic conflict.

Plot

The chain of events or actions in which the characters are involved, and during which the dramatic conflict develops, comes to a climax and is eventually resolved.

Setting

The place(s) and time(s) during which the action takes place.

Theme

The emotional focus of the drama. The theme reflects a universal moral value or emotion that is understandable to all people at all times, such as truth, courage, love, fear, greed, or envy.

Message

Entertainment–Education dramas have a fifth component, which is not normally found in dramas designed purely for entertainment, and that is a specific message or lesson for the audience, which is related to the theme. For example, a drama based on the universal theme of the joy of parenthood might also contain the health message that both fathers and mothers need to be alert to their children's health needs and even willing to forgo other activities in order to provide their children with proper care.

THE STRUCTURE OF A DRAMA

The plot of every story and, therefore, every drama, is built on the same five-part structure:

Introduction

The beginning of the drama, during which the major character appears, perhaps along with one or two other characters, the plot (action) is initiated, the dramatic conflict is begun or hinted at, and the theme is foreshadowed.

Development (with conflict)

The main body of the drama, during which the plot advances and dramatic conflict develops.

Climax

The point where the dramatic conflict becomes so intense that something must happen to end it.

Resolution or dénouement

The final portion of the plot, in which the dramatic conflict is resolved or the problem solved. The conflict may be resolved in an unpleasant manner, for example, by divorce,

Figure 11.1

THE STRUCTURE OF A DRAMA

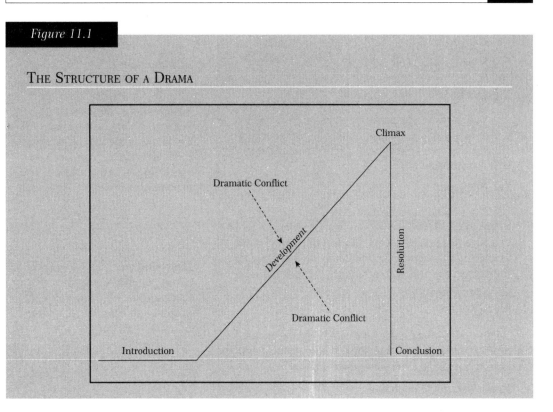

murder, war, or death. Alternatively, the conflict may be resolved amicably or even in an amusing way. In an Entertainment–Education drama, a negative resolution demonstrates what can happen if the prosocial message is ignored; a positive resolution shows the rewards of a message learned and practiced.

Conclusion

The ending, during which the loose ends of the story are tied up, either by the writer or the audience. Some cultures enjoy "dilemma tales," in which the action stops just before the conclusion to allow audience members to fill in the ending for themselves. In an Entertainment–Education drama, the resolution and conclusion underscore the relevance of the message to the listening audience.

For example: The following short story—one of Aesop's fables—illustrates the five-part structure of a drama. It provides a good example for Entertainment–Education writers, because fables traditionally contain an educational message as well as the other four components of a story. Script samples later in this book demonstrate how this story structure is maintained even when a more complex social message is added.

THE BUNDLE OF STICKS

Introduction

A wise farmer was greatly distressed because his three sons were always quarreling with one another. He tried in vain to reconcile them by pointing out how foolish they were.

Introduction: The **characters** are introduced, and the personality of the main character is established. The **setting** is indicated by the work of the main character. The **plot** and **dramatic conflict** are established. The **theme** is foreshadowed.

Development

Then one day the farmer called his sons to his room. Before him lay a heap of sticks which he had tied together in a bundle. Each son in turn was told to take up the bundle and break it in two. They all tried, each son trying to outsmart the other, but all the sons tried in vain.

Development: The conflict among the sons continues. The foolishness of the sons is now also in "conflict" with the wisdom of the father.

Climax

When the sons finally gave up, the farmer untied the bundle and gave his sons the sticks to break one by one. This, of course, they did easily.

Climax: The conflict comes to a head and is resolved by the father's wisdom.

Resolution and Conclusion

Then the father said, "My sons, by this test you can see that as long as you remain united, you are strong enough to resist all your enemies. Once you quarrel and become separated, then you are destroyed."

Moral: Unity is strength.

This story was presented in narrative form, with the storyteller relating the characters' tale for them. In drama, the characters tell—or reveal—their own story. The following dramatized version of the same fable shows how, in radio drama, everything must be revealed through what the characters say and by some occasional, appropriate sound effects. A study of the two versions of the fable will show how dialogue is used to reveal in the drama all the details that are given by the storyteller in the narrative version. Characters, structure, and dialogue are considerably more complex in an Entertainment–Education drama than in this short fable, but the fable demonstrates simply and clearly the building blocks of every story whether told in narrative or dramatic form.

Fables of Our Time **Episode 10: The Bundle of Sticks** Writer: Aesop/Hall	Page 1 of 3 Final Version Date: Jan. 16, '99

1. FX. FARM ANIMAL NOISES IN BACKGROUND, COWS, CHICKENS, ETC. MIX WITH

2. FX. THREE TEENAGE BOYS QUARRELING

3. SONS: (QUARRELING AD-LIB) I did not!
You always do!
It's all your fault.
Well, if you weren't so stupid, it
wouldn't ... Are you calling me stupid?
Just you wait!

*Introduction: The central characters and their personality traits are introduced. The **plot** and **dramatic conflict** begin. The **theme** is foreshadowed.*

4. FARMER: (CALLING LOUDLY) Boys ...
boys ... Stop that quarreling.
How can we ever get any work done
on our farm with the three of you
arguing all day long?

5. SON 1: But it's all HIS fault.

6. SON 2: It is not! THEY started it!

7. SON 3: No ... I'm the one who's been trying
to stop it.

8. FARMER: It's not important who started it and
who tried to stop it. I just don't want
to hear the three of you quarreling like
this again. Arguing is a foolish waste of
time. It is not the behavior of wise folk.
Now come along ... (GOING OFF)
Let's get on with our tasks.

9. MUSIC. BRIEF SCENE CHANGE THEME. CUT.

10. SONS: (QUARRELING AD-LIB). I did not!
You always do!
It's all your fault.
Well, if you weren't so stupid, it
wouldn't ... Are you calling me
stupid? Just you wait!

*Development: The **conflict** continues.*

(Continued)

(Continued)

Fables of Our Time **Episode 10: The Bundle of Sticks** Writer: Aesop/Hall	**Page 2 of 3** **Final Version** Date: Jan. 16, '99

11. FARMER: (LOUDLY INSISTENT) All right.
That's enough. Come with
me, all three of you. (GOING OFF)
I want to show you something.

    The conflict comes to a **climax** *where something must happen to end it.*

12. SON 1: (FOLLOWING) Where are we going?

13. SON 2: (FOLLOWING) I don't know. We'll
have to follow him and see.

14. FARMER: (COMING IN) Come in here to my
room ... all of you. What do you see on
the floor in front of you?

15. SON 3: (CONFUSED) A bundle of sticks.

16. FARMER: Exactly! A bundle of simple sticks.
Now I want to see if any one of you
can pick up that simple bundle of sticks
and break it in two.

17. SON 1: Easy! Any fool can break those
little old sticks. Watch me, Father,
I can do it.

18. FX. CLATTER OF STICKS BEING MOVED
19. SON 1: (GRUNTING) Uh ... it's not ...
so easy ... Uhh!

20. SON 2: Don't be so stupid. Anyone can
break those sticks. Come on, let me
do it. I'll show you I'm the strongest.
Father ....

21. FX. CLATTER OF STICKS BEING MOVED

22. SON 2: (GRUNTING) What's ... the
matter ... with these ... stupid sticks?
They should break easily ... Uhh!

(Continued)

(Continued)

Fables of Our Time	Page 3 of 3
Episode 10: The Bundle of Sticks	Final Version
Writer: Aesop/Hall	Date: Jan. 16, '99

23. SON 3:   Just pass them over here to a really strong man. You'll see how easy the job is. Obviously, Father, I am strongerthan the others.

24. FX. CLATTER OF STICKS BEING MOVED

25. SON 3:   (GRUNTING) What have you done to them ... you two? You put ... stones in them ... otherwise, I could break them easily ... Uhh!

26. FARMER: All right, my sons. Stop ... all of you. Put the bundle of sticks on the floor.

27. FX. CLATTER OF STICKS BEING DROPPED ON FLOOR

28. FARMER: Now then, let me untie the bundle.

29. FX. CLATTER OF STICKS BEING UNTIED AND DROPPED

Resolution and Conclusion:
The conflict is resolved through the personality of the farmer: his wisdom.

30. FARMER: Here, I will give you one stick each ... one for you ... one for you ... and one for you. Now then, each of you, break the stick you are holding.

31. FX. THREE SEPARATE STICK SNAPS

32. FARMER: And so, my sons, by this test you can see that as long as you remain united, you are strong enough to resist all enemies. Once you quarrel and become separated, you are vulnerable and can be destroyed.

*The lesson (**message**) is understood by the charac-ters and by the audience.*

Moral: Unity is strength.

TYPES OF RADIO DRAMA

Radio drama, which follows the same basic principles as all other drama, can be presented in three different styles: as an independent drama, as a series, or as a serial.

The independent drama can be likened to a short story. Like the dramatized fable earlier, it tells the complete story in one broadcast, usually lasting no longer than one hour. It can be shorter, as short as five minutes, for example, when the drama is broadcast as a brief segment on a 30-minute radio magazine program.

The drama series is a **collection of independent dramas** that use the same major characters in each program. For example, the characters of the father and his three sons from the fable above could appear in further dramas, with each presentation telling a different story, underscoring a different theme, and teaching a different message. Extra characters might appear in these follow-on stories, and some might appear in more than one story, but none would appear as regularly as the farmer and his sons. Each drama in the series would be completed in one program. Some of the program titles for such a series might be:

- The Farmer and his Sons and the Plague of Rats
- The Farmer and his Sons Build a Big Barn
- The Farmer and his Sons and the Terrifying Bandits

A situation comedy, also frequently termed a "sitcom," is a series that is intended to be amusing or, at least, to have a happy ending. Situation comedies are now more frequent on television than on radio and tend to be popular with the audience—even when they make use of exaggerated or far-fetched plots.

The drama serial is an ongoing story that continues from one broadcast to another. Each episode is open-ended, and the story is picked up and continued in the next episode. A serial can be likened to a novel, where the story is divided into chapters, with each chapter leading into the next. A serial may be as short as six 15-minute episodes, aired weekly, or it can continue on a daily basis for decades without end. A continuing drama that is presented in fewer than six episodes is usually referred to as a miniseries, or a "two-" or "three-part" drama.

If the fable of "The Bundle of Sticks" were to be made into a serial, the story would not end where it does. Rather, it would continue into more episodes with other characters and other plots introduced to enrich the story.

For example, one son might find it impossible to do as his father suggested and take himself off to the city to set up a business of his own, where he could work independently. The other two sons might work happily together until they both marry and then discover that their wives do not get along. Thus, the story could continue for a long time, following the various adventures of the brothers and their wives.

THE MULTIPLOT NATURE OF A SERIAL

The serial is the drama format that most reflects real life, because it "constructs the feeling that the lives of the characters go on during our absence" (Ang, 1985). Serial drama, therefore, can be most effective as a means of reaching and affecting a wide audience with a story that has all the appearances of reality, while being fiction. One major advantage of the serial is its **multiplot structure**. Several stories are woven together: a central story (the **main plot**) and several additional stories (**subplots**). A serial that runs for 52 episodes typically has three or four subplots accompanying the main plot. Each plot has its own characters and its own dramatic conflict, suspense, climax, and resolution, but all the plots are interrelated in some way. Frequently, a serial, like a series, has a central uniting character who connects the various plots without having a strong, separate plot of his or her own.

For example: The following plot outline, of a serial entitled *Too Late, Too Bad*, includes a main plot and three subplots. The brief outline shows how each of the plots is separate, yet connected with all the others, and how the central uniting character, Dr Peter Moss, helps tie the plots together. The outline also shows how the message is brought in as part of the lives of the various characters; it is not the central or only event of importance to them.

Advantages of Multiple Plots in an Entertainment–Education Serial

The outline of *Too Late, Too Bad* shows how the various plots in a serial fit together and demonstrates some of the advantages of the multiplot approach in dramas used to promote social development. These advantages include the following:

The serial can appeal to a wider range of audience members. While the characters involved in one plot may appeal only to some audience members, characters from other plots—who have quite different lifestyles—can attract other audiences.

Suspense can be maintained throughout all the episodes. As the writer moves from one plot—and its mix of conflict, suspense and crisis—to another, the audience is kept in a constant state of questioning and suspense. This constant, but changing suspense helps maintain their emotional involvement.

The story is enriched by a wide range of characters, and the action becomes more complex as the subplots weave in and out. The ability to suspend the action of one or more plots for a while also helps to enrich the story. Similarly, the movement from the crisis of one plot to the crisis in another helps prevent a frequent problem of poorly constructed Entertainment–Education serials: the suggestion that everything in life follows a predictable course and works out neatly in the end.

A serial can be more emotionally powerful than a single-plot story, because multiple plots allow for a wider variety of people interacting in very different ways and expressing both positive and negative emotions. Since emotional involvement is what attracts and holds listeners, multiple plots increase the chances of attracting and holding the emotions of a wide audience.

Message relevance can be shown through a variety of characters. It is clear that "people cannot learn much ... unless they attend to, and accurately perceive, the relevant aspects of modeled activities" (Bandura 1986). If only one set of characters communicates the social message of a drama, listeners may believe that the message applies only to people in those circumstances. Subplots can show, subtly and naturally, that the message is relevant to a variety of people in differing situations.

The message can be repeated easily and unobtrusively. It can be incorporated into several different plots, presented in a number of different ways, and viewed from different angles.

Multiple plots provide a greater opportunity for message relief. The message can be set aside briefly in one or more of the plots while other elements that enrich the story are developed.

The various Steps to Behavior Change (Chapter 2) can be demonstrated naturally in different plots. The characters in one plot, for example, may be at an early stage in the process, just becoming aware of the need for behavior change. Those in a second plot may be at the point of deciding to take action. Still other characters in a third plot may have adopted the new behavior already and begun advocating it to other family and community members.

PLOT OUTLINE FOR *TOO LATE, TOO BAD**
Central Uniting Character: Dr Peter Moss

Main plot	Subplot A	. Subplot B	Subplot C
Major Character Steven Stan, a wealthy man who lives in Sunville. His family has been feuding for years with the Twigg family over which is the wealthier and more influential family in the district. There is constant friction between the two families. Their hatred of one another is often revealed in their conversations with the local doctor, Peter Moss, who is the family physician for both families.	**Major Characters** Carla and George Brown, a young couple who have moved recently to Sunville. They are expecting twins. George is a builder and is trying to get started in his own business. He is having trouble finding work, and things are very hard for the young couple. Mr Stan has told George several times that he will have some work for him "soon" but these promises so far have come to nothing.	**Major Characters** Hedda and Harry Jones. They live several hundred kilometers from Sunville. Hedda is a home-visit nurse, who devotes a lot of her spare time to helping young people understand sexuality and family planning. Harry is a dreamer and schemer who has no real profession, but who has a strong ambition to make a lot of money in a hurry. He is a distant relative of the Stan family, so he decides to borrow money from them to start a business. He and Hedda come to Sunville to request a loan.	**Major Characters** Mr and Mrs Jadd who work for the Stan family, she in the kitchen and he in the garden. They are uneducated and had more children than they could afford before they learned about family planning. They have four surviving children. Several others died in infancy because the Jadds did not know how to care for them. Mr and Mrs Jadd are working hard to provide for their surviving children and are encouraging them to plan and provide for their own futures.
Conflict comes to a head when Brian Twigg (25) announces that he is going to marry Patty Stan (27). The Twiggs believe Brian is too young to marry and that he has more education and more training to complete before taking ·on the responsibilities of marriage. They blame the Stan family for encouraging Patty to seduce their son, Brian, just to get their hands on the Twigg wealth.	Because of the financial difficulties she and George are having, Carla seriously considers having an abortion. Dr Moss persuades her against this, and although her pregnancy is difficult, she eventually begins to look forward to her child. George does, too, although he is increasingly concerned about how he will support his family.	Hedda visits Dr Moss to find out how she can volunteer to help young people in the Sunville area. At his request, she goes one night to the local hospital to visit a young pregnant girl who is afraid she might have HIV/AIDS.	The Stan family has promised to pay for the university education of the Jadds' eldest son, Bob, who is a hardworking student. He wants to become an obstetrician. Because of what his mother suffered with so many children, Bob wants to work with the community on improving maternal and child health conditions in the area.

(Continued)

*The outline of each plot, as it is presented here, is incomplete; it is intended only as a quick example of how the plots are separate, yet united.

(Continued)

Main plot	Subplot A	Subplot B	Subplot C
Shortly before the wedding date, the Stan mansion burns to the ground. Several people are injured, including some fire fighters and Patty Stan, who is badly burned.	Carla unexpectedly goes into labor on the night of the mansion fire. George cannot locate Dr Moss so he rushes Carla to the hospital, afraid that she might lose the babies—and even her own life.	Harry, meantime, goes to the local bar and, after a few drinks, starts boasting to the strangers around him about his wealthy relatives and their house full of rich goods. One of the strangers in the bar is a thief who decides to enhance his own wealth through a visit to the Stan mansion. It is he who sets fire to the house as he is trying to rob it.	Dr Moss encourages Bob's activities, even taking him with him when he goes to visit patients in their homes. Because of this habit, Bob has come to know George and Carla quite well. He overhears George one day, suggesting to Carla that if he doesn't find work soon, he will have to do something drastic to create a need for his services.
Dr Moss and his nurse, Jane, are called to a nearby house to assist with those who have been injured in the fire, or who are suffering from smoke inhalation.			
During his examination of Patty, Dr Moss discovers that she is pregnant and threatened with a miscarriage as a result of her injuries in the fire.		When Harry returns from the bar—quite drunk—he banishes Hedda from the house, believing that she must have contracted the AIDS virus while visiting the hospital, and that she will infect him if she so much as breathes on him.	When the Stan home burns down, the Jadds are left wondering if this will make a difference to the family's promise of assistance to Bob. They wonder about asking Dr Moss whether he can help if the Stan offer falls through.
		Hedda turns to Dr Moss for advice on how to assure Harry that neither she nor he is in any danger of contracting AIDS as a result of her visit to the hospital.	

The Structure of a Radio Serial Episode

Each program in a serial is called an **episode**, and episodes of all serials are structured in a similar way, whether they are created purely for entertainment or for education as well as entertainment. The typical structure of an episode is:

Signature (or theme) tune: The first sound the audience hears when tuning in to a radio serial is music—the signature or theme tune. This alerts listeners that today's episode is about to start and gives them a few seconds to prepare themselves for the listening experience. The signature tune serves another important function in places where the radio signal is not always clear. It gives listeners a little time in which to tune the radio correctly so that the actors' voices come through clearly when the drama begins. Note that in some cultures, the opening signature music is referred to as "Music: intro."

> **Box 11.1**
>
> STRUCTURE OF THE EPISODE FOR
> ENTERTAINMENT–EDUCATION DRAMA
>
> 1. Signature tune (Intro)
> 2. Standard opening
> 3. Narrator's recap of story to date
> 4. 3–4 scenes
> 5. Narrator's closing comments
> 6. Signature tune (outro)
> 7. Standard closing announcement
> 8. Signature tune to end

Standard opening: When the serial is funded or supported by a government ministry, outside sponsor, or other organization(s), it is usually necessary to acknowledge this with a standard opening, presented by an announcer, immediately after the opening theme music. (See example below.) The standard opening can be prerecorded and copied onto the beginning of each episode during recording.

EXAMPLE: STANDARD OPENING

MUSIC: THEME MUSIC UP 10 SECONDS. HOLD UNDER ANNOUNCER.

ANNOUNCER: The Ministry of Health with support from Johns Hopkins University,

Bloomberg School of Public Health brings you the next episode of *A Better Life*.

MUSIC: THEME MUSIC UP 10 SECONDS. FADE UNDER DIALOGUE.

Brief recap of the previous episode: It is common practice at the start of each episode to remind listeners of what has happened in the story so far, or in the most recent episodes. This recapitulation should be done as briefly as possible, so that the action of the new episode can begin right away.

The recap is usually read by a **narrator** who is like the main storyteller. The audience becomes accustomed to the voice of the narrator as a friendly "guide" to the story.

EXAMPLE: OPENING NARRATION

1. MUSIC. SIGNATURE MUSIC :10. FADE UNDER ANNOUNCER

2. ANNOUNCER: The Family Planning Division of the Ministry of Health, in association with Pathfinder International presents *A New Tomorrow*.

3. MUSIC. SIGNATURE MUSIC UP :05. FADE UNDER NARRATOR

4. NARRATOR: In our last episode, Jofra, our bad-tempered, uncaring husband, stormed out of his home in anger because his mother-in-law had criticized him for once again spending so much money on alcohol. His wife, Judy, is left alone with three small children and a furious mother. Let us join them to see what will happen.

5. MUSIC. SIG. MUSIC UP :05. CROSS FADE TO FX.

6. FX. CHILDREN CRYING IN BACKGROUND

7. MOTHER: (SHOUTING) And if you'd listened to me before you married that idiot, this would never have happened....

8. JUDY: (PLEADING) Mother, please ... the children ....

9. MOTHER: (INTERRUPTING) Don't you "Please" me, young lady. You should listen to me.

ETC.

In place of opening narration, some writers like to use "clips" from previous episodes, as can be seen in the following sample (see next page) from an episode of a well-known Indian Entertainment–Education serial drama *Tinka Tinka Sukh*.

1. ANNOUNCER:	Serial "Tinka Tinka Sukh" sponsored by Prime Time.	
2. JINGLE:	**Advertisement for "Prime Time Media Service"**	
3. ANNOUNCER:	Come, let us listen to the 6th episode of Tinka Tinka Sukh.	
4. MUSIC:	**THEME SONG**	

> *When the day speaks, I agree*
> *When the night speaks, I listen.*
> *In this world of joy and woe*
> *We weave shade to shelter us*
> *From the harsh rays of the sun.*

5. ANNOUNCER:	Listeners, do you remember the accident that occurred in the last episode?
6. CLIP	**(Replay of accident scene from Episode 5)**
7. ANNOUNCER:	Yes, Suraj and Jumman were involved in an accident and the entire village sympathized with them.
8. CLIP	**(Replay from Episode 5)**
9. ANNOUNCER:	Champa and her friends visited Suraj to enquire about his recovery.
10. CLIP:	**(Replay from Episode 5)**
11. ANNOUNCER:	And now, let's listen to the 6th episode to see where the story takes us.
12. MUSIC	
13. GAREEBO:	Nandini, please shut the window. The wind has really picked up. Could you please get me a glass of water? My throat is parched. Oh, God!
14. NANDINI: etc.	Mother, please drink some water ….

Three or four scenes: To keep the serial active and exciting, there should be at least three separate scenes in each 15- to 20-minute episode. This is easily done if various plots have been mapped out in advance and outlined in a full synopsis (treatment). The synopsis is written and approved before any scriptwriting begins. (Information on developing the full plot synopsis can be found in Chapter 12 and Appendix D.)

Closing comments from narrator: Typically, the narrator makes a closing comment about the story and invites the listeners to tune in next time. The narrator's closing comments should be kept brief so that the audience is left on the note of suspense with which the episode concluded.

EXAMPLE: CLOSING COMMENTS FROM NARRATOR

NARR: And so ends today's episode of *Happily Ever After*. What will become of the health worker now that the whole community seems to have turned against her? Do you think she will be able to persuade the community members to bring their babies for vaccination? Be sure to tune in at the same time next Thursday to find out if she is successful.

Signature tune: After the narrator's final words, the signature tune is played to signal the end of the episode. Sometimes referred to as the "outro," this tune can be different from the "intro", ending perhaps on an upward beat of excitement.

Some dramas like to make use of an original theme song at the end of each episode— a song that has both a catchy tune and a reminder of the main theme of the drama. This approach was used in *Tinka Tinka Sukh* where a verse like the following was used to introduce each episode:

The wise, when in the water
Check carefully for currents,
Lest they be swept away.
The wise ensure that their musical instruments
Have all the strings they need
Before they play beautiful music.
The wise, when they reach for the sun,
Use caution, knowing that although it brings glory
The sun has harsh rays, capable of scorching one.

Closing announcements: The station announcer ends the program with a brief announcement similar to the one that opened the program. The announcer may also tell listeners, during this closing announcement, how to obtain support materials, encourage them to write to the radio station, or take other actions related to the program.

If the same information is to be given each time, the closing announcement can be prerecorded and added to the tape or CD of each episode. If the drama is part of a longer program, such as a magazine or a distance learning program, the closing announcements may not immediately follow the drama, but come at the end of the entire program.

EXAMPLE: CLOSING STANDARD ANNOUNCEMENT

14.   ANNOUNCER: You have been listening to another episode of *The Wisdom of Youth*, brought to you by the Ministry of Education in association with UNICEF. We remind you that an information brochure about adolescence and how young people can grow up to be healthy and wise can be obtained by writing to the program. Our address is:

The Wisdom of Youth
P.O. Box 679, X town.

Remember to listen next Wednesday at this same time, 7:30 p.m, for the next exciting episode of *The Wisdom of Youth*.

15.   MUSIC. SIG. MUSIC TO END

Brief repeat of signature tune: The whole program ends with another 5–10 seconds of signature music. If the episode runs short, the music can be extended.

Optional cuts (OC): Many, if not most, radio stations insist that every serial episode be of a very specific length to fit into their allotted program spaces. Even with the most careful writing, it is not always possible to ensure the exact timing of a script. Sometimes the acting interpretation will lengthen or shorten the recorded time. If an episode is a little too short, the time can be filled up with closing music. If the episode is over time, however, it can be a problem. This problem is especially troubling with Entertainment–Education dramas because of the danger of vitally important information or modeling being cut during the recording in order to fit the drama into the available time. For this reason, writers should indicate in the margin of the script those lines that can be cut safely without interfering with the message. These optional cuts can be indicated by putting square brackets around them and marking *OC* (optional cut) in the margin.

EXAMPLE: OPTIONAL CUT

VODA: Look at all the rubbish in this pond! No wonder your children are sick all the time. There must be millions of germs growing in that filthy mess.

OC   [[Anyway, Jodi, that's not even your land. You don't even have any right to throw your rubbish over there.]]

12

Blending Story and Message
in the Drama Plot

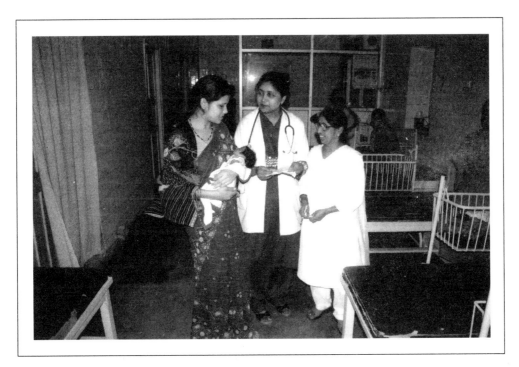

Messages must come into the story naturally.

Topics

- *The Ten Aims of Plot Development*
- *Combining message and Story*
- *Creating Original Plots*
- *Guidelines for Creating Original Stories*
- *Steps in Full Plot Development*
- *Guidelines for Plot Development*

THE TEN AIMS OF PLOT DEVELOPMENT

A successful Entertainment–Education drama depends on a strong plot that fulfills the following 10 aims:

Create an Emotional Experience

Emotional involvement in a drama allows listeners to live out their own hopes and fears vicariously. Most adults do not freely give vent to their emotions, but keep them bottled up inside. Characters in dramas can express strong emotions "on behalf of" audience members, who then experience an emotional release or *catharsis*. It is this emotional experience that makes drama so powerful. The added advantage of serial drama is that the characters in its multiple, ongoing plots can demonstrate realistic ways for listeners to achieve personal—not just vicarious—relief from their own problems.

The other major advantage of the multiple plots of serial drama is that the writer can construct each plot to appeal to

Box 12.1

THE TEN AIMS OF PLOT DEVELOPMENT

1. Create an **emotional** experience
2. Tell a **people** story
3. Work within the **culture**
4. Convey **ideas** rather than words
5. **Show** rather than tell
6. Use **humor**
7. Motivate **positive** change
8. Create **trust**
9. Encourage **advocacy**
10. Be **original**

Source: "Strategies for Improving a Treatment," in *Script Writing for High Impact Videos* (John Morley).
Points 8, 9, and 10 are added for Entertainment–Education writers.

a different audience if necessary. Many, if not all, Entertainment–Education serials use messages designed to appeal to more than one audience. The serial drama allows for one plot to be specifically designed, for example, to appeal to adolescents, while another might be designed to appeal to community leaders, and a third to married couples.

Tell a People Story

People are interested in other people. Dramatic details about the tragedies and triumphs in the lives of other people, who are just like themselves, will always attract listeners. It is people, not messages, who make drama. Serial dramas must focus on the characters who demonstrate the message as they go about their daily lives. In the episode of *Life in Hopeful Village* (page 255–66), for example, the audience pays attention to the serial's message on literacy, because they are gripped by the story of what happens to Littlejohn as a result of his inability to read and write.

Work within the Culture

The drama should reflect the customs of the audience for which it is intended. In some cultures, for example, young people customarily address their elders with terms of respect rather than their names; elsewhere, names are used. In some cultures, people always remove their shoes before entering a house or offering tea to visitors. Other cultures emphasize praying before undertaking any new venture. Nearly all cultures have traditional holidays or days of celebration that are observed in special ways. These cultural norms should be reflected in the drama.

Including local colloquial expressions also enhances the drama's attraction for listeners. The writer should become aware of religious expressions, proverbs, fables, and other colloquial expressions that are widely known and commonly used by the community. (Further information on the use of language is included in Chapter 15.)

Some projects are tempted to believe they can reuse a successful behavior change serial in a different country. Usually, this is not successful. Even in cultures that seem similar on the surface, there are subtle differences which must be acknowledged and reflected if the serial is to be effective as a model for behavior change. Throughout the serial, the writer must acknowledge the local culture and make use of its habits and idiosyncrasies. It is here that the audience profile and the writer's personal knowledge of the audience become so important.

Convey Ideas not Words

One reason for using drama rather than a lecture format is to get away from didactic words. Because it is the medium of the imagination, radio is an ideal instrument for conveying ideas, as long as the writer conveys these ideas through the lives and conversations of realistic characters, not through didactic speeches.

Show Rather than Tell

A major strength of the dramatic serial is its ability to *demonstrate* or *model* what life is like when new attitudes and practices are adopted. In learning situations, demonstration is always more effective than talk. The writer should create characters who can act as role models for listeners by demonstrating a growing understanding of the new ideas presented and by showing listeners how to adopt desired behaviors. One strong role model is worth a thousand words of didactic instruction.

Use Humor

Everybody enjoys a touch of humor in life. While a story need not be uproariously funny all or even part of the time, it helps to have occasional amusing scenes. Humor differs markedly from culture to culture, so the writer must know and appreciate the types of situations and characters that the intended audience finds amusing. Some writers find it useful to create a comic character who has a great sense of humor or is frequently involved in funny situations. An important rule, however, is, *do not deliver a serious message through the words of a comic character*. Since listeners are accustomed to laughing at comic characters, they are not likely to take the words of comics seriously when they deliver a valuable educational message.

Be Positive

While a drama may include difficult, even nasty, characters who are opposed to new ways, the overall thrust of the story should be positive. It is difficult, if not impossible, to educate people by telling them only what they should *not* do. Sometimes, even mentioning the negative side of a situation reinforces—however inadvertently—the very behavior that the story is aiming to replace. Telling listeners not to believe a rumor that vasectomy causes impotence, for example, may plant the notion even more firmly in their minds.

Create Trust

Creating trust in the listening audience is critical to bringing about social change through radio drama. Listeners must have confidence in the story and in the message. To give the drama a sense of authority, role model characters should resemble closely the type of people whom listeners respect in their community. Trust is further enhanced by presenting accurate, appropriate, and consistent information. This can be ensured by constant reference to the writer's brief, which contains the precise message information to be included in the drama as well as definitions of key words and phrases.

Encourage Advocacy

Even though a radio serial can reach many people in a community, it alone is not sufficient to "spread the word." By involving the listeners emotionally, however, the serial can motivate them to pass on what they hear to their families and friends. The writer can encourage this by demonstrating through role models in the serial how listeners who have already adopted the desired behavior can help others understand the new ways and change their behavior.

Be Original

The writer should try to avoid a stereotyped story that follows a predictable pattern, even when dealing with a problem that results from a known and finite set of causes, such as AIDS. The typical drama dealing with AIDS, for example, features a young man who behaves irresponsibly in the belief that he could not possibly contract the disease. Inevitably he succumbs to the disease, and all the "good" characters learn from his demise. An alternative approach might be to focus on an AIDS victim who is not all "bad." Although he may have contracted AIDS from promiscuous, unprotected sex, he might have improved a friend's life—not by warning him against AIDS, but, for example, by bequeathing the friend a bicycle that allows him to earn a living as a messenger. This differentiates the story from others on the same topic and gives it a positive thrust despite the tragic situation.

The multiplot nature of the serial gives the writer the opportunity to fulfill all 10 aims of plot development. While no single plot will achieve every aim, the combination of the main plot and various subplots can encompass all 10 aims comfortably and create a foundation for a successful blending of plot and message.

COMBINING MESSAGE AND STORY

The success of a radio serial for behavior change purposes depends as much on creating an exciting, emotional story as on the presentation of behavior change messages. At the same time, the message cannot be overlooked. Perhaps the biggest challenge facing the writer is successfully blending the message with the story. From the outset, writers should have a perfectly clear understanding of the vital points of message information that are listed in Box 12.2. Writers should keep these points in mind throughout all stages of plot, scene, and development. They should not have to force them into the story at the last moment. A well-constructed story is a good story anywhere in the world.

Even though particular cultural references may not be understood everywhere, a story built on the classic pattern can be enjoyed universally.

There are no hard and fast rules about how original plot development should begin. Different writers work in different ways. Before scripting commences, however, the writer must have the full story in mind and be able to clearly define how the story will develop from the first to the last episode. The overall story must be presented in a full narrative synopsis that shows how each plot will develop, how the plots will interrelate, and which parts of the message will be expressed at what point through each plot. At the same time, it is important that the story is fresh and new in its approach and does not simply repeat the message in a boring way.

Box 12.2

VITAL POINTS OF MESSAGE INFORMATION

The writer should have a clear understanding of:

- The changes the overall radio project hopes to achieve in audience behavior and social norms (measurable objectives).
- The approach to be taken in the drama to assist the audience to reach these goals (purpose).
- The lifestyle of the audience and their current attitudes and practices with regard to the new behavior.
- The overall message of the radio serial.
- The theme or emotional focus of the serial.
- The scope and sequence of the message.
- Glossary definitions to be used for specific technical terms.

CREATING ORIGINAL PLOTS

Finding a way to make a message new and compelling presents a special challenge when the topic has already been addressed previously on radio and in other media. The detailed message content will influence the writer's choice of conflicts in a story, but *relying on message content alone tends to result in stereotyped stories* that may bore the audience and dissuade them from listening. Messages relating to Adolescent Reproductive Health, for example, typically suggest a story that contains the following situations:

- An adolescent girl is ignorant of the meaning of the bodily developments she has undergone during puberty.
- She is attracted to an adolescent boy and he is attracted to her. The girl believes this means that he is in love with her and that one day they will marry.
- She agrees to meet him in a secluded place one night, believing that he is going to propose marriage to her.

- The boy has other ideas and forces himself on the girl even though she says "no."
- The girl becomes pregnant and her life is destroyed because she must drop out of school. She considers having an illegal abortion (or, she actually has an illegal abortion and dies as a result).

While such events do occur in real life, they have been put into stories many, many times. The writer needs to find a way to make each drama serial new and fresh—even when it communicates messages and events that have been covered by other writers in other times and places. The guidelines can be helpful in avoiding stereotyped stories:

Guidelines for Creating Original Stories

Base the plot, characters, and conflict of the drama on the realities of the audience members' lives. Visit and find out what problems of real and lasting concern currently exist in the listeners' community. Use one of these problems as the main plot of the serial, even if it is unrelated to the behavior change the project is addressing. Almost always, the writer can find a way of weaving the message into the action of a plot based around some aspect of the lives of the audience. Basing the main plot on whatever problem is currently of greatest concern to the audience will attract and hold the listeners' attention.

Find out what types of stories and characters the various audiences enjoy. Observe which types of people community members admire and which types they dislike. Discover what type of humor appeals to them, which behaviors they find amusing, and which people they like to copy. Base the drama's characters on these types.

Examine the audience's physical environment closely. Consider whether something in this environment could give rise to a crisis and dramatic climax instead of relying on the message to provide the conflict.

For example: The story could revolve around a young couple who are expecting their first child. The pregnancy has gone well, but on the day the young mother goes into labor, there is a ferocious rain storm. The baby's father is working in the

---

Box 12.3

GUIDELINES FOR CREATING
ORIGINAL DRAMAS

1. Base the drama on the realities of the lives of audience members, including:

   - their current problems,
   - stories types and characters that appeal to them (e.g. mystery, action, love stories, etc.), and
   - their physical environment.

2. Create realistic characters whose lives extend beyond the scope of the message.
3. Include suspense and unexpected twists in the story of each plot.
4. Be creative and think up a plot that no one else has used.

fields, and by the time he decides to go home, the river has broken its banks. He is scared and upset, knowing that his wife is very close to her delivery time. The swollen river also makes it unlikely that the young mother will be able to get to the clinic, or that the health worker will be able to reach the young mother to attend to the birth. The event of the pregnancy and the birth are used to demonstrate important lessons about pre- and postnatal care, but the crisis and climax of the story do not rely on the stereotypical event of something going wrong with the birth itself. Rather the real attraction of the story is on whether or not the father will survive the storm, and if the baby will be born safely. This story could have several endings, so the audience is kept in suspense as they try to guess which way the story will go.

Create characters whose lives extend beyond the topic being addressed by the serial. If the central uniting character is a female health worker, for example, the story should not show her only in the health clinic and in conversation with her clients, and always behaving perfectly.

   She should also have a private life—perhaps with a husband and children—and personal problems with which the audience can sympathize.

Create unusual or unexpected twists in the plots. To make the drama more exciting, first lead listeners in one direction and then change the direction. In *Too Late, Too Bad* (an extract of which was given in Chapter 11), for example, initially it seemed that George might have been responsible for the fire in the Stan mansion. After all, he did complain to Carla that if he could not find a job, he would have to do something drastic to create work for himself. The plot changed direction; however, when it was discovered that Harry's boasting at the bar had been indirectly responsible for the fire.

Be creative and original. Think about the stereotypical approach to the topic, and then use your imagination to think of some other, original—but appropriate—ways to deliver the message. Test new and unusual ideas before using them in the serial by creating a few pilot scripts and inviting some members of the chosen audience to listen to them and comment. It is best to record the test episodes with the actors, music, and sound effects that you plan to use, so that the test audience is judging the drama as it will actually be heard. If this is beyond the budget, however, test episodes can be presented quite effectively in a reading. (Some suggestions for pilot testing story ideas are given in Chapter 10.)

STEPS IN FULL PLOT DEVELOPMENT

The mark of good writing is the ability to create—at the same time—a sense of familiarity and originality. The most successful radio dramas for social development achieve this balance while blending the message harmoniously into the story. Writers might find it easier to develop exciting and appropriate plots if they follow the steps below.

Create a main story (plot) that is likely to appeal to the chosen audience and that is exciting and enjoyable to write. This means knowing the audience very well, knowing the types of stories they like, and also, very often, knowing who in the family is the one who decides which radio programs will be listened to. In some areas, men will not listen to programs which are obviously about women's health. If, therefore, the main message of a drama serial is to be about maternal health, it is important to embrace the message in a story that will truly attract the men who choose the programs for family listening.

For example: The Ghana drama *He Ha Ho is* a mystery in which a man is killed during a wedding ceremony. Whether or not anyone has actually seen the murderer becomes a topic of heated discussion among the villagers. At the same time, even while the murder mystery is evolving, a young schoolgirl claims that she has been raped by the headmaster of the school. And this headmaster has always been a highly respected leader in the community; one whom everyone admires. So there are two challenging mysteries running through this story, both of which will appeal to male listeners. Inevitably, people in the story begin to take sides, for or against the headmaster, and for or against the young man who is ultimately arrested for the murder.

Once the audience was well and truly gripped by the story lines, the writer, Celestine Ndanu, was able to blend in the messages carefully and subtly. Even as villagers were standing around proclaiming their own opinions of what had happened, there were obvious places where messages could be brought in.

Some parents find excuses to take their children out of school, on the pretext that the children are ill. After all, school is a dangerous place now! When the village nurse insists on examining the "sick" children, she finds nothing wrong. But, she is able to use the occasion to educate the parents (and the audience) on signs and symptoms that *do* indicate illness. Furthermore, she can take these opportunities to educate parents (and listeners) about vital points of child health. The main messages on women's health are brought in when one of the central characters becomes pregnant. The husband has to decide between taking his pregnant wife for her antenatal checkup and going to the court house to hear the latest news on the murder suspect. It is one of the attendants at the courthouse who insists that the husband must go back home

---

Box 12.4

STEPS IN CREATING THE
FULL PLOT OUTLINE

1. Create a main story (plot) with audience appeal.
2. Develop the subplots.
3. Write a brief outline of all plots.
4. Develop a full synopsis of all plots together, indicating where the messages come in.
5. Create character profiles.
6. Have synopsis reviewed.
7. Commence scriptwriting.

immediately and escort his wife for her antenatal checkup. He warns the husband that, unless he takes proper care of his wife, he too could be guilty of murder!

The wife of the once highly-respected headmaster was herself someone whom everyone in the village admired. Even while her husband is under suspicion for a cruel and hideous act, she remains true to her character and continues to guide and advise the women of the village on the best ways of caring for themselves and their families.

Develop the subplots, allowing each subplot to carry a separate message (if several main messages are involved) or a different aspect of the main message (perhaps involving a different group of people, representing a specific segment of the audience—such as adolescents).

In developing each of the plots, the writer must keep in mind:

- The action, dramatic conflict, suspense, climax, and resolution of the plot
- The time that elapses from beginning to end of the plot
- The emotional focus
- The aspect(s) of the message to be covered
- The setting
- The major character and his or her predominant personality trait
- Other characters and their relationships to the major character

The characters may be developed in full at this stage, with the completion of a profile for each main character, or profile development can be postponed until later, after the treatment is completed but before scriptwriting commences.

Write a brief outline of all the plots.

Develop a full synopsis (treatment) of every episode, showing how the subplots will come in and where the message will come into each episode, and ensuring that the time lines of all plots match comfortably. The full synopsis of each plot can be done in a chart form (as was done with *Too Late, Too Bad*), or it can be done in a paragraph format, as can be seen in the extract from the synopsis of the Ethiopian serial drama *Journey of Life,* provided in Appendix D.

Develop character profiles for the main characters in each plot (including the central uniting character). Full details of character development and character profiles are given in Chapter 13: Character Development.

Have the synopsis and the character profiles reviewed by both a drama expert and appointed members of the design team who will check to ensure that the messages are being brought in appropriately.

Begin scriptwriting. Once the synopsis and the character profiles have been approved, the writer can begin the writing of complete episodes.

GUIDELINES FOR PLOT DEVELOPMENT

Writers should follow these general guidelines when developing plots for Entertainment–Education serials:

Focus on one or two characters. While several characters may take part in each plot, the story should concentrate on the personality, actions, and interactions of one or two major characters.

Include a clearly identified dramatic conflict in each plot that differs from the dramatic conflicts featured in the other plots. The dramatic conflict should lead to a crisis as a result of the actions and personality of the major character. While a single plot may include several minor crises, there should be one major crisis in each plot that leads to a dramatic change (whether positive or negative) in the life of the major character. This crisis—as it develops—should raise questions in the minds of the audience. Which way do they want the crisis to be resolved? What would they do under similar circumstances? Do the characters truly deserve what is happening to them? How and when will the crisis be resolved?

Link each plot with the others. Each of the plots in a serial should connect in some way with the others, particularly with the main plot. As in life, so in a radio serial, the resolution of a conflict in one plot can create repercussions, either negative or positive, in another plot. The central uniting character also helps strengthen the connection between plots by playing an important part in each one.

Have a clear and consistent time line. The writer must establish a firm time line for the serial as a whole, so that the behavior of all the characters in all the plots is logically possible within the given period of time. If the main plot covers a 12-month period, for example, it would be impossible for a woman in one of the subplots to give birth to three children during the course of the serial, unless she had twins or triplets. Inexperienced writers and writers who do not prepare a full treatment before scripting often lose track

---

Box 12.5

GUIDELINES FOR PLOT DEVELOPMENT

- Focus on one or two characters.
- Include a clearly identified dramatic conflict.
- Link each plot with the others.
- Have a clear and consistent time line.
- Be logical.
- Keep to one main setting.
- Reflect a predominant emotion.
- Maintain cultural and linguistic integrity.

of the time line. Regular listeners, however, rarely do, and, once they detect inconsistencies in time, they will quickly lose trust and interest in the serial. The careful adherence to a specified and limited period of time in a serial is sometimes referred to as **unity of time.**

Be logical. Even imaginative and exaggerated fiction must be logical if listeners are to take it seriously. All too frequently, family planning dramas present a husband and wife who are suffering severe economic and emotional hardship as a result of their large number of children. A common mistake is to show their economic and emotional woes disappearing almost overnight when they agree—after many years of hesitation—to adopt family planning. This is illogical and virtually impossible. They still have the large family to support. Moreover, it is misleading, because it suggests that no matter how many children a couple have, as soon as they agree to plan their family, everything will work out all right. Listeners will suspect that the drama is distorting reality for the sake of the message, and they will no longer trust the program's message.

Another frequent mistake in behavior change dramas, is suggesting that a character becomes perfect in every respect once he or she adopts the recommended new behavior. Consider an adolescent who is portrayed as a school dropout, a spendthrift, and a drug addict, who belongs to a gang and is living under the impression that he has the right to have whatever he wants in life. During the course of the drama, he learns from a young woman—to whom he is very attracted—that the only reliable way to succeed in life is to take responsibility for all your actions even during your adolescent years. Immediately, he gives up drugs and his addiction disappears overnight. He gets a top level job with a big firm (even though he apparently had no qualifications) and sets about preparing for his marriage to the young woman of his choice. While this outcome is theoretically possible, it is neither logical nor believable! Even fiction must be logical.

Establish a main setting for each plot. Each plot should have its own unique, established setting; this is referred to as **unity of place**. While characters can visit a new location whenever the plot demands, it is easier for the audience to follow the story if most of the action in each plot takes place in an established setting, which can be identified with a simple, but consistently used sound effect.

Reflect a predominant or characteristic emotion. In a serial of limited duration (that is, 52 episodes or fewer), each plot should evoke one predominant emotion rather than try to cover a range of emotions. The major character of each plot, and his or her actions, must evoke some degree of recognition and response from audience members, even if they dislike the character. The aim is for the audience to experience *emotional involvement* with the developing crisis in the character's life. The emotional response of the audience can be negative or positive, anger or fear, pity or love, but a plot that fails to arouse a particular emotional reaction in the audience will fail to hold their interest or influence their behavior.

Maintain cultural and linguistic integrity. Each plot is different from all the rest. While the characters in some plots may share similar backgrounds and lifestyles, the characters in other plots may live under quite different circumstances. The writer must ensure that the characters in each plot remain true to their circumstances, speaking and acting in accordance with their background and life style. Maintaining the cultural and linguistic integrity of each plot heightens the reality of the story.

In a serial designed to convey the value and accessibility of higher education, for example, one plot might be set in a city university. To make this plot believable, the writer should ensure that the characters use language appropriate to urban university students. The writer must also provide clear word pictures to enable a rural audience to experience the city university and its personnel in a believable way. (Some guidelines on the creation and use of word pictures are included in Chapter 15.)

13

Character Development

Characters are chosen to suit the audience montage.

Topics

- *The Importance of Characters*
- *Guidelines for Character Creation*
- *Selecting Characters*
- *Creating Characters and Profiles*
- *Bringing Characters to Life*

THE IMPORTANCE OF CHARACTERS

A story cannot exist without characters to carry out the actions of the plot. Each plot in a radio serial drama, including the main plot and each subplot, has its own action, dramatic conflict, and climax, and its own set of characters. Choosing these characters is a challenging task in Entertainment–Education drama, because they must be both entertaining and well suited to the demonstration and delivery of the message to the chosen audience.

The detailed creation of characters for a serial begins as the plots start to take shape and depends on a thorough understanding of the writer's brief. The guidelines given here can help writers fully develop Entertainment–Education characters.

GUIDELINES FOR CHARACTER CREATION

All characters created for an Entertainment–Education serial should be:

Realistic and believable: Nobody is perfect, and no one possesses a perfectly balanced personality. All radio drama characters must exhibit dominant personality traits or characteristics that help make them who they are. There are many personality traits (characteristics)—both good and bad—that characters in a drama can exhibit. Some common ones are:

> ### Box 13.1
>
> #### CHARACTER CREATION
>
> Characters in a radio serial for social development should be:
>
> - Realistic and believable
> - Appropriate to the message
> - Appropriate to the audience
> - Varied in personality
> - Limited in number
> - Adults rather than children

innocence	laziness	ambition
nervousness	shyness	pride
egoism	rudeness	energy
insecurity	stubbornness	honesty
curiosity	dishonesty	reliability
slyness	creativity	thoughtfulness

It is these personality traits, whether negative or positive, that frequently trigger the action in a drama. The major character's dominant personality trait should cause the dramatic conflict and crisis in the story and also shape its resolution. It is important, therefore, to determine the major character's personality traits at the outset and decide how they will affect the other characters.

Many stories fail because the writer creates a main character who is wholly good, without any flaw or personality quirk. This is unrealistic, and such characters are generally boring. They can become more interesting and realistic, however, if, for instance, their good personality traits inadvertently land them in trouble.

For example: The leading character of an Indian drama is Amitra, a beautiful and intelligent young woman. She is polite and modest, but her modesty is exaggerated to the point of extreme shyness and self-effacement. She is a high-school student and would like to have a professional career that continues even after she marries. Amitra has had no education about sexual matters, and her crippling shyness makes it impossible for her to discuss such things with her family, her friends, or even the local health worker.

It is easy to see how Amitra's exaggerated shyness could lead to problems, such as conflict in her married life, and ultimately to a serious crisis. If she does not overcome her shyness and learn how to delay the birth of her first child, for example, she will undoubtedly become pregnant soon after marriage. If she does not learn to speak openly with her husband, she may have child after child without any idea of how to space them correctly—at the cost of her professional plans. If Amitra can overcome her shyness, however, the whole shape of her life may well be different.

As the audience comes to know, love, and respect Amitra, they become increasingly eager for her to maintain her attractive traits of politeness and modesty but to gain control over the extreme shyness which could ruin an otherwise promising life.

A serial must establish the dominant personality trait of the major character in each plot early on, so that the audience can begin to anticipate what will happen as a result. Listeners everywhere are excited when they think, "Uh oh, I can guess what's going to happen now." They enjoy the feeling that they can anticipate what is going to happen even before the character does because they can predict how the character will respond to a certain situation. This feeling of knowledgeable anticipation is possible only if the audience is given the opportunity to know and understand the characters so well that they seem like part of their lives.

Realism also demands that major characters be given roles in life that make it believable for them to affect the lives of many people. For example, in the drama *Too Late, Too Bad* (which was introduced in Chapter 11), the major character in the main plot is Steven Stan, a wealthy, powerful man who, because of his position in the town, can and does influence the lives of many of Sunville's residents.

Appropriate to the message of the serial, so that the characters can be involved naturally and believably with the message content. For example, doctors and nurses are obvious choices as characters when the message is health-related. Other characters also should be considered, however, such as a builder who can encourage men to construct latrines to protect their families' health; a young girl, who teaches other children in her community how to keep their hands and bodies clean, or, as in the case of *He Ha Ho*, when various influential community leaders, such as the clerk at the courthouse and the headmaster's wife become powerful advocates for behavior change.

Appropriate to the audience: The audience should recognize the characters' culture, life habits, and general standard of living. If the audience is largely rural and poor, then at least some of the drama's characters who eventually demonstrate the new behavior must also fall in the same category. It is not always the obvious characters who should be the strongest demonstrators of the appropriate behavior change.

Varied in personality: By varying the personalities of the characters involved in the serial's many plots, the writer makes it easier for listeners to quickly identify the characters in each scene of the story. Clearly different personalities also create an opportunity for a wide range of emotional interactions to be displayed in the story. A variety of personality types, from pessimistic and grumpy to lighthearted and outgoing, also increases the likelihood that listeners will find at least one character who is similar to someone they know.

Limited in number: No more than three or four characters should appear regularly in the main plot, and two or three in each of the subplots. While extra characters can appear occasionally, regularly appearing characters in all the plots in a serial should total no more than 12 to 15. This makes it easier for the audience to remember who is who. It also facilitates the casting of actors and lowers production costs.

As few as two or three characters can create excitement, emotion, and action. Moreover, the writer can create the illusion that more people are present by referring to or discussing characters who do not speak.

For example:

4.   FX. GENERAL BACKGROUND NOISE OF PEOPLE AT A MEETING

5.   BO: Looks like a great gathering here tonight. There's Grandpa Jones over there. Do you know what he thinks of this forest conservation idea?

6.   MO: I certainly do. I spoke to him only last night. He's totally against the idea. For obvious reasons … he makes all his money from cutting down the forest. It'll be interesting to hear what he says on the platform tonight.

Grandpa Jones is not heard speaking in this scene, or in any other scene of the drama. It is other characters who always report on what he is doing and saying.

Adults rather than children: It is wise to avoid child characters, because they are difficult to cast and cannot always be relied upon to come to the studio for recording when needed. While it may be necessary to include some child characters in a series on child care or family health, their appearance should be limited. For radio, it may be possible to find adult actors who can make their voices sound like adolescent and preadolescent children. It is difficult, however, to find actors—either children or adults—who can play the roles of children under 10 years of age convincingly. Frequent references to child characters, who are not actually heard, can make them seem "real" to the audience and eliminate the need to hire an actor to play the part.

For example: In the following scene, the child, Amila, is referred to several times, giving the audience a sense of her presence, even though she is never heard speaking.

14.   KANIZ: He's got terrible diarrhea …. I just can't make it stop.

15.   MOTHER: What are you giving him?

16.   KANIZ: Nothing … every time I give him anything, he has diarrhea again.

17.   MOTHER: Did you give him some salt and molasses mixture?

18.   KANIZ: No … what's that?

19.   MOTHER: It will prevent your baby from being dehydrated. I'll tell you how to mix it.

20.   KANIZ: What do I need?

21.   MOTHER: Clean boiled water. And salt. And molasses.

22.   KANIZ: Molasses? I don't have any molasses. Could your little Amila run to the market and get some for me?

23. MOTHER: Of course Amila can go. She knows the way. But I'm afraid it won't do any good. Old Sam has been forgetful again. He didn't get in any supplies of molasses.

24. KANIZ: Then what am I to do? How can I help my baby?

25. MOTHER: I have plenty of molasses. My mother-in-law gave me several jars two weeks ago. (GOING OFF) Come on inside, Kaniz, we'll make the mixture together. Amila can help. It is time she learned to do these things. (COMING IN) Let's see. First, we need a clean, washed container. Amila, get that basin over there please and wash it for me.

26. FX. SOUNDS OF WATER BEING POURED, SCRUBBING OF BASIN. WATER BEING EMPTIED.

Selecting Characters

The writer should select characters who can fulfill all the requirements of the message in a natural manner. Listeners find a serial more attractive when the characters are distinctly different from one another. A wide range of character types also allows the message to be presented and repeated more naturally. Because an effective Entertainment–Education serial can be motivating change of several kinds, it is helpful to include characters who represent the various Steps to Behavior Change—that is, knowledge, approval, intention, practice and advocacy. Writers should consider the following character options, including both heroes and villains.

Heroes and Heroines

These characters possess positive values and respond constructively to the recommended behavior change. Each hero or heroine must have a dominant personality trait or characteristic that makes him or her unique and that might bring happiness to, or even cause problems for, other people.

Box 13.2

RANGE OF CHARACTERS FOR ENTERTAINMENT–EDUCATION DRAMA

Heroes and Heroines

1. individual hero or heroine
2. older, reliable person or couple
3. counselor, advisor, religious leader (where appropriate)
4. seeker
5. comic

Central uniting character

Villains or Message Antagonists

1. Individual evil person
2. Doubter, skeptic
3. Wayward youngster

The suffering hero or heroine: This is a person who is essentially good, but who becomes involved in a conflict through no fault of his or her own. This person usually suffers as a result of a personality characteristic that is exaggerated, such as being too trusting, or because of a personality weakness, such as being careless about small details. In the long run, however, heroes and heroines—in spite of their human characteristics—prevail against evil forces because of their wisdom and outstanding moral virtue.

The influential hero or heroine: These are people who, in spite of what is happening in their own lives, are able to make a positive impact on the lives of others. Even though these characters may not start out with the intention of being a good influence, they have a positive impact anyway. Like all characters in a drama, these heroes or heroines must be realistic rather than perfect. It is the small imperfections or differences in people that make them unique and interesting.

Older reliable person or couple: In almost any community throughout the world, it is possible to find a "senior citizen" or even a "senior couple" who are respected and admired by everyone. Such characters, therefore, can be very influential in a drama, especially if they start out with traditional, if not old-fashioned ideas, and gradually move into the new behavior. Once the new behavior is accepted by the respected older people, it is highly likely that their example will be followed. The older people are also those in whom younger people very often confide, so they can provide effective modeling of how older people can influence the young.

Counselor, advisor, religious leader: In many societies religious leaders or tribal elders are held in high respect. In other societies it is the trained counselors who are often called upon to provide wisdom and guidance. Including an appropriate character from this category can provide an excellent opportunity to bring in message information in a fairly straightforward manner, while also modeling the idea that it is perfectly acceptable to seek advice for personal problems in life.

Seeker: The seeker represents members of the audience who, consciously or unconsciously, are looking for something better in life. Not uncommonly, the seeker comes under the influence of one of the villains and may appear, for a time, to lose his or her good intentions. Eventually, however, strong personality characteristics save the seeker, who triumphs in the end. The seeker can be used to express the kinds of doubts and misunderstandings that many members of the audience experience with regard to the desired behavior change.

The comic: Often not really a hero or heroine, this character has certain "failings" such as clumsiness, forgetfulness, or brainlessness that listeners find endearing, even when they lead to foolish or amusing behavior. The successful comic displays, in a somewhat exaggerated fashion, a weakness that most or all humans possess but would rather not acknowledge. The comic need not be a separate character in the drama. Instead, comic characteristics can be incorporated into the personality of one of the other characters, such as the seeker or the doubter. In some dramas, the comic, although regarded by other characters as foolish, is the one who demonstrates the fundamental truths of life, and a greater understanding of the desired behavior change better than any other character.

Villains and Message Antagonists

Villains are the people who oppose, conflict with, or make life difficult for the heroes and heroines. They are not always actually wicked by nature, but their personalities bring harm to other characters and impede the progress of behavior change. Message antagonists are those who stand in the way of the desired behavior change, either deliberately or unconsciously, and either permanently or temporarily.

The evil villain: This character opposes the major hero or heroine openly and dramatically. He or she usually does have evil intentions and usually will remain evil throughout the drama, ultimately coming to a bad end.

The doubter or skeptic: This initially antagonistic character is intelligent enough to understand the value of the recommended behavior changes, but is egotistical to the point of believing that nobody else could have ideas of equal value to his or her own. Consequently, this negative doubter tries to point out every little thing that might go wrong with the new behavior in order to block its adoption by others. This character, who frequently becomes the most popular in the story, is especially valuable in behavior change communication by expressing the doubts and fears that might nag listeners. The eventual conversion of the doubter, who ultimately supports and begins to practice the new behavior, creates trust and belief in the listeners.

  As these doubters are not inherently evil and do not deliberately hurt other people, listeners are instinctively attracted to them and find themselves silently cheering for their success. Perhaps the truth is that most people are skeptical or stubborn about some aspects of their own lives, so these doubters allow listeners to feel a little better about their own weaknesses. The character of Littlejohn in *Life in Hopeful Village* (see Chapter 17) is a classic example of the skeptic who attracts the sympathy of the audience.

The wayward youngster: The rashness of youth leads this character to challenge both traditional beliefs and new (adult) ideas and therefore to make foolish mistakes, sometimes with serious negative results for other people. It can be that this character gains wisdom slowly, if somewhat painfully. By the end of the drama, the wayward youth can become a hero or heroine, but the change must be gradual and logical. Listeners are usually attracted to this character as they recall the foolish moments of their own youth. This type of character is particularly valuable in dramas or plots designed to appeal to adolescents.

While heroes and heroines might attract the sympathy of listeners, it is very often the villains the listeners most enjoy. A converted villain frequently makes a more convincing role model than does a near-perfect heroine. Most people identify more easily with the imperfections of a villain than with the flawlessness of a perfect hero or heroine. With this in mind, the writer should remember to make even the greatest heroes and heroines human to the point that they are not perfect or stereotyped.

Creating Characters and Profiles

Every story in the world revolves around one major character who is sometimes referred to as the protagonist (from two Greek words: *prōtos* meaning "first" and *agōnistes* meaning "actor"). Other characters will be involved directly and indirectly with this person and with the action of the story, but it is the protagonist who experiences the main action, dramatic conflict and climax. The personality and behavior of the protagonist, therefore, is of paramount importance to the development and success of the story. The protagonist of the main plot is critical to the serial's ability to attract and hold the appropriate audience.

To make the major character and all other characters come alive for listeners, the writer must first become familiar with every detail of the characters' lives. One of the surest ways to gain this familiarity is to base the most important characters on real people that the writer already knows, or finds in the process of getting to know the audience. The next vital step is writing up a detailed **profile** for each character. The writer must constantly refer to this profile while creating the drama to ensure the consistency of each character. Some writers keep the profile information on file cards; others use a notebook or computer; others like to use photographs or sketches hanging on the wall as reminders. Each profile should contain at least the following information about the character:

- Position in the family (e.g., sister, in-law, grandparent, husband)
- Job
- Life's ambition
- Level of education
- Time lived in present place (e.g., all through life or recent arrival)

- Age
- Religious beliefs
- Attitude towards change and new ideas
- Appearance, including height, weight, color of eyes, hair color and style, and other physical characteristics
- Interests or hobbies (even in poor communities, people can develop special interests; e.g., music, painting, or gardening)
- Animals owned (for profit or as pets)
- Favorite food
- Favorite color
- Habits (e.g., smoking, drinking, oversleeping, laughing a lot, forgetting things)
- Personality trait or weakness that distinguishes this person, and contrasts (or conflicts) with the personalities of other characters
- Personal fear or dislike (e.g., hates insects, scared of deep water, afraid of the dark)
- Speech characteristics (e.g., speaks quickly, drawls, or speaks in brief broken sentences)—speech difficulties, such as stuttering, should never be made fun of.
- Commonly used remark or "catch phrase" (e.g., the catch phrase of the famous American cartoon character, Bugs Bunny, "er … what's up Doc?")—repetition of a certain phrase is especially helpful in establishing a comic character.

While not every item in the profile will be mentioned or demonstrated in the drama, it is important that the writer fill out the details as fully as possible before drafting a script. The list of characteristics evokes a clear sense of what a character would be like in real life; how he or she would behave and react to various people and situations. The detailed profile also helps ensure that each character is different from all others and is portrayed consistently throughout the drama. In addition, the profiles—especially the dominant personality traits of each character—can suggest directions the plots can take and how various characters could interact.

Writers should strive to create characters that inspire listeners to say, "I know somebody just like that," or "that reminds me of …." In some cases, characters in serial dramas have become so real to listeners that they will send gifts to a favorite character who becomes ill or marries or celebrates a special event as part of the story. Having the audience recognize the characters as personal friends is a big step in ensuring continued listening.

Sample Character Profiles

The profiles outlined here are taken from the draft treatment of a proposed Indian serial *Heart to Heart*, show how characters become increasingly real as details are combined.

CHARACTER PROFILES: *HEART TO HEART*

Dr Amit	Kamal	Renu	Wardboy (Raju)
(Doctor in charge of clinic. Central uniting character)	(Older male role model. Advocate of new behavior)	(Kamal's wife, with same interest in advocating new behavior)	(The seeker)
Age: 40–50 years Education: MBBS Degree (Bachelor of Medicine, Bachelor of Surgery)	Age: 37–38 years. Has a limp from polio contracted as a child because his parents did not have him vaccinated.	Age: 33 years Education: Grade 8 pass. Beautiful, a little plump.	Age: 20–22 years Education: Failed 8th grade in school.
He has had some training in communication and is a good communicator.	Practical, wise, serious, yet very caring; loves his wife and his two daughters.	Happy and healthy. Modest, neat, clean, and tidy.	Skinny and lanky; not very strong physically.
Is an excellent teacher and enjoys helping people learn. Has done some traveling in his own country and closely observed how other doctors in charge of clinics perform their duties.	No regrets for not having a son. Chose to have only two children because he suffered from being one of seven, and saw his mother suffer from having so many children. She actually had more than seven, but several babies died.	She likes all food and sometimes objects to what her husband calls "healthy foods." Outgoing, sociable and willing to talk to other women in the community who would like to know how to be like her.	Grew up in a large family with an irresponsible father and was not properly cared for. Ran away from home and was involved in a traffic accident outside the clinic. He was taken in for treatment and has remained there ever since (3 years).
He is a little plump; he really enjoys his food. Going grey, but a full head of hair. Height: 5′9″ Moustache, also going grey. Disciplined in his work, and very clear in the way he presents things.	Owns a general store which his wife runs most of the time, while he works part-time in a typing shop. Eats sparingly and has a passion for what he calls "healthy foods." Slightly bald and beginning to go grey.	Supportive of her husband and her daughters. Works in the shop that she and Kamal own. She works long hours and is always willing to talk to people who come to the shop for goods or to drink tea.	Devoted to the doctor and his wife. Wears a uniform to work, but off duty likes to wear T-shirts and crazy caps, especially if they are bright red. Energetic off the job. Good at fixing things.
Always dedicated to helping people through his profession. His only fear is letting down his clients or not doing his job well. Occasionally	Slim to the point of being skinny. Has a strong dislike of dirt and untidiness.	Loves to watch street theater and to sing. She has a favorite song which she often sings or hums while working in the shop.	Ignorant about "the facts of life." Questions clinic personnel or listens in as they talk to their clients.

(Continued)

(Continued)

Dr Amit	Kamal	Renu	Wardboy (Raju)
he is short-tempered with staff members who are unprofessional on the job.	Has graduated from high school and would like to have more education, but cannot afford the time or the money for it.	Personality trait: Maintains some traditional reticence. Although she can talk to other people, she cannot bring herself to talk openly to her own daughters about sex and related matters.	Likes to "spy on" the nurse and the male health worker (the love interest in the drama).
Married. His wife teaches music and dance at the local school.	Determined that both daughters will have a good education.		Naughty at times when his youth and high spirits get too much for him.
They have an adopted child. They have suffered the disappointment of infertility, but adore their adopted daughter.	Determined to give his family a good life.		Personality trait: Lazy on the job and has to be reminded of his duties.
Always punctual and is irritated by people who cannot be on time.	Personality trait: Impatient to the point of rudeness with people who cannot see the sense in regulating family size.		Frequently says, "I'm sorry. I'm sorry," even before he has been accused of anything.
Personality trait: He is forgetful in his personal life (although never forgetful on the job).	Together with Renu, fills the role of highly respected member of the community and role model to the audience.		Owns a small goat that he rescued from drowning in a drain.
He sometimes forgets his tie or he wears shoes that don't match or he forgets where he puts his keys.			
Fills the role of teacher and counselor in the drama.			

Bringing Characters to Life

Listeners discover the personalities of radio serial characters in the same four ways that they learn about people in everyday life. That is, they take into account:

- What the person does
- What the person says
- What others say about the person
- How the person reacts to particular circumstances

Radio is an ideal medium for revealing both what a person says and what others say about him or her. The following short dialogue between a farmer and a storekeeper

(Fred) reveals something of the natures of each of them without either of them making any comment about the personality of the other.

1. FX. SHOP DOOR OPENING AND CLOSING

2. FARMER: (OFF) 'Morning, Fred.

3. FRED: 'Morning.

4. FARMER: (COMING IN) I haven't seen you in a long time, Fred. (ON MIC) Mind you, that doesn't mean I've been going to any other store.

5. FRED: True.

6. FARMER: But now, suddenly, I seem to need all sorts of things. Mind you, that doesn't mean I've come into money or anything.

7. FRED: Right.

8. FARMER: Let's see. I need some fencing wire ... Er ... was there something else? Mind you, I could use a new shovel.

9. FRED: Shovel. Right. You planting this year?

10. FARMER: Yes. Potatoes I think. I've heard good things about potatoes. Mind you, one can't believe everything one hears.

11. FRED: True ...

Listeners frequently learn about characters by hearing what other characters say about their behavior. Because a listening audience only *hears* and does not *see* what a radio character does, it is the dialogue that must make the character's behavior and actions clear.

14

Developing the Setting

Each plot in the story requires a specific setting.

Topics

- *The Importance of Setting*
- *Time*
- *Establishing Time through Dialogue and Sound Effects*
- *Maintaining Real Time*
- *The Use of Flashbacks*
- *Location*
- *Establishing the Drama's Locations*
- *Sketching the Setting*
- *Conveying Location to the Radio Audience*
- *Using Sound Effects to Establish Location*

THE IMPORTANCE OF SETTING

The word "setting" refers, in drama, to both time and place. The radio audience has a better chance of accepting the reality of the drama if they know both when and where the action is taking place.

TIME

Establishing Time through Dialogue and Sound Effects

Time can refer to the hour, day, month, season, year or even to an era of history. Establishing the hour or the day is relatively easy on radio, because a character can make a passing reference to the time in the course of normal conversation. For instance, a character might say, "Good morning, neighbor. Looks as if it will be a hot day, judging by that sunrise." Some other examples might be, "Hello Namilla. Did you have a good weekend?" or "So ends another week. Man, am I glad tomorrow is the weekend!"

When dramas are set in rural areas, sound effects also can help establish the time. The natural sounds of insects and birds mark day and night. The sound of a rooster crowing, for example, is a universal sign of early morning; while in some areas, the sounds of crickets or other insects indicate that it is evening. For some cultures, church or temple bells or the sounds of prayer can be clear indicators of the time of day.

Seasons can be suggested by passing references to the weather, crops, festivals, holy days or school vacations. Sound effects and seasonal music can also help establish the time of year.

In most radio scripts it is not necessary or even wise to establish the seasonal time too precisely, however, unless it is of immediate relevance to the script. Once a script has indicated a precise time, the writer must be careful to remain faithful to that time in the remainder of the episode and in following episodes.

Maintaining Real Time

Maintaining "real time" in a serial drama has two meanings. First, it refers to the passage of time over the course of the entire serial. Second, it refers to the passage of time within an individual episode. The writer must maintain a balanced time spread from the time the story starts to the time it ends. When writers fail to prepare a full treatment of all plots in advance of ongoing writing, time problems can occur. The writer may be forced to speed up the story in the closing episodes to bring it to a satisfactory conclusion. Many unplanned serials start out slowly, allowing, for example, four or five episodes to go by between the time a woman is taken to the hospital to deliver and the actual birth of her baby. Then, suddenly, about two-thirds of the way through the serial, the writer realizes that time is running out and is forced to leave gaps of three, six or even 12 months between one episode and the next in order to bring the story to its planned conclusion.

Similarly, when the treatment is not fully developed, it is too easy for time lapses in the various plots to get out of sync. While the action of one plot clearly occupies a full year of the characters' lives, a secondary plot just as obviously requires two or more years to complete all its necessary action. Careless writing like this can leave listeners less than convinced about the reality of the story. If they doubt the story, they are also more inclined to doubt the message!

Equally important is the necessity of maintaining real time *within* in an individual episode. Real time means that within any particular scene or episode, listeners have the sense that they are present for the whole of the specific "story" or action, or that they are well aware of how and why additional time has passed. The following scene shows the confusion that is created when real time is ignored.

---

1. **FX. SOUND OF DOOR OPENING**

2. DR: Good Morning, Mama Jeno. Please come in. I am happy to see you this morning.

3. JENO: Good Morning, Doctor. I am sorry to bother you. I shall take up only a few minutes of your time. I hate to be a bother to you.

(Continued)

(Continued)

4. DR: (PATIENTLY) My time is your time, Mama Jeno. What can I do to help you?

5. JENO: It's not me. It's my baby. He throws up all the time. That's why I didn't bring him with me. I was afraid he would throw up in here and mess everything up. But my sister is bringing him. She will be here any minute now.

6. DR: That's good, Mama Jeno. I think it would be better if I could see him. Then I can examine him and see what the problem is.

7. JENO: Yes, doctor. Shall I see if she is here yet?

8. DR: Yes, do. You and I have been sitting here talking for 30 minutes. She surely should be here by now.

9. JENO: I'll look.

10. FX. DOOR OPENS. CLOSES.

Listeners realize that nowhere near 30 minutes has elapsed from the time the door opened at the start of the scene until the time Mama Jeno went to see if her sister had arrived. They are left wondering if part of the story has been omitted or if they have missed something by not paying attention. There are simple devices, however, that can indicate passage of time within an episode or scene and that sound comfortable and natural to the listeners. The following script makes a simple adjustment to the earlier sample and clarifies the passage of time.

---

1. **FX. SOUND OF DOOR OPENING**

2. DR: Good Morning, Mama Jeno. Please come in. I am happy to see you this morning.

3. JENO: Good Morning, Doctor. I am sorry to bother you. I shall take up only a few minutes of your time. I hate to be a bother to you.

4. DR: (PATIENTLY) My time is your time, Mama Jeno. What can I do to help you?

5. JENO: It's not me. It's my baby. He throws up all the time. That's why I didn't bring him with me. I was afraid he would throw up in here and mess everything up. But my sister is bringing him. She will be here any minute now.

6. DR: That's good, Mama Jeno. I think it would be better if I could see him. Then I can examine him and see what the problem is.

(Continued)

(Continued)

  7.   JENO: Yes, doctor. Shall I see if she is here yet?

  8.   DR: Yes, do. In the meantime, I shall go into the next room to see one of my other patients. Please knock on the door when your sister arrives with your baby.

  9.   JENO: (GOING OUT) Thank you, Doctor.

10.   *PAUSE 5 SECONDS ... (Brief MUSIC could be added here if preferred)*

11.   <u>FX. GENTLE KNOCKING ON DOOR</u>

Time—even a fairly long period of time—can pass between one episode and the next and be made clear to the audience in a few simple remarks by one of the characters in the opening scene.

---

  2.   DR: Hello, Mrs. Green. You're looking well. I can't believe it's already a month since I last saw you. I hope everything is going well.

  3.   MRS G: I'm fine thank you, Doctor. Time might be passing quickly for you, but I feel as if I've been pregnant forever. I hope the next four months don't go as slowly as the last one.

The Use of Flashbacks

A flashback is a dramatic device in which an earlier event is inserted into present time.

---

  5.   AIDA: I shall be back later, Mama. I'm going to a meeting at the clinic now.

  6.   MOTHER: Clinic? What is this clinic? I never went to a clinic when I was having babies.

  7.   AIDA: That's true, Mama. But things are different now. When you were a young woman living in the village, there was no clinic nearby.

(Continued)

(*Continued*)

8.   MOTHER: And we managed perfectly well without it, thank you. Why, I can remember when you were born.... (FADING OFF MICROPHONE) My sister came....

9.   **FX. ECHO SOUND INDICATING FLASHBACK**

10. MOTHER: (AS A YOUNGER WOMAN) (BREATHING HEAVILY) I think it's nearly time for my baby to come.

11. B.A*:   Lie still, now. We must put some green camphor leaves on your belly to make sure the baby stays the right way round. Then you'll feel better.

12. MOTHER: (GROANING) Oh ... This is so painful. I do hope everything is all right.

13. B.A.*   Of course it is. Let me put these charms around your neck. That will help. (*The scene continued in this fashion for two minutes as the Mother's past experience revealed how she was treated during childbirth. Then it continued as follows.*)

30. **ECHO SOUND. COMING OUT OF FLASHBACK.**

31. MOTHER: And look at you today. And look at me. We're both as healthy as can be. So, where's the need for all these clinics?

---

*B.A. are initials for Birth Attendant.

As a rule, flashbacks should be avoided. They can easily confuse listeners who are not accustomed to them, or who have not been following the story regularly. A good writer can weave in necessary information naturally without having to use a flashback. In the scene between Aida and her mother, the mother could easily have recalled her pregnancy in conversation with her daughter without using a flashback.

LOCATION

Establishing the Drama's Location

Establishing in the minds of the audience the place *where* the story is happening is even more important than establishing the time. Because radio is not a visual medium, it can be tempting to think that graphic details of a scene's location are of no great importance. In fact, the opposite is true. If the audience is to believe in the drama serial as an expression of real life, it must be able to visualize clearly the surroundings in which the characters live and work.

The writer should strive to create settings that are:

1. Familiar to the audience or that can be made familiar: A rural audience, for example, would be generally more accepting of a drama set in a small village than one set in a big city business office. An unfamiliar setting, however, can be exciting and add interest to the story as long as the writer gives sufficient detail to enable the audience to imagine it clearly.

Box 14.1

GUIDELINES FOR CREATING DRAMA LOCATIONS

Locations should be:

1. Familiar to the audience
2. Suitable to the message
3. Limited in number
4. Standard for each plot
5. Identifiable by sound

---

2. Suitable to the message: Writers should choose locations that allow the message to be presented in a natural manner, even though the story does not center on the message. Locating the entire main plot in a big city, for example, would make it difficult to naturally bring in messages or modeling relating to rural health clinics.

3. Limited in number: Listeners feel more comfortable if they are taken to the same familiar settings on a regular basis rather than being moved from one new location to another frequently. Just as in real life, listeners might enjoy occasional visits to exotic places, but they always like to return to those familiar places with which they feel most comfortable.

4. Standard for each plot: It is easier for listeners to recognize where a scene is taking place if each plot has an established, standard setting. The standard setting for the main plot of a rural drama, for example, might be the interior of the family home, while one of the sub-plots is routinely set in a farmyard and another in a local garage. Any of the plots could move, occasionally, to a different location if the story requires it, but relying on standard settings simplifies writing and helps make the story coherent and believable to the audience.

5. Identifiable by sound: Each standard setting can have some brief sound that identifies it, so that listeners can recognize the location immediately without the need for explanation in the dialogue or by the narrator. The sound of utensils being moved around and a fire crackling could be used to identify the interior of the rural family home, the sound of animals could identify the farmyard, and sounds like automobile engines revving, horns and tools being used could identify a garage.

The selected sound effect can be heard at the beginning of a scene to establish the setting, held under softly through the opening lines of dialogue in the scene, and then gradually faded out. Some sound effects can be made live in the studio (utensils being moved and tools being used, for example), or they can be prerecorded and edited in (animal sounds and automobile engines, for example). More information on the use of sound effects can be found later in this chapter and in Chapter 15.

Sketching the Setting

For a television drama, new settings, or "sets," as they are called in the trade, are drawn in detail by an artist so they can be prepared (or built) prior to filming. Even though listeners will never see the radio settings will with their own eyes, these settings should be sketched. The drawings, however, need not be as detailed or professional as those required for television. Writers can make their own simple sketches that indicate where various objects are within the set. The sketch helps the writer create references in the script that eventually build up, in the minds of the listeners, a complete picture of the location.

If, for example, the standard location for one plot is a room, the writer should make a sketch, like the one here that shows what is in the room and the relationship of one object to another. It also helps if writers keep written notes of the details of the standard locations so that references to them will be in all scripts.

Drawn by Daniel Volz

Some writers like to prepare maps of the villages or towns where main scenes are set. This helps them avoid inconsistencies in detail, such as how long it takes a character to travel from one place to another. The map shown on the next page outlines details of the small village of Kyerewodo, where most of the action took place in the Ghanian behavior change serial drama, *Family Affair*.

Based on the map, the writer can decide questions, such as:

- How long would it take the principal character, Ogidigi to walk to the main road?
- Could people in the clinic hear a child in trouble in the pond?
- Could someone in the clinic hear a car going up the village road?
- Could someone creep up on Dr Mandus's bungalow without being seen by anyone in the village?
- Could Auntie Katie see from her house someone arriving at the clinic?

Without the map and a clear understanding of the village layout, the writer could easily confuse or contradict details from one episode to the next. When the writer is confused, so is the audience.

Sometimes one plot in a drama serial will be set in a location far distant from the locations of the other plots. The stories within the drama call for characters from the distant location to visit other characters in the nearby locations. In such cases, the writer should keep notes on travel to and from the distant location. The writer should consider:

- How far away is the distant location from each of the other locations in the serial? (1 kilometer, 25 kilometers, 100 kilometers?)
- What method of transport do the characters in the story use to get to this distant place? (bus, train, bicycle, foot?) How much does public transportation cost?
- Is travel ever restricted, or made impossible by weather conditions? Is transport available on a restricted basis only? Only on market days, for example, or only when the local store owner drives his truck to the city to pick up supplies?
- How long does it take to get from this distant location to each of the others?
- Where do people stay when they visit this distant location?
- What sound(s) do people hear immediately on arriving in this distant place? (city traffic, farm animals, birds in the forest, water running?)
- How do the geography, climate, social life and the economy of the distant location differ from those in other settings?

Conveying Location to the Radio Audience

While the writer can look at sketches and maps of the various settings, the audience cannot. Graphic details of the settings must be conveyed to listeners through the medium of sound alone. Sound includes dialogue, sound effects, narration and music.

The Village of Kyerewodo (pop. 2000)

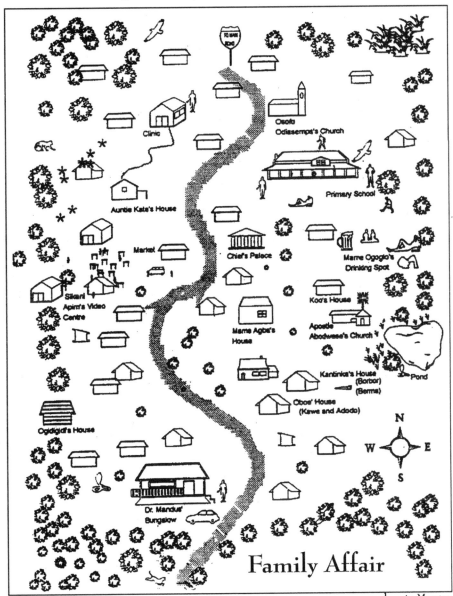

Family Affair

map by win Morgan

← 1 Km →

Dialogue is the most reliable source of details about setting. Indeed, some settings such as the room sketch on page 217 cannot be conveyed through sound effects or music. In such cases, the writer must rely on dialogue, allowing the characters to reveal a picture of their surroundings as a natural part of their conversation.

The following 14 lines of dialogue open a scene located in the room in the sketch. (The term "line" in radio drama refers to whole speech or technical direction as indicated by the number in the lefthand margin.) This scene is taken from a drama designed to encourage greater use of and respect for community health volunteers (CHVs). On this occasion, the CHV comes to visit an old man who has been ill. As well as moving the action of the story forward, the dialogue gives a clear picture of where the client lives and what type of person he is. It also subtly introduces an important message.

FX. KNOCK AT DOOR—DISTANT

2.   MAN: (CALLING) Come in. (LOUDER) Be careful of the door. (ON MIC) The stupid hinges are broken.

3.   CHV: Good morning, Mr. Jones. I'm Sally. I've come to see how you are. And I've brought some medicines for you. Where shall I put them? On this ... er ... table?

4.   MAN: (GRUFFLY) That's not a table. It's a fish trap! Can't you smell it?

5.   CHV: Well, yes I can. So ... where...?

6.   MAN: Over there. By the sink.

7.   CHV: Right. (OFF SLIGHTLY) Um ... there's something ... What?...Where?

8.   MAN: Don't tell me the cats have been up there again. What did they leave behind this time? Last week it was a frog. Not even quite dead when they dropped it in the sink. Okay, just bring the medicines here. I'll keep them under my pillow.

9.   CHV: (ON MIC. PERPLEXED) Your what?

10.   MAN: It's a pillow to me. I know ... it's really an old saddle, but you'd be surprised how comfortable it is if you beat it a bit. I asked my daughter to get me a real pillow, but ... well, she's just too busy with all those children.

11.   CHV: How many does she have?

12.   MAN: Four I think. Doesn't know how to stop, obviously.

13.   CHV: Perhaps I can help her. I'd be happy to speak to her about it. But right now, I must take your temperature. Where can I wash my hands?

14.   MAN: There's water in the sink. It's probably still clean.

In this scene between Mr Jones and Sally, the description of the setting is woven into the dialogue so naturally that it does not delay the action. Brief snatches of the overall appearance of the room are presented in the way that a first time observer would see it. The listeners' imaginations can fill in other details and complete the picture for themselves.

Using Sound Effects to Establish Location

Radio writers can also rely on sound effects to establish locations. For example, adding the sound of crashing waves and the call of sea birds to suggest the ocean, or the noise of traffic to suggest a city street. In cases like these, it is important to ensure that the recorded sound effects are culturally correct. The sound of traffic in a London street where there are cars, taxis and many buses, is entirely different from the sound of traffic in Hanoi, Vietnam, where traffic is almost exclusively motor cycles.

In the following scene extract, the chosen audience of Nepalese village people can easily visualize the rural wedding that is taking place, from the sound effects that are added.

1. MUSIC. LOUD WEDDING MUSIC. START IN DISTANCE. MOVE IN

2. FX. WEDDING CROWD NOISES. HOLD MUSIC AND FX UNDER

3. SHERSINGH: (OFF) The auspicious time is elapsing. We must start the ceremony now. (COMING IN) Where is Dambar? At this rate it will be nightfall before we reach the bride's place?

4. SHYAM: (OFF. GIVING ORDERS) Carry the stretcher. Musicians—you go in front, please!

6. FX. TRUMPET BLOWING. WEDDING MUSIC AND CROWDS SLOWLY MOVE AWAY AND FADE OUT.

7. FX. WEDDING POEMS BEING RECITED QUIETLY IN THE BACKGROUND. FADE UNDER NEXT LINE.

8. PUTALI: (COMING IN QUIETLY) Beli, I have brought with me Sister Health Worker. She has come from the bridegroom's place with the wedding procession. She would like to speak to you before you take your wedding vows.

While sound effects, including appropriate music, can help create the picture of a location in the listeners' minds, they should be used carefully and sparingly. An overload of "noise" can destroy a radio picture just as easily as appropriate "sound" can create it. (See "Guidelines on the Use of Sound Effects" in Chapter 15.)

15

Writing for the Ear

Sound effects are used to provide location.

Topics

- *The Golden Rule of Writing for Radio*
- *Guidelines for the Use of Dialogue*
- *Creating Word Pictures*
- *Similes and Metaphors*
- *Analogies*
- *Proverbs and Sayings*
- *Guidelines for the Use of Sound Effects*
- *Guidelines for Using Music in Radio Drama*

THE GOLDEN RULE OF WRITING FOR RADIO

The golden rule of writing for radio is to write everything for the listener's ear. Unless the listener can understand the setting, the characters, the action, and the message of the drama simply by listening to it, the drama will not succeed in its mission. Adherence to this golden rule requires that the writer strive for clarity and simplicity in every aspect of the serial. Simplicity, however, should not be misunderstood. It is the illusion of simplicity for which the radio writer strives. In fact, writing a successful radio drama calls for close attention to many details simultaneously in order for the audience to understand what they are hearing.

Since radio drama is delivered by sound alone, particular attention must be paid to dialogue, sound effects and music. In a well-written radio drama all three of these elements work together harmoniously. None should predominate; all should fit together to create a complete picture in the imaginations of the listeners.

GUIDELINES FOR THE USE OF DIALOGUE

Entertainment–Education radio dramas rely on words to keep the audience informed of the:

- **Action** that is going on, together with the dramatic conflict that arises from the action
- **Place and time** in which the action is occurring

Box 15.1

GUIDELINES FOR WRITING DIALOGUE

- Dialogue should be fully scripted
- Dialogue should be natural
- Dialogue should suit the character's personality
- Pace the dialogue to suit the action
- Use names in dialogue
- Avoid use of soliloquy

- **People** involved in the action and how they either cause it or react to it
- **Emotion** being evoked
- **Message** including modeling

Most of the words in a radio drama take the form of dialogue, that is, conversation between two or more people. Writing convincing dialogue is, therefore, one of the writer's most essential skills. The following guidelines can help a writer create convincing dialogue:

Dialogue should be fully scripted: In a drama written strictly for entertainment, radio actors sometimes ad-lib some of their lines. To "ad-lib" means to change the words in the script into language that they find easier to say or that they believe are more appropriate to the characters they are portraying. In Entertainment–Education dramas, ad-libbing can cause real problems. Even a small change in wording can confuse the meaning of a message or make information inaccurate. For this reason, the writer should take care to script all dialogue exactly as the actors should present it.

In some countries, it is difficult to find actors who are sufficiently literate to read scripts accurately and convincingly. In this event, it is better to have the actors learn the correct lines ahead of the recording date rather than to have them read badly or ad-lib as they go along.

Even in Entertainment–Education drama, however, there are a few occasions when ad-libbing can be permitted, but these should be handled carefully. In the following example, line 6 asks for everyone in the cast to ad-lib general comments of congratulation. This type of ad-libbing is perfectly acceptable.

For example:

5. FATHER: And it is with great pride that I ask you all to join me in congratulating my daughter on becoming the first person in our family to graduate from high school.

6. **AD LIB.** EVERYONE CHEERING, MAKING CONGRATULATORY REMARKS, CLAPPING, ETC.

Dialogue should be natural: The most important consideration in creating natural dialogue is that it should reflect the conversational habits of the culture to which it will be broadcast. In many parts of the world, everyday conversation is not expressed in full and grammatically correct sentences. Rather, people tend to use incomplete sentences and interrupt each other. Radio dialogue should be so natural that audience members believe they are listening in on an actual conversation.

The following dialogue is completely unnatural. The speeches sound more like lectures than normal conversation. The sentences are long and formal and there is no sense of spontaneity in the language.

---

1. MOTHER: My daughter went to the clinic today and the health worker told her all about the advantages and disadvantages of this Norplant implant that so many people have been talking about. She said that the advantages are that it works for up to five years; that it works immediately after insertion; that it can be used by breastfeeding women, and that you can get pregnant right after you stop using it. Doesn't that sound like something that you would like to use, Maggie?

2. MAGGIE: It does sound interesting, but perhaps you would be good enough to tell me a little more about it. I would really like to know more about it before I decide.

In the following example, the same characters present the same message, but they converse naturally. They interrupt each other and their thoughts are expressed in fragments rather than in formal sentences. Note the use of ellipses (a series of full stops or periods) to indicate to the actor that the speech should be read as a series of disjointed statements, rather than as a single straightforward sentence. Ellipses are used at the ends of speeches also to indicate that the next character should interrupt before the speech is complete, as can be seen in line 5.

---

1. MOTHER: My daughter went to the clinic today, Maggie. She's been saying for ages that she wanted to find out about this Norplant thing ... I was ....

2. MAGGIE: Norplant implant I think it's called, sister.

3. MOTHER: Right. Some of her friends have had it put in their arms. Jenny ... of course ... had to find out about it. I mean, she's a follower. We know that. She says there are lots of good things about this Norplant ... what did you say ... implant?

4. MAGGIE: (SCORNFULLY) Such as?

5. MOTHER: I can't remember everything. The health worker said it works very well .... Up to five years .... That sounds pretty good.

6. MAGGIE: Maybe, sister, maybe.

(Continued)

(*Continued*)

7. MOTHER: (GOING RIGHT ON) And ... oh yes ... she said it works right away ... not like some of those contraceptives that you have to ... um ... stay away from your husband for a few weeks before they work. You know what I mean.

8. MAGGIE: No sex, you mean! .... So .... Norplant works right away. But what about when you WANT to get pregnant. I'll bet you have to wait six months after the thing's been removed.

9. MOTHER: No, no. I remember that ... um ... Jenny said you can get pregnant quite soon after having it removed. So what do you think Maggie? Sound like something you could use?

10. MAGGIE: I don't know ... maybe.

Not only does this dialogue sound more natural to the culture for which it was written, it also allows the audience to absorb the message more slowly and it reveals something of the personality of the characters.

Suit the dialogue to the character: The style and tone of the dialogue must be adapted to suit the personality of each character. While the actors can employ appropriate accents and voice tones for individual characters, it is the writer's responsibility to create dialogue that reveals the true nature of each character. A highly educated professional city-dweller, for example, is more likely to use sophisticated language, including scientific terminology, than is a rural person with little formal education.

Even when characters come from similar backgrounds, they often have individual speech patterns and idiosyncrasies that reveal their personalities. The capable writer uses dialogue artfully to assist in the depiction of character. In the Nigerian youth radio program *Ku Saurara*, the visiting doctor who was on the program each week had a habit of saying "Do you follow me?" The youthful audience began to anticipate when she would say this, and joined in with her every time.

Pace the dialogue to suit the action: The characters' dialogue must be paced to fit the action of the drama. Two people chatting over a cup of tea speak in a more leisurely way and use longer sentences than do people who have just discovered that their house is on fire. The listeners can feel the mood of a scene through the pace of the dialogue.

The following scene starts off in one mood and shifts to another. The change in the **pace** of the dialogue as well as the words used, trigger the emotional response of the audience.

This short scene demonstrates an extreme change in pace and mood. Not all scenes will be as dramatic as that, but the pace of dialogue should quicken whenever excitement rises in a scene. This is best accomplished with short speeches and quick interchanges between the characters.

1.   TREY: (AS IF DROPPING INTO A CHAIR) Ahh, that feels good. There's nothing like it, Nessa ... sitting on your own porch at the end of the day, watching the sun go down.

2.   NESSA: It's a good life, Trey. We've worked hard, but we've also been lucky .... Many things to be grateful for. If I had my life to live over again, I wouldn't change it.

3.   TREY: No ... could use a bit more free time, perhaps, but, on the whole, no complaints. Now then, Nessa, dear wife, can I pour you a nice cup of....

4.   FX. TELEPHONE RINGS OFF. HOLD UNDER TILL TREY ANSWERS

6.   NESSA: Why does it always ring while we're sitting down?

7.   TREY: I'll get it. (GRUNTS AS HE GETS OUT OF THE CHAIR)

8.   PAUSE ... TELEPHONE STILL HEARD IN BACKGROUND

9.   TREY: (OFF) Hello ... who? (SOUNDING DOUBTFUL) Oh yes, officer .... What can I do? What? Oh God, no!

10.   NESSA: (COMING IN) What is it, Trey? What's wrong?

11.   TREY: It can't be ... but he ... yes, yes officer ... yes I'll come.

12.   FX HANGS UP TELEPHONE

13.   NESSA: (TERRIFIED) Trey .... Trey .... What's wrong?

Use characters' names in dialogue: This scene also illustrates one slightly unnatural feature of radio drama dialogue: the characters use each other's names more often than they would in normal conversation. This helps the audience identify who is speaking and to whom. This use of names is particularly important in the early episodes of a serial when the listeners have not yet grown completely accustomed to the voices of the actors who portray the various characters.

Avoid the use of soliloquy: A soliloquy is a speech in which the character talks to herself or himself; in effect, thinking out loud. On radio, where the character cannot be seen by the audience, it is difficult to make soliloquy sound convincing. On television, the character can be shown thinking and the thoughts are presented as a "voice over" without any suggestion that the character is speaking aloud. Obviously, this is not possible on radio. So, it is generally better to have the character speak the thoughts to someone or something.

In the following short scene, Bongani, who has just been jilted by the girl he loves, expresses his misery to his dog!

1. FX. DOOR CREAKS OPEN. CLOSES WITH A BANG

2. BONGANI: (SIGHING) Hi there, Jojo. What are you wagging your tail about?

3. FX. DOG PANTING. WHINING HAPPILY

4. BONGANI: It's all very well for you. You can find a girlfriend whenever you want one. You don't have to care if she loves you or not. But humans are different, Jojo. I can't believe she'd do that to me. I mean, we were going to be married and everything. I love her. I THOUGHT she loved me. I'll bet there's someone else.

5. FX. SLAPPING DOG ON NECK

6. BONGANI: Yeah, but who? Hey, you know what Jojo? Maybe I'll go away somewhere .... South Africa maybe. Then she'll be sorry ... when I'm not here anymore.

As this excerpt shows, characters can speak to animals, or even plants, to reveal their feelings. In countries where trees are thought to house spirits, it is natural for people to speak to trees. Alternatively, a mother can speak her thoughts to her very young baby, who cannot respond, but who can be, quite naturally, the target for her mother's heartfelt outpourings.

CREATING WORD PICTURES

Creating good radio dialogue requires the writer to think in pictures, to become the listeners' eyes, and to see the world as the listeners would see it if they were present at the scene. Throughout the entire serial, the writer reveals mental pictures of characters and scenes subtly, almost coincidentally, as part of the dialogue. While it is essential for radio writers to create **word pictures**, this does not mean using the exaggerated figures of speech and poetic style often encouraged by writing teachers. Radio drama must be written to reflect the way real people speak. Creating pictures in the minds of listeners is best accomplished with dialogue that refers to locally familiar sights and situations. For example, listeners will understand immediately when a character announces, "The wind was so strong, it nearly blew me over." Employing an unfamiliar simile, "The wind was as strong as a turbo engine," would, in many cultures, only confuse matters.

Similes and Metaphors

The radio writer should be extremely careful about using similes and metaphors in dialogue to create pictures of people and places. The writer should use only figures of speech that would be used naturally by the characters in the story. Similes are likely to be heard in everyday speech in virtually every culture. For example, "He's as strong as an ox." "She's as pretty as a flower." "It's as hot as fire today." Comparison with unknown things, however, no matter how beautifully written, will make dialogue sound less realistic.

The following speech creates a vivid picture of the setting, but it is hardly the type of language the average person uses, although it might be used by a character who is a poet!

> Look, Thabo, we have arrived at a magnificent sweeping plain. It is an enormous magic carpet spread before my feet. Just as Adam must have felt on first beholding the Garden of Eden, so I feel as I view this plain.

A more believable response to the sight of the plain, using the same simile, but in a more natural way, could be:

> Wow, Thabo, look at this plain. It's huge! It goes on forever. Wow, I feel like Adam discovering the Garden of Eden. It's magnificent!

In creating word pictures, the writer should always choose language that is suitable to the character and comfortable for the audience. Remember, writing radio serial drama for social development should not be viewed as an attempt to win a prize for great literature.

Analogies

An analogy is a type of comparison that suggests that if two things are similar in some ways, they are likely to be similar in others. Analogies can be extremely helpful in clarifying a new idea for a listening audience.

In the following scene from the Tanzanian radio drama, *Awake*, the health worker, Shada, uses an analogy to help Mama Jeni understand that some contraceptive users experience side-effects and so need to be kept under observation.

1. SHADA: Oh, Mama Jeni, so it is already three months since your last injection. Let me see your card, please. O.K. March, April, May. It's all right. How is your body adopting this new method?

2. JENI: What do you mean, adopting?

(Continued)

(*Continued*)

3. SHADA: You know human bodies are all naturally different from one another. Some like their tea with a lot of sugar. Others can tolerate just a very small amount of sugar.

4. JENI: Yes, that's very common.

5. SHADA: Some people are upset by medicines like chloroquine, while others are not.

6. JENI: My husband always scratches himself after taking chloroquine. I don't.

7. SHADA: Because of these differences, it is good to monitor any new phenomenon in the body to see how well it is adopted by the body.

8. JENI: That's right. My daughter is allergic to perfumed soaps. They cause rashes on her body.

9. SHADA: In the same sense, when people start using a certain modern family planning method, we must follow up and monitor how each body has adopted the new method.

Proverbs and Sayings

Yet another way to enrich the language of a radio drama and to create pictures in the minds of the listeners is to use local proverbs, expressions or sayings.

The following excerpt from the Australian agricultural serial *Dad and Dave* demonstrates that familiar expressions reflecting the norms of one culture may not be understood by another. At the same time, it shows how the use of local expressions can enrich the characterization and the story while providing evocative word pictures.

8. DAD: Well, look at you, Dave. You've grown into one long cold drink of water, you have. You're even taller than I am. (LAUGHING) You'll have to have a party in your shoes and invite your trousers down. What you up to these days?

9. DAVE: Not much. Can't get a job or nothing. Think I'll have to become a beggar.

10. DAD: If you ask me, becoming a beggar's got long white woolly whiskers on it. No bloke who calls himself a man ever goes out begging.

11. DAVE: That's all very well for you to say. You've got the farm.

12. DAD: So what? You think that means I can sit around all day playing with the lambs? The farm's like anything else. You gotta work for it to make it work for you. Hard work never hurt nobody. Hard work works, I tell you. Hard work is guaranteed never to rip, tip, wear, tear, rust, bust or fall apart at the seams.

Life in Hopeful Village
Episode #36
Writer: Elaine Perkins

123. LJ: Stand back! Give me room.

124. ROY: (EAGERLY) Yes … yes.

125. MISS B: I told you he would come, Mass Roy.

126. FX. COW MOOS
     OCCASIONALLY THROUGHOUT

127. LJ: Good girl. Good girl. That's it! That's it!

*The **resolution** of the immediate crisis of this scene ends with safe birth of the calf.*

128. FX. 30 SEC. AD LIB AS COW
     GIVES BIRTH. ENCOURAGING
     WORDS FROM ALL THREE.

129. MISS B: (HAPPILY) It's a little bull, Littlejohn.

Nevertheless, the crisis of Littlejohn's refusal to learn to read has still to be met.

130. ROY: (IN WONDER) A champion!

131. LJ: Don't talk too soon.

132. ROY: (LAUGHS HAPPILY) It works,
              Littlejohn. Artificial insemination
              works!

133. LJ: Make sure the calf can get up before
              you start boasting.

134. ROY: (ANXIOUSLY NUDGING CALF) Come
              on, son, stand up …. Stand up!

135. FX. CALF MAKING EFFORT

136. MISS B: Ooh, look at him. He's rising up! He's
              standing.

137. ROY: (ENCOURAGING CALF) That's it.
              Rock and come back, baby. That's my
              boy. (HAPPILY) Look at the markings,
              Littlejohn. That is what you call
              a first rate, upgraded Holstein. Look at
              the size of the back leg. My mother
              Jemima! What have you got to say
              about artificial insemination of cows
              now, my boy? Eh? What have you got
              to say about this injection calf?

*The scene ends on a very positive note, and a sense of joy …. **BUT** …*

138. LJ: I reserve my opinion.

139. ROY: You learned a thing or two here today, eh?

FINAL NARRATION

142. NARR: In no time at all, the news of Roy's bull calf spread all around town, from Tydedixon to Mount Moria, from Salem to Glengoffe. Next day, the Extension Officer was back in the office. Everyone wanted to hear more about the injection calf. People came to look ... to stroke their chins ... and marvel. Littlejohn was not among them. For early the next morning, before the cock started to crow to call the morning, before the dew left the grass, he harnessed the mules and rode quietly away through the morning mist. Rode away to town!

And it wasn't until weeks later that everybody realized what Littlejohn was up to. By that time ... for certain people ... it was too late.

In the final narration two new questions are raised: Why has Littlejohn gone to town? What to do the final words of the narration imply?

The audience is left wanting to know WHAT WILL HAPPEN NEXT?

144. MUSIC. SIGNATURE MUSIC TO END

END OF EPISODE.

Original Version

This is the opening of the same episode (#36) as it was originally written in Jamaican dialect

1. NARR: Now imagine a thing as this! Litigation upon litigation. Not five minute after the judge decide de case against him last week, Littlejohn step straight downstairs to the clerk o'court and file an appeal. Yes! This will make the fourth time him and Sawyers fight law over dar little slip of land that divide them two property. Talk about bad feelings. Remember last week when the two of them buck up in the bar across the way? (FADE OUT)

2. TAPE: LAST MINUTE OF PREVIOUS EPISODE, WHEN LITTLEJOHN COLLARS SAWYERS. SCUFFLES. SHOUTS. ETC. MIX WITH PRE-RECORDED FX BAR. VOICES. PEOPLE BREAKING UP THE FRAY. OVERLAP WITH FOLLOWING.

3. LJ: You are an unconshanable tief!

4. SAW: (SHOUTING) If you wasn't so illiterated.

5. MISS B. Make them stop noh Mass Roy, I appeal to you.

6. ROY: Come on, Mass Littlejohn

7. LJ: Let me go Mass Roy.

8. ROY: You is my friend, man. I am talking to you. Stand steady.

9. LJ: Dis man Sawyers move my land-marker. Tief land dat my old people dead and left. He poison my dumb things.

10. SAW: You goat was nyaming dung my young peas.

11. LJ: Down to the star-apple tree my navel string bury under. He chop dung. Root out. And turn round obeah the Judge to mek him rule against me. Well, so help my Almighty God. No Sanky don't sting so. If it is the last farthing I have. If I have to sell out me shop.

12. MISS B: Don't tek no oath, Littlejohn.

13. LJ: (CONTINUING) If I have to starve me belly ... walk around in sackcloth and ashes.

Success of Radio Entertainment–Education Programs

Quality radio programming can make a positive contribution to family health and happiness.

ENTERTAINMENT–EDUCATION AND SOCIAL CHANGE

There is ample evidence around the world that radio Entertainment–Education (E–E) dramas can have a positive effect on social change.

Australia was one of the first countries to make effective use of this medium. A country with a large geographic area—some 7,682,300 square kilometers—Australia had in 1944 a very small population of under five million people. In that year, The Australian Broadcasting Commission (ABC) went on the air five days a week with *The Lawsons*, a 15-minute-long serial drama, designed originally to help farmers adjust to new farming methods required to help the country survive World War II. In 1949 the name of the drama changed to *Blue Hills*, which ran uninterrupted for 27 years!

Following on the ideas developed by the ABC, the BBC launched their famous serial *The Archers* in 1951, with the initial aim of encouraging British farmers to adopt new methods to help overcome the dreadful food and produce shortages created by World War II. *The Archers* continued on the air for over 8,000 episodes.

Since then, serial drama has been used successfully in many parts of the world to have a positive effect on behavior change. In India, one of the radio E–E dramas was the 104-episode serial drama, *Tinka Tinka Sukh* ("Happiness Lies in Small Pleasures"), which ran from 1996 to 1997. It is estimated to have reached about 40 million listeners from 27 local stations covering seven Hindi-speaking states. In 1997, as a result of listening to this serial, a young tailor in the village of Lutsaan, North India, encouraged the people in his community to form radio listening clubs. Gradually the community became more and more interested in and influenced by the behavior change being modeled in the drama. They began planting trees, building pit latrines, and—most impressively—increasing the enrolment of girls in schools and discouraging dowry marriages.

In 1994, Nepal introduced a synergistic radio series, reaching two audiences with two different programs. One serial drama, *Cut Your Coat According to Your Cloth*, was designed for a general audience, with the hope of encouraging everyone in Nepal to have a small well-planned family. The other program series, *Service Brings Reward*, was designed as a Distance Learning (DL) series to train health workers to effectively counsel couples in choosing an appropriate family planning method. The DL programs presented the topics a few weeks ahead of the same topics being presented to the general public. The effect of this synergistic approach was extremely positive and resulted in a marked increase in the number of couples learning about and accepting modern family planning methods.

Soul City, which began life in 1992 as a 13-part TV drama, is known throughout the world now for its extraordinary reach and effect. It soon became apparent that, because radio reaches 65 percent of the target audience for the proposed behavior changes messages, it would be wise to put the programs on radio as well as TV. *Soul City* continues to build, with its programs now being produced in many different languages, and with the development of support materials (comics, audiotapes, etc.) and a multimedia series (radio and television) for children—*Soul Buddyz*. The *Soul City* model has reached out across the world, and even in its home country—South Africa—it is still the series that many people claim has the greatest influence on their behavior change.

Zambia produced *Our Neighbourhood* as a dramatized Health Volunteer workshop which also contained an intriguing mystery. Ghana reached out to female health volunteers with the radio series *The Front Liner*, and Senegal, Guinea, Haiti, and Indonesia all used the radio E–E format to increase the knowledge and improve the services of health workers and midwives. Nepal began broadcasting a new DL series, *Service is Dharma*, in 2004 to reach out to Female Community Health Volunteers.

Detailed analysis of a number of E–E radio dramas and programs can be found in a report entitled *Institutional Review of Educational Radio Dramas* submitted by Mary Myers to the Center for Disease Control and Prevention in Atlanta, USA.

In the last decade, the use of E–E dramas has increased greatly, both on television and radio. In many developing countries, radio remains the widest-reaching medium, and so is used extensively for encouragement of positive behavior change. Increasingly, the radio E–E format is being used for DL programs to upgrade the skills of health workers in remote areas.

The art of Entertainment–Education is still relatively new, and still developing. There is, however, no doubt that high quality E–E programming is now universally accepted as a powerful means of encouraging positive social change. Already, the Entertainment–Education approach is being introduced to internet teaching programs. The future success of this methodology, no matter what the medium, lies in the ability of more and more designers, writers, and producers to understand it and use it well. It is hoped that this book will assist all those engaged in Entertainment–Education programs for radio to improve the quality of their work.

CREDITS

The following list shows the names of dramas from which extracts have been taken for this book, together with the name of the writer, and the country where the writer works:

Tinka, Tinka Sukh by Chandra Dutt Indu, India

Heart to Heart by Parvez Imam, India

Cut Your Coat According to Your Cloth by Kurber Gartaula, Nepal.

Family Affair by Fred Daramani, Ghana

He Ha Ho by Celestine Ndanu, Ghana

Journey of Life by Almaz Beyene Kahsay, Ethiopia

Tale of a Village by Humayun Ahmed, Bangladesh

Life in Hopeful Village by Elaine Perkins, Jamaica

Sample Design Document

DESIGN DOCUMENT
FOR
26-EPISODE RADIO SERIAL DRAMA
FOR THE PEOPLE OF UTTAR PRADESH, INDIA

CREATED AT THE DESIGN WORKSHOP
HOTEL TAJ GANGES
NADESAR PALACE GROUNDS
VARANASI

ORGANIZED BY:
STATE INNOVATIONS IN
FAMILY PLANNING SERVICES
AGENCY (SIFPSA)

NOTE: In its original form, this design document followed the complete outline presented on page 37 of this book. It also contained a list of the names and contact numbers of all those on the design team, and a complete index.

The following pages present points 1–10 of the document and only **some** of the message content pages from this design document, as an example of how these pages should be prepared and presented.

The original design document also included the following important notes to the writer:

- Please follow the messages in the design document faithfully.
- If there is anything you are unsure of, please contact a member of the script support team.
- Words that are marked with an asterisk (*) have a Hindi definition in the Glossary. These Hindi definitions from the Glossary should be used throughout your writing of this series of programs.
- Please ensure that the Health Service Providers you include in your programs always present a friendly, caring attitude and that they reflect positive self-esteem.

THE DESIGN DOCUMENT CONTENTS

Part 1: Background and Overall Description

1. Justification for the Project

Background: State Innovations in Family Planning Services Agency (SIFPSA) has been implementing Behavior Change Communication (BCC) programs as part of the Innovations in Family Planning Services (IFPS) Project. The IFPS Project, supported by the United States Agency for International Development (USAID), is designed to revitalize the family planning program in Uttar Pradesh by improving the access to and quality of health and family planning services. The Health Communication Partnership/Johns Hopkins University is providing technical assistance in the domain of behavior change communication for the project. The project approach is to translate family planning into a people's program.

SIFPSA formulated a communication strategy for health and family planning in Uttar Pradesh in mid-1995. An overarching campaign was developed with the aim of bringing the hitherto taboo subject of planning families out into the open and to trigger dialogue across audience groups: between spouse(s), between the service provider and client, between policymakers and implementers.

Articulation of the theme was in the form of a call to action 'Aao Batein Karein' (Come, Let's Talk). *Tota* and *Mynah*, birds linked to popular folklore on crosstalk, banter and wisdom, were used as visual cues to illustrate the theme.

A statewide communication campaign was developed and implemented to promote contraceptive methods used for birth spacing. With a focus on specific methods, messages were developed in continuity with the umbrella theme (Aao Batein Karein). Campaign components included mass media, local media, community media and interpersonal communication. The campaign was supported by orientation and training of outreach workers. In addition to the campaign promoting Spacing methods, SIFPSA has also implemented statewide campaigns on age at marriage and Tetanus Toxoid (TT) immunization.

(At this point the document included a detailed presentation of the SIFPSA Communication Strategy.)

2. Information about the Chosen Audience

(The following information was collected and discussed with regard to each of the audiences to be addressed in the series. Before completing the document, the team sought and found answers to those areas of information labeled "What do we need to know?")

(I) Rural men
What do we know?

- Myths and misconceptions on FP prevalent among them.
- More comfortable talking with peers.
- Decision-making now increasingly shared amongst spouses.
- Hesitation to accompany wife to health care facility ("too much of a women's affair").
- Hesitation to talk and seek information; put wife forward to get information.
- Sex uppermost in mind.

What do we need to know?

- Satisfied beneficiaries of vasectomy on the increase.
  - ➢ Places where contraceptives could be picked without embarrassment.
  - ➢ Soft sell of vasectomy camps has helped to create a positive environment.

Why do they have current behaviour?

- Men are reticent by nature.
- Programs and media are more womencentric.

What are the main motivators for change?

- Sense of companionship is being discovered. We need to cash in on that.
- Hope for prosperity is on the rise. Desire to have better life.

(II) Rural women
What do we know?

- Illiterate/low education level.
- Financially dependent.

- Little exposure outside peer group.
- Low aspirations.
- Wish to prove fertility.
- Son preferred.
- Low self-esteem.
- Influenced by traditions/myths.
- However: positive changes due to exposure.
- Unmet needs high.
- Inertia
- Custom and ritual bound
- Lack of knowledge

What do we need to know?

- Who/what influences them the most.
- Barriers.
- Motivational factors.

Why do they have current behaviour?

- Low education level.
- Tradition/social norms.

What will motivate them to change?

- Promise of a better life for their family; promise of good health.
- Lessening of economic insecurity by reducing number of children.
- Dispelling myths.

A similar examination was made of each of the other audience groups specified for this radio serial drama: Other Family Members (Mother-in-law, Father-in-law, Sister-in-law, Mother), Local Influentials and leaders.

3. Justification of the Chosen Medium: RADIO

Radio is an important component of mass media with a reach of 27 percent across rural Uttar Pradesh, thus offering a unique media edge both in terms of cost effectiveness and reach. This is more so in the context of rural audiences, which are the largest and most critical segment of our program's target groups.

It is thus planned to air 26 episodes of a radio drama serial for the general public.

Advantages of radio

1. It is portable.
2. One can listen and work at the same time.

3. It is cheap.
4. No electricity is needed.
5. Cost per message is low.
6. Cost per listener is low.
7. Radio is the medium of the imagination.
8. Wider access to radio possible because it is cheap.
9. People learn more from listening to the radio.
10. There is better recall of message from radio. No distractions (unlike TV and its constantly moving images).
11. No channel clutter.
12. Easy to reproduce and replicate on audio tapes. NGOs/others can playback the cassettes or distribute them.
13. More people listen to the radio than watch TV.

Possible limitations

1. Radio, an audio only medium, is not suitable for some things that are better explained when you actually show them.
2. Everything depends on dialogue and sound effects. Silent scenes are not possible.
3. Need for support materials and supplementary materials.
4. Channel reception issues.
5. Radio listenership declined but now it's on the rise again.
6. Not a medium that people in the rural areas aspire to have.
7. People don't know the schedule of programs.
8. It's a one-way medium. But radio can be made interactive by including quiz questions, etc.

4. The Overall Measurable Objective(s)

The overall measurable objectives for this series as a whole are:

Family planning

There will be a measurable *increase* in the number of

1. couples seeking FP methods,
2. couples seeking FP counseling,
3. couples discussing FP together,
4. people who have correct knowledge of all methods.
5. couples adopting appropriate FP practices.

There will be a measurable *decrease* in the number of

- people who believe in myths on FP.

RTI/STI/HIV and AIDS

There will be a measurable *increase* in

1. The number of people who have correct knowledge of RTIs/ STIs and HIV and AIDS including knowledge of service delivery points for advice and treatment,
2. The number of people (men and women) who seek appropriate services of all types of reproductive and sexually transmitted diseases.

Age at marriage

There will be a measurable *increase* in

1. The number of audience members who have correct knowledge of the benefits of delaying marriage until appropriate age,
2. The number of audience members willing to accept and abide by the legal age of marriage.

Maternal and child health (MCH)

There will be a measurable *increase* in

1. The number of couples who know the facts about the importance of MCH issues and services including service delivery points,
2. The number of families adopting appropriate practices with regard to maternal and child health.

5. The Overall Purpose(s)

The overall purposes of this series as a whole (how the program must allow the audience to reach its objectives) are:

Family planning

1. To educate people and reinforce knowledge of FP.
2. To demonstrate couples talking comfortably talking about FP.
3. To motivate people to get the facts about FP from a reliable source and trust only the facts.

RTI/STI/HIV and AIDS

1. To remind people about the dangers of HIV and AIDS.
2. To teach people how to protect themselves from this fatal infection.
3. To educate people about signs and symptoms of RTIs and STIs.
4. To motivate them to seek and complete treatment.

Age at marriage

1. To educate listeners about the consequences of early marriage.
2. To reinforce their knowledge of current policies and rules about marriage.
3. To motivate them to abide by the guidelines against early marriage and encourage others to do the same.

17

The Finished Script and
the Writer's Checklist

Every script must be carefully reviewed for quality and accuracy.

Topics

- *Putting the Serial Episode Together*
- *Writer's Checklist of Essential Features in a Well-constructed Episode*
- *Message Presentation*
- *Characters in* Life in Hopeful Village
- *One Episode from* Life in Hopeful Village
- *Original Version*

PUTTING THE SERIAL EPISODE TOGETHER

This chapter presents an episode from the Jamaican radio serial *Life in Hopeful Village* by the outstanding Jamaican writer, Elaine Perkins. It demonstrates how all the elements of good scriptwriting discussed in this book are combined to create an episode that is both entertaining and educational. Elaine Perkins wrote the drama to promote the overall message that people can help themselves to a better standard of living. This particular episode examines two different ways that people can improve their lives: by becoming literate and by trying new agricultural techniques, such as the artificial insemination of their livestock with better breeds.

Life in Hopeful Village was written originally in Jamaican English. The episode presented here has been translated into standard English, but an excerpt from the original script (page 267) gives readers a flavor of the original language.

Annotations on the right hand side of each script page analyze the important elements of the script. The episode exemplifies all the following essential features of a drama serial episode designed for behavior change purposes.

WRITER'S CHECKLIST OF ESSENTIAL FEATURES IN A WELL-CONSTRUCTED EPISODE

Entertaining main plot: The main plot in this drama revolves around a conflict that has no direct connection with the message: an argument between two neighbors, Littlejohn and Sawyers, over land rights. The audience is intrigued by the fight between the two characters and tunes in to the serial week after week to find out who will win. At the same time, this plot allows the serial's message—improvement comes through self-help—to be introduced naturally.

Relevance: Through what happens to Littlejohn, the audience can see the value of being willing to improve one's own life.

Hook: The episode starts with a hook—a short line or action that commands listeners' attention. The hook uses an element of surprise or an unanswered question to intrigue the audience and keep them listening.

Scenes: The episode is divided into five scenes, so that it can explore more than one plot and more than one stage of the same plot. Most of the message information is presented in the middle portion of each scene, where the speeches tend to be longer and move more slowly. The opening and closing speeches of each scene are short and quick.

Scene links: The scenes are smoothly linked together to make it easy for the audience to keep track of events and actions. Likewise, the first scene is linked to the end of the previous episode.

Settings: The settings of the various scenes are quickly and easily established, either with sound effects or with a few descriptive words in the dialogue.

Character personality: Listeners can quickly recognize the predominant personality trait of each character, even if they have heard no previous episodes of the drama. Personalities are revealed through what characters say, what they do, what others say about or to them, and how they react to situations.

Names: Characters address each other by name, especially in the opening lines of a scene, so the audience is left in no doubt as to who is speaking to whom.

Action: The episode opens with action: action recalled (last week's court decision and bar fight), action anticipated (the continuing court case), and immediate action (the argument between Littlejohn and Sawyers).

Emotion: The overall theme of the episode is the universal emotion of love: the love between husband and wife, and the loving support of community members for one another. At the same time, each scene evokes its own emotion, such as pride or fear. These changing emotions keep the audience involved and interacting with the drama throughout the episode.

Message: The episode's two messages—the importance of literacy and the value of new scientific farming methods, are introduced naturally, subtly, and gradually.

Cultural appropriateness: The settings, the story, the characters, the language (see the original script on page 267), and the message presentation are suited to the audience for whom the serial is designed. At the same time, the characters and conflict of the story have universal appeal.

Narrator: The narrator introduces and closes the episode, but does not bridge scenes or explain actions during the episode; that is done naturally through the dialogue.

Music: Music is used sparingly—at the beginning and at the end of the episode and when there is a major scene change. There is no need for mood music because the dialogue indicates the emotional tone of each scene.

Sound effects (FX): Sound effects are used judiciously and naturally, not as a decoration to make the serial more attractive. The drama's attraction comes from the personalities and actions of the characters. Where sound effects are essential, as in the final scene of the episode, they are all the more effective because they have not been overused in earlier scenes.

Cliffhanger: The episode ends with a cliffhanger—a suspenseful finale that leaves the audience eager to know what is going to happen next. This motivates listeners to tune in to hear the next episode.

Word pictures: Throughout the episode, the writer uses evocative word pictures to help the audience visualize the scene and follow the action. Some of the characters use similes and local proverbs in a perfectly natural way.

MESSAGE PRESENTATION

The messages in this episode of *Life in Hopeful Village* adhere perfectly to the 7Cs of message presentation.

Correct

The importance of literacy is obvious and the information about artificial insemination is simple but correct.

Complete

The references to the Agricultural Extension Officer let the audience know where they can turn if they want more information about artificial insemination of cattle.

Concise

The messages are powerful but presented naturally and are not overpresented.

Consistent

The messages are consistent throughout—learning to read is advantageous; upgrading one's cattle is a new and perhaps frightening experience, but it is worth investigating.

Clear

There is no doubt at all about what the messages are saying to the audience.

Culturally Appropriate

This drama is addressing rural people in Jamaica who are poor and who lack education. The messages—like the story and the language used—are completely appropriate to the chosen audience.

Compelling

The message of literacy is made compelling by the fact that Littlejohn could lose his land because he does not know how to read. The message of artificial insemination is made compelling by the fact that Roy could lose his only cow if the method fails. When the calf finally stands and moves, Roy—and the audience—are aware that he has done the right thing.

Characters in *Life in Hopeful Village*

The following characters appear in this episode of *Life in Hopeful Village*. This list gives the names and a brief description. The personality of each character will be apparent as the script is read.

John Littlejohn (main character): a middle-aged farmer living in a poor rural area of Jamaica.
Miss Birdie (main character): his wife.
Roy (main character): a longtime friend of Littlejohn; also a farmer living in the same rural area

Sawyers: enemy of Littlejohn. Same age and living in the same area. The two are fighting over ownership of a piece of land.

Voice: this can be male or female. A member of the crowd outside the courthouse.

Narrator: can be male or female.

Cow! This would be done with a sound effects disk during actual recording, but can be performed by an "actor" during a demonstration reading.

Life in Hopeful Village
Episode #36
Writer: Elaine Perkins

Page 1 of 12

OPENING NARRATION

1. NARR: Imagine that. Litigation upon litigation. Not five minutes after the judge decided the case against him, last week, Littlejohn went straight to the clerk of courts and filed an appeal. Yes! This will make the fourth time that he and Sawyers have been to court over that little slip of land that divides their two properties. Talk about bad feelings! Remember last week, when the two of them scuffled in the bar across the way (FADE OUT).

The opening line immediately "hooks" the attention of the audience.
This is followed by a brief summary of the previous episode and a reminder of the main characters, before moving directly into the action of the new episode.

SCENE 1

2. (Cut in tape—last minute of episode 35. Mix with FX)

Scene begins with ACTION.

3. <u>FX. SCUFFLES. SHOUTS. PEOPLE BREAKING UP A FIGHT.</u>

4. LJ: You are an unconscionable thief!

5. SAW: (SHOUTING) If you weren't so illiterate ....

6. MISS B: Make them stop, Mr Roy. I appeal to you.

7. ROY: Come on, Littlejohn.

8. LJ: Let me go.

9. ROY: You're my friend. I'm talking to you, keep still.

10. LJ: This man Sawyers moved my land marker. It's inherited land that my parents left me when they died. He poisoned my animals.

Message (illiteracy) introduced naturally and then dropped temporarily.

Personality traits of characters are revealed.
***Littlejohn** (major character): headstrong, proud, victim of his own pride and circumstances;*
***Sawyers** (villain): takes advantage of Littlejohn's weaknesses: pride and illiteracy;*
***Miss Birdie** (Littlejohn's wife): wise counselor and loving supporter;*
***Roy** (friend): practical; self-controlled.*

Life in Hopeful Village
Episode #36
Writer: Elaine Perkins

11. SAW: Your goat was chewing down my young peas.

12. LJ: Downed the star apple tree where my umbilical cord is buried. He chopped it down! Rooted it out! And worked black magic on the judge to make him rule against me. Well, so help me, Almighty God, there's no hymn that allows that. If it costs me the last cent I have ... if I have to sell my shop ....

Culturally appropriate references to traditions that the audience understands.

Bulk of information given in the middle of the scene, with slower, longer speeches.

13. MISS B: Don't swear an oath Littlejohn.

14. LJ: (CONTINUING) If I have to starve .... Walk around in sackcloth and ashes.

15. SAW: (OFF) Illiterate old fool. Couldn't even read the summons.

Message is revealed through natural events. The main conflict is not over illiteracy but over land.

16. VOICE: Go away, Mr Sawyers. (PULLING HIM AWAY) The judge gave you the verdict. Go away!

17. SAW: (GOING) Illiterate and ignorant. You shall pay for your rudeness.

Emotion: Predominant emotion is anger.

18. LJ: (GOING AFTER HIM) We'll see who'll pay.

19. MISS B: (ALARMED) Littlejohn! Hold him, Mr Roy.

20. ROY: Control your temper, man. (CALLING OFF) Hey! Go on your way Mr Sawyers. It takes two to make a quarrel.

21. MISS B: Yes, and whom God blesses, no man can curse.

22. VOICE: Come now, Sawyers. You have the upper hand. Don't throw it away.

23. LJ: (CALLS) Every unfair game has to be played over. You hear me, Sawyers. Run from me if you like, but you can't run from God!

Scene ends on a note of suspense. The conflict between Littlejohn and Sawyers has not been resolved.

Life in Hopeful Village
Episode #36
Writer: Elaine Perkins

24.	MISS B:	That's right!
25.	FX. FOOTSTEPS FADING OUT. PEOPLE LEAVING	*Scene transition is marked by the fading footsteps indicating that everyone has left this place and gone somewhere else.*

SCENE 2

26.	ROY:	(RELIEVED) Well, sir, what a performance. It's enough to send up my blood pressure. Let's have a soda. Barman!	*Roy's words immediately identify the setting.*
27.	FX. RAPPING ON BAR COUNTER	*Tension drops after the excitement of the first scene.*
28.	LJ:	Don't want anything to drink. I'm going to my place.
29.	ROY:	All right. Pick up his bag and come along, Miss Birdie. We have to stop at my place first.
30.	LJ:	I'm not stopping anywhere. I have my own business to attend to.
31.	ROY:	Remember your promise to give me a hand today. My cow's set to drop her calf anytime.	*The second message is introduced very subtly.*
32.	MISS B:	Yes, Littlejohn. You did promise.
33.	LJ:	I don't have the mind to do anything like that today.
34.	ROY:	I left her this morning lowing like thunder corked up in a grave.	*Figure of speech (simile) is typical of people in this culture.*
35.	LJ:	I've never yet heard of or seen a cow serviced with an injection. Bound to give birth to a seven-foot monster or a thing with three heads. It can't be good.	*Subplot and secondary message (artificial insemination) continue to be revealed gradually and subtly.*
36.	ROY:	Well the man from the Agricultural Department said ....
37.	LJ:	Cha! White collar type! Like the judge there! What do they know about anything? I told you to make that cow with my Redpole bull .... Then you would be sure of	*A new **conflict** is introduced—between Roy and Littlejohn.*

Life in Hopeful Village
Episode #36
Writer: Elaine Perkins

		getting a first rate calf. But no! Artificial insemination, hah! But maybe you believe what Sawyers says … that I'm illiterate. That's why you never count on my advice.	*Longest speeches and bulk of information are contained in the middle of the scene.*
38.	ROY:	Illiterate? Littlejohn? You? Hie, Miss Birdie, bear me witness. Doesn't the entire district of Tydedixon hang on every word from this man's mouth?	**Characters** *reveal themselves further. Littlejohn is the* **doubter** *as well as being stubborn. Roy is the* **seeker** *after new information. Miss Birdie's support of Littlejohn encourages the audience to see the good in him.*
39.	MISS B:	On the word of the Bible! Littlejohn was born brilliant. His mother ate nothing but fresh fish when she was carrying him.	
40.	ROY:	Just the same, the Bible says you're never too old to learn. And I want to upgrade my stock … get a better breed. Understand me, Miss Birdie?	**Overall theme** *of improving your own life is repeated.*
41.	LJ:	I'm going to lodge a complaint about what took place here today .... with the Supreme Court. We'll see whose illiterate … when I sign my name. Hmm! Have you got the court order, Birdie?	**Emotion** *of pride is present throughout the scene.*
42.	MISS B:	Right here in my purse.	
43.	LJ:	Let's go then. I have to study it from top to bottom.	
44.	ROY:	So what about my cow, Littlejohn?	**Tension** *mounts towards the end of the scene. The conflict between the two men is unresolved and the audience is left with the question, "Will Littlejohn help his friend or not?"*
45.	LJ:	The Extension officer got you into this. Let him get you out. Come on Birdie.	
46.	MISS B:	You go on. I'll catch up with you.	
47.	LJ:	(GOING OFF) He who won't listen must suffer!	
48.	FX. DOOR BANGS IN DISTANCE		*The* **scene transition** *is marked by Littlejohn banging the door behind him. It is clear that Miss Birdie and Roy did not leave the scene.*

SCENE 3

49.	MISS B:	Allow him to cool his temper, Roy. You know how he blows hot and cold.	*A short scene that re-establishes the two conflicts that are occurring, with Miss Birdie at the center of each. Predominant* **emotion** *is fear.*

Life in Hopeful Village
Episode #36
Writer: Elaine Perkins

50.	ROY:	Why is he taking his anger with Sawyers out on me, Birdie?	
51.	MISS B:	Littlejohn loves you like his own flesh and blood, but ….	
52.	LJ:	(WAY OFF. CALLING) Birdie!	
53.	MISS B:	(CALLING) Coming. (TO ROY, QUICKLY) Send a message if anything happens.	
54.	ROY:	(SIGHS) I only want to improve my stock. And I believe the extension officer. But so many people are waiting to laugh me to scorn. And now Littlejohn is joining them, and I'm starting to doubt myself. Worrying that I'm making a mistake … that my only cow is going to die.	*Roy expresses the doubts that would be in the minds of many of the listeners as they contemplate the new behaviors the drama is recommending.*
55.		FX. DOOR BANGS AS BIRDIE LEAVES	
56.	ROY:	All right. (TO HIMSELF. UPSET). The Bible says that a good friend is better than a pocketful of money, but I guess He never had to deal with Littlejohn. Barman, serve me a soda. Then I've got to hurry and find that extension officer.	*A touch of humor as Roy admits that probably even God wouldn't know how to deal with Littlejohn.* *Scene ends with unanswered question of whether Roy has done the right thing or not.*
57.		MUSIC. BRIDGE MUSIC UP. :05. CROSS FADE TO FX IN SC. 4	***Music*** *is used here to bridge the scene. Because the next scene is the major scene in the episode.*

SCENE 4

58.		FX. DOOR OPENING. FOOTSTEPS ENTERING ON WOODEN FLOOR	*After the quietness of the previous scene, the action picks up immediately. The FX suggest several things happening at once.*
59.	MISS B:	(COMING IN) I am going to open the shop, Littlejohn. Don't want them to think we're ashamed or hiding because you lost the court case.	
60.	LJ:	No! Tell them to go and buy from Mr Chin Fah.	***Conflict*** *begins right away as Littlejohn refuses to open the shop.*

Life in Hopeful Village
Episode #36
Writer: Elaine Perkins

61. MISS B: There's no sense in turning away business like that all the same.

62. LJ: I can just see Sawyers bawling out to the crowd that I don't know A from B.

63. MISS B: You've only yourself to blame for that.

64. LJ: Look here, Birdie!

65. MISS B: (PLUCKING UP COURAGE) Littlejohn, no one can calculate dollars and cents like you. You can pick and pluck and add and subtract. All you need is a little polishing. But you just stiffen your neck and stop up your ears. Look, even four and five year old children can spell C-A-T, cat and R-A-T, rat. And read "Dan is the man in the van." You could do it, too, and better. But, no. You are too big! Look at when the literacy program started. Look how many people I have taught. Old men walking with canes. Miss Katy with her back bent with age.

66. LJ: Look here, my love ....

67. MISS B: (CONTINUING) Twenty years ago ... from the time we got married ... I bought books ... I bought pencils ... I've been down on my knees to you.

69. LJ: It wasn't a thing I could decide so simply.

70. MISS B: False pride! That's what's in your way.

71. LJ: A man can have a good life ... make money; get respect for himself from other people ... without having to be able to read and write.

This scene delivers the major part of the message: helping yourself to a better life—in this case through literacy—in a natural, non-didactic manner. Miss Birdie takes 5 approaches with Littlejohn, stressing the message in different ways:

1.   *She appeals to his pride.*

Life in Hopeful Village
Episode #36
Writer: Elaine Perkins

72. MISS B: Your mouth says one thing. Your heart says another.

73. FX. RAPPING ON DOOR. VOICE CALLING FOR SERVICE

74. MISS B: Did you hear that?

75. LJ: (IMPATIENT) Hypocrites!

76. FX. FOOTSTEPS FADING OFF. THEN DOOR OPENING

77. LJ: (WAY OFF. ANGRY) Shop's locked. Call tomorrow.

78. FX: DOOR SHUT. FOOTSTEPS COME IN. CHAIR DRAGGED ACROSS FLOOR

79. LJ: (SITTING. SIGHS WEARILY) I don't know ... I just don't know.

80. MISS B: I don't think it makes much sense to spend good money to go through all that constant pushing and pulling. Every time the lawyer writes you a letter you have to dip into your pocket, just to take Sawyers to court over three feet of land ... year after year. Do you think it's worth it?

    2.   *She appeals to his pocket.*

81. LJ: I stand on principle, Birdie.

82. MISS B: For Jesus' sake, husband. Think about it. Don't throw good money after bad.

83. LJ: That man shamed me to my face.

84. MISS B: You behaved shamefully this morning. If you would let me teach you to read and write, you wouldn't have a secret to hide. Remember how I held your hand and taught you to write your name? Do you remember, Littlejohn? All the promises you made to continue, you never kept. Yet you claim to believe in progress.

    3.   *She appeals to his sense of honesty.*

85. LJ: I never wanted anything in life that I couldn't get with my own hands.

Life in Hopeful Village
Episode #36
Writer: Elaine Perkins

86. MISS B: God's truth! But suppose you could read better, eh? Imagine the heights you could reach. Imagine! With your brains! Reading all those books like the ones in Parson's library. Getting all those ideas ... those up ....

4. She appeals to his intelligence.

*This scene evokes a wide range of **emotions**: anxiety, anger, pride, love.*

(THINKS QUICKLY). You know, Parson has a book ... "Six and Seven Books of Moses." I've heard that the Pope in Rome has one just like it in his palace. Oh yes, and that's why those men are so smart and powerful. They know about the Seven Keys to Power from their reading.

87. LJ: Cha!

88. MISS B: There's not a man in the world who can beat you when it comes to brain power, Littlejohn. A little book learning put with your natural brilliance, and millions of people could come to this little island just to look at you. Even school children in England know that much. You didn't hear what Roy said this morning, did you?

5. She appeals to his self-esteem.

The audience recognizes that Littlejohn's real problem is his stubborn pride. They recognize a typical human frailty and they are eager for him to overcome it.

89. LJ: (SNEERING) Roy, ha! (AMUSED) Watch how he's going to lose that cow today!

90. MISS B: The dog barks for his supper. The pig howls for his life. Even the frog is not amused when he sees his life at stake.

91. LJ: You've gone too far now. Stop!

92. MISS B: Stop? When I can feel in my heart that you really don't want to stop. Stop? When I see your eyes, your whole face in church? When Parson calls out the Bible verse, and you start to fumble all over the page, moving your fingers up and down as if you were blind. Rolling your eyeballs like bone dice ... pretending! Feeling ashamed. Feeling less than other people.

*The first **climax** of the episode is reached when it seems that Miss Birdie will not be able to find a way to make her husband change his behavior.*

Life in Hopeful Village
Episode #36
Writer: Elaine Perkins

93. LJ: Ah, don't break your neck over it. Go and get the court paper.

But the tension of this main scene builds even further as the second climax of the episode is revealed: Littlejohn's apparent willingness to desert his friend in his hour of need.

94. MISS B: You're a hard man, Littlejohn. Hard and cruel to yourself. But as people used to say: You can lead a horse to water, but you can't make it drink. Now where on earth is my purse? (SEARCHING) I thought I put it here.

Miss Birdie makes one last appeal to Littlejohn and then leaves him in disgust.

95. FOOTSTEPS FADING OUT

96. ROY: (OFF. CALLING DESPERATELY) Littlejohn! For God's sake!

97. MISS B: (OFF) It's Roy!

98. LJ: Don't worry about him. Find the court paper.

99. ROY: (CALLING. OFF) You're going to be the death of my only cow.

100. LJ: (DISGUSTED. CALLING BACK) Call the expert. I'm not a cow doctor.

101. MISS B: (URGENT PLEA) From Tydedixon to Salem, not a man can handle calf birthing better than you, Littlejohn. Besides, you and Roy go a long way back. He helped you dig your mother's grave.

102. ROY: (OFF. DESPERATE) Littlejohn!

103. MISS B: I'll go!

104. LJ: Birdie!

105. MISS B: Now people will know you really are ignorant.

107. MUSIC. BRIDGE TO NEXT SCENE. CROSS FADE TO FX

The scene ends on a point of high tension. How will Littlejohn react to his wife's insult and his friend's need?

Life in Hopeful Village
Episode #36
Writer: Elaine Perkins

SCENE 5

108. FX. COW MOOING LOUDLY. ROY STRAINING TO DELIVER CALF. MISS BIRDIE BREATHING HARD AS SHE TRIES TO HELP. CONTINUE FX THROUGHOUT SCENE.

The excitement begins immediately with the opening lines of this final scene.

The suspense builds and builds as the audience waits to learn if the calf will be born safely without Littlejohn there to help.

109. Miss B: Did you call the extension officer?

110. ROY: Yes, but he's traveling outside the parish. Hold the rope hard.

111. MISS B: I am holding it.

112. ROY: (TO COW) Bear up. Daisy. Bear up. We'll soon deliver you.

You'll soon get some relief. (TO BIRDIE) It's her first calf and she's scared.

The audience sides with Miss Birdie and Roy as they struggle to manage without Littlejohn. At the same time, the audience experiences a sense of severe disappointment that Littlejohn has let himself down so badly with his best friend.

113. MISS B: It's the same thing with women. I remember when I had my first baby. It was the same time of day as this ... I was barely seventeen years old ... and ....

*The **sound effects** are essential to this scene to convey the picture of the suffering cow and the human beings struggling to help her.*

114. ROY: Wait! I think it's coming. It's coming. Hold her!

115. FX. COW IN LABOR. BIRDIE AND ROY STRAIN HARDER

116. MISS B: (STRAINING) Ohhhiee! It looks as if it's too big, Roy. She doesn't have the strength to deliver it.

*The **climax** of the scene. If something doesn't happen right now to save the cow, she will die, and all Roy's dreams will be destroyed with her.*

117. ROY: Pull!

118. FX. COW STRAINING, MOOING, ETC. THEN SILENCE.

119. ROY: Oh, Father in heaven. You mean I'm going to lose my one cow?

120. LJ: (STRIDING IN) Move over there! This is my job!

The tension lets up slightly as Littlejohn arrives. The listeners are delighted that he has overcome his personal stubbornness and come to his friend's rescue. But the question still remains: Has he come in time?

121. MISS B: (RELIEVED) Littlejohn! I knew you would come!

122. ROY: Thank you, Jesus!

Life in Hopeful Village
Episode #36
Writer: Elaine Perkins

123. LJ: Stand back! Give me room.

124. ROY: (EAGERLY) Yes ... yes.

125. MISS B: I told you he would come, Mass Roy.

126. FX. COW MOOS
     OCCASIONALLY THROUGHOUT

127. LJ: Good girl. Good girl. That's it! That's it!   *The **resolution** of the immediate crisis of this scene ends with safe birth of the calf.*

128. FX. 30 SEC. AD LIB AS COW
     GIVES BIRTH. ENCOURAGING
     WORDS FROM ALL THREE.

129. MISS B: (HAPPILY) It's a little bull, Littlejohn.   *Nevertheless, the crisis of Littlejohn's refusal to learn to read has still to be met.*

130. ROY: (IN WONDER) A champion!

131. LJ: Don't talk too soon.

132. ROY: (LAUGHS HAPPILY) It works,
                Littlejohn. Artificial insemination
                works!

133. LJ: Make sure the calf can get up before
                you start boasting.

134. ROY: (ANXIOUSLY NUDGING CALF) Come
                on, son, stand up .... Stand up!

135. FX. CALF MAKING EFFORT

136. MISS B: Ooh, look at him. He's rising up! He's
                standing.

137. ROY: (ENCOURAGING CALF) That's it.   *The scene ends on a very positive note, and a sense of joy .... **BUT** ...*
                Rock and come back, baby. That's my
                boy. (HAPPILY) Look at the markings,
                Littlejohn. That is what you call
                a first rate, upgraded Holstein. Look at
                the size of the back leg. My mother
                Jemima! What have you got to say
                about artificial insemination of cows
                now, my boy? Eh? What have you got
                to say about this injection calf?

138. LJ: I reserve my opinion.

139. ROY: You learned a thing or two here today, eh?

Life in Hopeful Village
Episode #36
Writer: Elaine Perkins

FINAL NARRATION

142. NARR: In no time at all, the news of Roy's bull calf spread all around town, from Tydedixon to Mount Moria, from Salem to Glengoffe. Next day, the Extension Officer was back in the office. Everyone wanted to hear more about the injection calf. People came to look ... to stroke their chins ... and marvel. Littlejohn was not among them. For early the next morning, before the cock started to crow to call the morning, before the dew left the grass, he harnessed the mules and rode quietly away through the morning mist. Rode away to town!

                  And it wasn't until weeks later that everybody realized what Littlejohn was up to. By that time ... for certain people ... it was too late.

144. <u>MUSIC. SIGNATURE MUSIC TO END</u>

In the final narration two new questions are raised: Why has Littlejohn gone to town? What to do the final words of the narration imply?

The audience is left wanting to know WHAT WILL HAPPEN NEXT?

END OF EPISODE.

Original Version

This is the opening of the same episode (#36) as it was originally written in Jamaican dialect

---

1. NARR: Now imagine a thing as this! Litigation upon litigation. Not five minute after the judge decide de case against him last week, Littlejohn step straight downstairs to the clerk o'court and file an appeal. Yes! This will make the fourth time him and Sawyers fight law over dar little slip of land that divide them two property. Talk about bad feelings. Remember last week when the two of them buck up in the bar across the way? (FADE OUT)

2. TAPE: LAST MINUTE OF PREVIOUS EPISODE, WHEN LITTLEJOHN COLLARS SAWYERS. SCUFFLES. SHOUTS. ETC. MIX WITH PRE-RECORDED FX BAR. VOICES. PEOPLE BREAKING UP THE FRAY. OVERLAP WITH FOLLOWING.

3. LJ: You are an unconshanable tief!

4. SAW: (SHOUTING) If you wasn't so illiterated.

5. MISS B. Make them stop noh Mass Roy, I appeal to you.

6. ROY: Come on, Mass Littlejohn

7. LJ: Let me go Mass Roy.

8. ROY: You is my friend, man. I am talking to you. Stand steady.

9. LJ: Dis man Sawyers move my land-marker. Tief land dat my old people dead and left. He poison my dumb things.

10. SAW: You goat was nyaming dung my young peas.

11. LJ: Down to the star-apple tree my navel string bury under. He chop dung. Root out. And turn round obeah the Judge to mek him rule against me. Well, so help my Almighty God. No Sanky don't sting so. If it is the last farthing I have. If I have to sell out me shop.

12. MISS B: Don't tek no oath, Littlejohn.

13. LJ: (CONTINUING) If I have to starve me belly ... walk around in sackcloth and ashes.

18

Success of Radio Entertainment–Education Programs

Quality radio programming can make a positive contribution to family health and happiness.

Entertainment–Education and Social Change

There is ample evidence around the world that radio Entertainment–Education (E–E) dramas can have a positive effect on social change.

Australia was one of the first countries to make effective use of this medium. A country with a large geographic area—some 7,682,300 square kilometers—Australia had in 1944 a very small population of under five million people. In that year, The Australian Broadcasting Commission (ABC) went on the air five days a week with *The Lawsons*, a 15-minute-long serial drama, designed originally to help farmers adjust to new farming methods required to help the country survive World War II. In 1949 the name of the drama changed to *Blue Hills*, which ran uninterrupted for 27 years!

Following on the ideas developed by the ABC, the BBC launched their famous serial *The Archers* in 1951, with the initial aim of encouraging British farmers to adopt new methods to help overcome the dreadful food and produce shortages created by World War II. *The Archers* continued on the air for over 8,000 episodes.

Since then, serial drama has been used successfully in many parts of the world to have a positive effect on behavior change. In India, one of the radio E–E dramas was the 104-episode serial drama, *Tinka Tinka Sukh* ("Happiness Lies in Small Pleasures"), which ran from 1996 to 1997. It is estimated to have reached about 40 million listeners from 27 local stations covering seven Hindi-speaking states. In 1997, as a result of listening to this serial, a young tailor in the village of Lutsaan, North India, encouraged the people in his community to form radio listening clubs. Gradually the community became more and more interested in and influenced by the behavior change being modeled in the drama. They began planting trees, building pit latrines, and—most impressively—increasing the enrolment of girls in schools and discouraging dowry marriages.

In 1994, Nepal introduced a synergistic radio series, reaching two audiences with two different programs. One serial drama, *Cut Your Coat According to Your Cloth*, was designed for a general audience, with the hope of encouraging everyone in Nepal to have a small well-planned family. The other program series, *Service Brings Reward*, was designed as a Distance Learning (DL) series to train health workers to effectively counsel couples in choosing an appropriate family planning method. The DL programs presented the topics a few weeks ahead of the same topics being presented to the general public. The effect of this synergistic approach was extremely positive and resulted in a marked increase in the number of couples learning about and accepting modern family planning methods.

Soul City, which began life in 1992 as a 13-part TV drama, is known throughout the world now for its extraordinary reach and effect. It soon became apparent that, because radio reaches 65 percent of the target audience for the proposed behavior changes messages, it would be wise to put the programs on radio as well as TV. *Soul City* continues to build, with its programs now being produced in many different languages, and with the development of support materials (comics, audiotapes, etc.) and a multimedia series (radio and television) for children—*Soul Buddyz*. The *Soul City* model has reached out across the world, and even in its home country—South Africa—it is still the series that many people claim has the greatest influence on their behavior change.

Zambia produced *Our Neighbourhood* as a dramatized Health Volunteer workshop which also contained an intriguing mystery. Ghana reached out to female health volunteers with the radio series *The Front Liner*, and Senegal, Guinea, Haiti, and Indonesia all used the radio E–E format to increase the knowledge and improve the services of health workers and midwives. Nepal began broadcasting a new DL series, *Service is Dharma,* in 2004 to reach out to Female Community Health Volunteers.

Detailed analysis of a number of E–E radio dramas and programs can be found in a report entitled *Institutional Review of Educational Radio Dramas* submitted by Mary Myers to the Center for Disease Control and Prevention in Atlanta, USA.

In the last decade, the use of E–E dramas has increased greatly, both on television and radio. In many developing countries, radio remains the widest-reaching medium, and so is used extensively for encouragement of positive behavior change. Increasingly, the radio E–E format is being used for DL programs to upgrade the skills of health workers in remote areas.

The art of Entertainment–Education is still relatively new, and still developing. There is, however, no doubt that high quality E–E programming is now universally accepted as a powerful means of encouraging positive social change. Already, the Entertainment–Education approach is being introduced to internet teaching programs. The future success of this methodology, no matter what the medium, lies in the ability of more and more designers, writers, and producers to understand it and use it well. It is hoped that this book will assist all those engaged in Entertainment–Education programs for radio to improve the quality of their work.

CREDITS

The following list shows the names of dramas from which extracts have been taken for this book, together with the name of the writer, and the country where the writer works:

Tinka, Tinka Sukh by Chandra Dutt Indu, India

Heart to Heart by Parvez Imam, India

Cut Your Coat According to Your Cloth by Kurber Gartaula, Nepal.

Family Affair by Fred Daramani, Ghana

He Ha Ho by Celestine Ndanu, Ghana

Journey of Life by Almaz Beyene Kahsay, Ethiopia

Tale of a Village by Humayun Ahmed, Bangladesh

Life in Hopeful Village by Elaine Perkins, Jamaica

Sample Design Document

DESIGN DOCUMENT
FOR
26-EPISODE RADIO SERIAL DRAMA
FOR THE PEOPLE OF UTTAR PRADESH, INDIA

CREATED AT THE DESIGN WORKSHOP
HOTEL TAJ GANGES
NADESAR PALACE GROUNDS
VARANASI

ORGANIZED BY:
STATE INNOVATIONS IN
FAMILY PLANNING SERVICES
AGENCY (SIFPSA)

> **NOTE:** In its original form, this design document followed the complete outline presented on page 37 of this book. It also contained a list of the names and contact numbers of all those on the design team, and a complete index.
>
> The following pages present points 1–10 of the document and only **some** of the message content pages from this design document, as an example of how these pages should be prepared and presented.
>
> The original design document also included the following important notes to the writer:
>
> - Please follow the messages in the design document faithfully.
> - If there is anything you are unsure of, please contact a member of the script support team.
> - Words that are marked with an asterisk (*) have a Hindi definition in the Glossary. These Hindi definitions from the Glossary should be used throughout your writing of this series of programs.
> - Please ensure that the Health Service Providers you include in your programs always present a friendly, caring attitude and that they reflect positive self-esteem.

THE DESIGN DOCUMENT CONTENTS

Part 1: Background and Overall Description

1. Justification for the Project

Background: State Innovations in Family Planning Services Agency (SIFPSA) has been implementing Behavior Change Communication (BCC) programs as part of the Innovations in Family Planning Services (IFPS) Project. The IFPS Project, supported by the United States Agency for International Development (USAID), is designed to revitalize the family planning program in Uttar Pradesh by improving the access to and quality of health and family planning services. The Health Communication Partnership/Johns Hopkins University is providing technical assistance in the domain of behavior change communication for the project. The project approach is to translate family planning into a people's program.

SIFPSA formulated a communication strategy for health and family planning in Uttar Pradesh in mid-1995. An overarching campaign was developed with the aim of bringing the hitherto taboo subject of planning families out into the open and to trigger dialogue across audience groups: between spouse(s), between the service provider and client, between policymakers and implementers.

Articulation of the theme was in the form of a call to action 'Aao Batein Karein' (Come, Let's Talk). *Tota* and *Mynah*, birds linked to popular folklore on crosstalk, banter and wisdom, were used as visual cues to illustrate the theme.

A statewide communication campaign was developed and implemented to promote contraceptive methods used for birth spacing. With a focus on specific methods, messages were developed in continuity with the umbrella theme (Aao Batein Karein). Campaign components included mass media, local media, community media and interpersonal communication. The campaign was supported by orientation and training of outreach workers. In addition to the campaign promoting Spacing methods, SIFPSA has also implemented statewide campaigns on age at marriage and Tetanus Toxoid (TT) immunization.

(At this point the document included a detailed presentation of the SIFPSA Communication Strategy.)

2. Information about the Chosen Audience

(The following information was collected and discussed with regard to each of the audiences to be addressed in the series. Before completing the document, the team sought and found answers to those areas of information labeled "What do we need to know?")

(I) Rural men

What do we know?

- Myths and misconceptions on FP prevalent among them.
- More comfortable talking with peers.
- Decision-making now increasingly shared amongst spouses.
- Hesitation to accompany wife to health care facility ("too much of a women's affair").
- Hesitation to talk and seek information; put wife forward to get information.
- Sex uppermost in mind.

What do we need to know?

- Satisfied beneficiaries of vasectomy on the increase.

    ➢ Places where contraceptives could be picked without embarrassment.
    ➢ Soft sell of vasectomy camps has helped to create a positive environment.

Why do they have current behaviour?

- Men are reticent by nature.
- Programs and media are more womencentric.

What are the main motivators for change?

- Sense of companionship is being discovered. We need to cash in on that.
- Hope for prosperity is on the rise. Desire to have better life.

(II) Rural women

What do we know?

- Illiterate/low education level.
- Financially dependent.

- Little exposure outside peer group.
- Low aspirations.
- Wish to prove fertility.
- Son preferred.
- Low self-esteem.
- Influenced by traditions/myths.
- However: positive changes due to exposure.
- Unmet needs high.
- Inertia
- Custom and ritual bound
- Lack of knowledge

What do we need to know?

- Who/what influences them the most.
- Barriers.
- Motivational factors.

Why do they have current behaviour?

- Low education level.
- Tradition/social norms.

What will motivate them to change?

- Promise of a better life for their family; promise of good health.
- Lessening of economic insecurity by reducing number of children.
- Dispelling myths.

A similar examination was made of each of the other audience groups specified for this radio serial drama: Other Family Members (Mother-in-law, Father-in-law, Sister-in-law, Mother), Local Influentials and leaders.

3. Justification of the Chosen Medium: RADIO

Radio is an important component of mass media with a reach of 27 percent across rural Uttar Pradesh, thus offering a unique media edge both in terms of cost effectiveness and reach. This is more so in the context of rural audiences, which are the largest and most critical segment of our program's target groups.

It is thus planned to air 26 episodes of a radio drama serial for the general public.

Advantages of radio

1. It is portable.
2. One can listen and work at the same time.

3. It is cheap.
4. No electricity is needed.
5. Cost per message is low.
6. Cost per listener is low.
7. Radio is the medium of the imagination.
8. Wider access to radio possible because it is cheap.
9. People learn more from listening to the radio.
10. There is better recall of message from radio. No distractions (unlike TV and its constantly moving images).
11. No channel clutter.
12. Easy to reproduce and replicate on audio tapes. NGOs/others can playback the cassettes or distribute them.
13. More people listen to the radio than watch TV.

Possible limitations

1. Radio, an audio only medium, is not suitable for some things that are better explained when you actually show them.
2. Everything depends on dialogue and sound effects. Silent scenes are not possible.
3. Need for support materials and supplementary materials.
4. Channel reception issues.
5. Radio listenership declined but now it's on the rise again.
6. Not a medium that people in the rural areas aspire to have.
7. People don't know the schedule of programs.
8. It's a one-way medium. But radio can be made interactive by including quiz questions, etc.

4. The Overall Measurable Objective(s)

The overall measurable objectives for this series as a whole are:

Family planning

There will be a measurable *increase* in the number of

1. couples seeking FP methods,
2. couples seeking FP counseling,
3. couples discussing FP together,
4. people who have correct knowledge of all methods.
5. couples adopting appropriate FP practices.

There will be a measurable *decrease* in the number of

- people who believe in myths on FP.

RTI/STI/HIV and AIDS

There will be a measurable *increase* in

1. The number of people who have correct knowledge of RTIs/ STIs and HIV and AIDS including knowledge of service delivery points for advice and treatment,
2. The number of people (men and women) who seek appropriate services of all types of reproductive and sexually transmitted diseases.

Age at marriage

There will be a measurable *increase* in

1. The number of audience members who have correct knowledge of the benefits of delaying marriage until appropriate age,
2. The number of audience members willing to accept and abide by the legal age of marriage.

Maternal and child health (MCH)

There will be a measurable *increase* in

1. The number of couples who know the facts about the importance of MCH issues and services including service delivery points,
2. The number of families adopting appropriate practices with regard to maternal and child health.

5. The Overall Purpose(s)

The overall purposes of this series as a whole (how the program must allow the audience to reach its objectives) are:

Family planning

1. To educate people and reinforce knowledge of FP.
2. To demonstrate couples talking comfortably talking about FP.
3. To motivate people to get the facts about FP from a reliable source and trust only the facts.

RTI/STI/HIV and AIDS

1. To remind people about the dangers of HIV and AIDS.
2. To teach people how to protect themselves from this fatal infection.
3. To educate people about signs and symptoms of RTIs and STIs.
4. To motivate them to seek and complete treatment.

Age at marriage

1. To educate listeners about the consequences of early marriage.
2. To reinforce their knowledge of current policies and rules about marriage.
3. To motivate them to abide by the guidelines against early marriage and encourage others to do the same.

Maternal and child health (MCH)

1. To educate and reinforce in all family members appropriate knowledge about MCH issues.
2. To motivate families to pay special attention to maternal and child health and make use of appropriate services.

6. The Overall Message and the Main Emotional Focus of the Message

The overall message of this serial as a whole is:

Everyone—women and men alike—has the right to good health. The basis of a happy family life is a small, healthy, and planned family, irrespective of boys or girls. A planned family gives all its members a better chance of good health, good education, and a higher standard of living. It is important that husbands and wives plan their family size and maintain good family health together, with the help of a health service provider where necessary.

The **main emotional focus** of the drama serial as a whole will be confidence in one's ability to take care of oneself and one's family as well as a sense of pride in being able to do so.

7. The Number of Episodes

There will be a total number of 26 episodes in this radio drama serial for the general public.

8. The Duration of each Episode

Each program will occupy a 30 minute radio slot—which means each will be about 25 minutes long.

9. The Message Scope and Sequence and the Number of Programs to be Devoted to each Topic

The following topics will be covered in the order given below, spread over 26 episodes:

1. Story introduction.

Family Planning

2. Child spacing; benefits of a small family—could improve quality of life/health.
3. Benefits of a small family regardless of the sex of the children; father responsible for sex determination of child—not mother.
4. The community perspective—involving gatekeepers, family influentials, religious leaders, PRI leaders.
5. Contraceptives: Oral contraceptive pills.

6. Contraceptives: Condoms.
7. Contraceptives: IUCDs.
8. Contraceptives: Female sterilization.
9. Contraceptives: Non-scalpel vasectomy.
10. Knowledge of RTIs/STIs: Transmission/avoidance.
11. Knowledge of HIV/AIDS: Transmission/avoidance.
12. RCH camps: Various types of services available, trained providers, free services, accessibility, etc.
13. Age at marriage and childbirth—awareness/impacts/consequences/delay in age at marriage/benefits.
14. Gender imbalances: Roles of community and individuals in addressing them.
15. Story development (without message).

Maternal and Child Health

17. Care during pregnancy: Good nutrition; husband, in-laws, other family members caring for the pregnant woman, sharing her workload, etc.
18. Antenatal care: Regular checkups, TT shots, iron supplements.
19. Preparing for safe delivery: Transport planning, skilled attendant at delivery, institutional delivery services in case of high risk.
20. Postnatal care: Importance and benefits.
21. Immunization: Immunization schedule, its importance and the dangers of not immunizing.
22. Breast feeding: Colostrum, benefits, duration, lactation problems.
23. Child nutrition: Introducing other foods—when, what, malnutrition, and weighing.
24. Diarrhea: What it is, causes, prevention, management, ORS.
25. Other childhood diseases, Vitamin A deficiency, pneumonia, worms, etc.
26. Summary program.

Runner themes

Throughout the entire serial, the following important themes will also be demonstrated:

- The role of the Health Service Provider (HSP).
- Appropriate behavior of health service providers.
- Reproductive and Child Health Camps.
- Male involvement and role in family planning and child care.
- Mother-in-law involvement and modern knowledge.
- Gender equality.

Part 2: Individual Program Message Content

*Episode #1**

Topic: Story Introduction

Measurement Objectives: After this episode, the audience will:

---

*Only some of the 26 episodes have been discussed here.

KNOW:

- That a new, exciting drama serial is beginning
- What time it will be broadcast each week
- Who the main characters in the story are

DO:

- Plan to listen to future episodes of the drama
- Inform friends and family members about the new, exciting drama serial

HAVE AN ATTITUDE OF:

- Eagerness to listen to future episodes

PURPOSE:

The purposes of this episode are:

- To introduce listeners to the main characters in the drama
- To attract their interest in the drama so they will continue to listen
- To advise listeners of when future episodes will be played
- To advise listeners that they can win prizes in the quizzes (if we decide to have quizzes)

CONTENT:

- The main plot and subplots of the serial drama will be introduced in this first episode of the serial drama.

The narrator or announcer will inform listeners of:

- The time of the broadcast each week.
- That there will be a quiz question each week.
- The address to which questions, comments and quiz answers should be sent.

Episode #2

Topic: Family Planning
Subtopic: Child Spacing*—benefits of a well planned family*
MEASURABLE OBJECTIVES: After listening to this episode, the audience will:

KNOW:

- What a well planned family* is
- What child Spacing* is
- Benefits of child Spacing* and a well-planned family
- Where to get more information and guidance on a well-planned family and child Spacing*

DO:

- Get more information on the joys and benefits of a well-planned family and child Spacing*
- Consider adopting methods to have a well-planned family
- Consider and practice child Spacing* as a viable and effective method of improving their lives

HAVE AN ATTITUDE OF:

- Appreciation of the advantages of a small family
- Sense of responsibility towards the welfare of their family
- Feel confident that they will be able to get information from the health service provider* on planning their family

PURPOSE:

The purposes of this episode are:

- To educate the audience about the definition of a well-planned family, the advantages of a well-planned family* and child spacing*
- To advise them on where and how they can access further information

CONTENT:

- A well-planned family is one in which the husband and wife discuss and decide together on:
  - ➢ The number of children they want to have (regardless of the sex of the child).
  - ➢ How they would space their children so there is at least 3 years' interval between the birth of one child and the next.
  - ➢ What FP method they will use.
- There are many ways by which one can have a well planned family* and a planned family provides opportunity for more resources and overall well-being of the family.
- Spacing the birth of the next child by three years helps a mother regain her health. She is healthier and hence able to pay more attention and care for her children.
- To access more information from the health service providers* and/or local health center.

Episode #3

Topic: Family Planning
Subtopic: Benefits of a well-planned family* regardless of the sex of the child; father responsible for sex of child
Measurable Objective: After listening to this episode, the audience will:

KNOW:

- What constitutes a well-planned family
- Why a well-planned family* is important
- That the well-planned family is complete irrespective of the sex of the children

- That biologically, it is the father's sperm that determines the sex of the child
- The importance of a girl child in the family and in the society

DO:

- Realize the value of a well-planned family*
- Initiate a dialogue between the couple and within the family, on having a well-planned family
- Appreciate the importance of the girl child
- Acknowledge that the father determines the sex of the child and therefore not hold mother responsible

HAVE AN ATTITUDE OF:

- Responsibility for a well-planned family*
- Respect for the girl child
- Respect for the mother for delivering a healthy child irrespective of the sex of the child

PURPOSE:

The purposes of this episode are:

- To sensitize the community* towards the benefits of the well-planned family*, regardless of the sex of the children
- To discourage the practice of blaming the woman for delivering a girl child
- To initiate and encourage discussion within the community* on having a well-planned family, regardless of the sex of the child.
- To educate the community* about the fact that the father's sperm determines the sex of every child

CONTENT:

- A well-planned family* is one in which the husband and wife decide together
  - ➢ How many children they can support.
  - ➢ How to space their children so that there is at least 3 years interval between the birth of one child and the next.
  - ➢ To determine (with the help of the service provider*) which family planning* method is right for them.
  - ➢ That daughters are every bit as valuable as sons.
- A well-planned family has greater opportunity to make the best use of what they earn. Everyone should know that it is the father's sperm that makes the baby a boy or a girl. The woman's body has NO influence on the sex of the child. However, neither the mother nor the father has any control/choice over the sex of the child to be born, so mothers are not responsible if the couple has only daughters.
- Daughters are the life of any home; they are caring and loving and continue to care for their entire family throughout their lives. Father and mother must love and appreciate their daughters. Without girls there would be no wives. Throughout the whole world, girls and women are being recognized and valued. It must be the same in India.

Episode # 4

Topic: Family Planning
Subtopic: Role of community* leaders

MEASURABLE OBJECTIVES: After listening to this episode, the audience will:

KNOW:

- The important role of community* leaders in encouraging small families
- The definition and importance of well-planned families
- The advantages of well-planned family for all couples
- The availability of resources/correct information/action points
- The options of services available

DO:

- Create a positive and supportive environment to initiate discussion at community* and family level
- Encourage the community* to adopt the appropriate family planning* methods
- Support government initiatives by providing space, infrastructure for services, and ensuring community* participation
- Co-ordinate with service providers* in maintaining correct data and create action plan in consultation

HAVE AN ATTITUDE OF:

- Responsibility towards society and the state as a whole on the issue of a small family
- Feel motivated to organize discussion forums and service camps
- Feel proud and have a sense of achievement in encouraging small families

PURPOSE:

The purposes of this episode are

- To give community* leaders the complete picture of population and health issues
- To provide knowledge of resources available to provide better health and family planning* services to the community*
- To encourage community* and religious leaders to understand the value/power of their word and include the well-planned family* issues into their work area

CONTENT:

- Uttar Pradesh (UP) contains one-sixth of all the people in India and the state's population is still growing rapidly every year.
- Consequences of this growth will be a reduction in resources to feed, educate, look after, provide jobs, places to live, and water to drink for everyone.
- The government is working hard to tackle this issue at village and individual levels.

- Community* leaders should take up the role of motivating and monitoring the program by organizing community* meetings, rallies, forums, and camps to promote planned families. They should also work with other NGOs in the area.
- Community* leaders should support initiatives by being present at and participating in the days of camps and meetings.
- Panchayati raj officials should activate village health subcommittees to keep and update their records on community* progress.
- At all community* forums, gender issues, benefits of small well-planned families, and issues regarding gender equality and general health and hygiene should be included.
- In talking with the community* use examples that can be well understood; local people can help to drive these points home.

  ➢ e.g., ever-increasing population will mean more number of houses for living, more land utilized for survival, thereby reducing the land available for cultivation.
  ➢ e.g., gender imbalance will leave many men unmarried, suppression of women, leading to imbalance in society.

Community* leaders, including religious leaders, can do a great deal to motivate their communities to understand the value of a small family, and to seek guidance and advice on how to have a small well-planned family.

Episode # 5

Topic: Family Planning
Subtopic: Contraceptive* Oral Pills
MEASURABLE OBJECTIVES: After listening to this episode, the audience will:

KNOW:

- That "Oral Pills" are a safe modern contraceptive for women
- How to take them
- Advantages of the Oral Pill
- Where to get Oral Pills

DO:
They will:

- Consider the Oral Pill as a reliable method for spacing children and limiting births
- Follow correctly the health service provider's instructions on how to take the Oral Pill

HAVE AN ATTITUDE OF:

- A positive image about the oral contraceptive pills as a way of helping a woman to have a planned life
- Husbands feel motivated to support their wives in continuing with the pills

PURPOSE:

The purposes of this episode are:

- To educate the audience about oral contraceptive* pills, their advantages and the importance of taking them correctly.
- To motivate the audience to seek more information from health service provider* (HSP) on all forms of contraceptive methods.
- To reinforce* correct and complete information about pills.
- To encourage men to support their wives to take oral pills as directed.

CONTENT:

- The Oral Pill is a safe, reliable modern contraceptive method that can be used by women who want to delay the birth of their first child and space subsequent births appropriately.
- A woman should use the oral pill to prevent* pregnancy ONLY after she has visited a service provider* to make sure the pill is suitable for her.
- The Oral Pill is highly effective when taken daily and is perfectly safe
- It can be taken regularly for a long time in accordance with the Health Service Provider's* (HSP) advice.
- Advantages

  ➢ It is convenient and easy to use and prevents pregnancy for as long as the woman wants to.
  ➢ After stopping the pill, the woman can conceive immediately.
  ➢ Many women taking the pill find they have fewer menstrual cramps.

- The health service provider* will instruct the woman on how to use the pill

  ➢ It is taken at the same time every day, such as bedtime.
  ➢ When a service provider* recommends the oral pill, ask her or him for all the details on how to take it correctly, and what to do if you forget to take the pill one day.

- Where to get the pill?

  ➢ The pills are available from the service provider*, in the market and at the health center.
  ➢ As soon as one packet is finished, the woman should start immediately on the next packet. So she should have a stock of at least two packets at home.

- Just as there are some temporary bodily changes when a woman gets pregnant, there are also some temporary bodily changes when a woman starts taking pills. These changes usually disappear after a few months. If these temporary changes worry her, the woman should seek advice from the health service provider*.
- If the woman is using the oral contraceptive* pill, her husband should give her support by making sure she takes the pill regularly every day.
- A well-planned family* offers every family member the chance of a better life.
- Using the oral contraceptive* pill is an easy way to space children and have a properly planned family.

Episode # 6

Topic: Family Planning*
Subtopic: Condoms
MEASURABLE OBJECTIVES: After listening to this episode, the audience will:

KNOW:

- What a condom is, how to use it correctly and the benefits of the condom
- How it should be stored and disposed
- Where it is available

DO:

- Use condoms or plan to use condoms correctly and consistently to avoid pregnancy, RTI*/STI*/HIV
- Communicate with partner about use and get more information from health services provider about correct use and disposal.

HAVE AN ATTITUDE OF:

- Men will accept responsibility for preventing pregnancy as well as RTI*/STI*/HIV
- Willingness to seek information, and procure and use condoms.
- Women will feel comfortable about asking their partner to use the condom to prevent pregnancy as well as to prevent RTI*/STI*/HIV

PURPOSE:

The purposes of this episodes are:

- To educate the audience about condoms and about the advantages of condoms
- To motivate audiences to seek more information from the health service providers* about correct use, storage, and disposal of condoms.
- To motivate people to use condoms appropriately and correctly

CONTENT:

- Condom is a protective cover made of thin latex that men use during intercourse to prevent* pregnancy and STI*/HIV .
- It is easy to use, and is a simple method of preventing pregnancy and infection.
- The condom is
  - ➢ safe and effective,
  - ➢ easily available everywhere,
  - ➢ easy to use,
  - ➢ reliable protection against pregnancy and against STI*,
  - ➢ a way to enjoy sex without the fear of pregnancy or STI*.

- Before using condoms it is important to know:

  ➤ There are instructions on the packet for correct use.
  ➤ Each condom can be used only once and a new condom must be used each time during intercourse (sex).
  ➤ The condom MUST be correctly and safely disposed of after use by burying or burning.

- Information on correct condom use can be obtained from the health service provider* or from a local health clinic. Read and follow instructions given on the pack for correct use.

Modern, responsible men take the lead in showing that they care for their wife and family by using condoms when appropriate. It is the only method that prevents* STI*, HIV infection, as well as pregnancy.

Episode #11

Topic: HIV/AIDS*
Subtopic: Knowledge of transmission and avoidance
MEASURABLE OBJECTIVES: After listening to this episode, the audience will:

KNOW:

- What HIV and AIDS* is
- How it is transmitted*
- How they can protect themselves and others from HIV and AIDS*

DO:

- Begin to take appropriate steps to protect themselves and others from HIV and AIDS*.
- Accept personal responsibility for doing everything they can to help prevent the spread of HIV and AIDS

HAVE AN ATTITUDE OF:

- Confidence that they know how to protect themselves
- Responsibility to protect themselves and others from HIV and AIDS infection

PURPOSE:
The purposes of this episode are:

- To educate people about HIV/AIDS* so that they can take appropriate preventive measures.
- To motivate people to realize the importance of accepting responsibility for protecting themselves and others from HIV/AIDS*

CONTENT:

- HIV/AIDS* is an infectious, fatal disease and worldwide there is no cure for it.
- It is not possible to know who is suffering from this infection by looking at them, as the infected person may look and feel healthy for many years, before becoming bedridden and gravely ill. However, those who know how this deadly disease is caused can protect themselves and others from it by responsible and careful behaviour.
- HIV/AIDS* is spread by the following ways:

  ➢ By having unprotected sexual intercourse*, because it is transferred from one partner to the other if one of them is infected (the risk is increased if one has multiple sexual partners)
  ➢ If infected blood is given in a blood transfusion.
  ➢ If one is given an injection with a syringe and needle which was used for giving injection to another person.
  ➢ By the use of blades/razor or tattoo needles etc., which have been used by another person.
  ➢ From infected mother to baby.

- It's everyone's responsibility to protect oneself and others from HIV/AIDS*. This can be done by:

  ➢ Avoiding sex before marriage.
  ➢ Being faithful to your partner after marriage.
  ➢ Using condoms if abstinence and faithfulness are not possible.
  ➢ Ensuring use of new disposable syringes and needles or those that have been properly sterilized by being boiled for 20 minutes in clean water.
  ➢ Use of new or properly cleaned blades and razors, etc.
  ➢ If you or your family members ever need blood transfusion, be sure to ask the blood bank for blood that has been tested and found to be free of HIV and AIDS*.
  ➢ If all of us take the responsibility upon ourselves towards protecting ourselves and others from this deadly infection, AIDS* will not be able to continue to spread.
  ➢ Those who do not use a condom when having sex before marriage or outside marriage are a menace to themselves and to others.

Episode # 12

Topic: RCH* Camps
Subtopic: Services available
Measurable Objectives: After listening to this episode, the audience will:

KNOW:

- What RCH* camps are and where they are held
- The variety of services available at the RCH camps
- That services at RCH camps are free and follow-up service is provided.

DO:

- Make use of services at camps as approved and needed.

HAVE AN ATTITUDE OF:

- Confidence in the services provided at the RCH camp and willingness to access the camp
- Responsibility towards one's self and one's family

PURPOSE:

The purposes of this episode are:

- To educate the audience about the services at the RCH* camps
- To reassure them about the availability/quality of friendly services
- To motivate everyone to make appropriate use of the camps
- To create an environment that will encourage the audience to demand quality services

CONTENT:

- Everyone in the community* has the right to good health.
- An arrangement of health services on a regular basis is available at RCH* camps at your block's government hospital with a team of skilled/trained doctors and other female health service providers.
- The services provided are:
  - ➢ Checkups for pregnant women and provision for iron tablets.
  - ➢ Immunization* for children and pregnant women.
  - ➢ Checkups for RTIs* and STIs*.
  - ➢ Pregnancy tests, counseling*, and provision of FP methods including sterilizations and IUCD insertions.
  - ➢ General health checkups.
- After sterilization, you can take advantage of free transportation to your village.
- Follow-up visits at the homes of the sterilization/IUD patients will be made by the ANMs (Auxilary Nurse Midwives).
- The services are provided free of cost.
- Contact your health worker about the services available closest to you and when the next camp will be.
- All families should learn about the RCH camps from their service provider*, so that they can take advantage of them to help keep all family members healthy.

Episode #15

Topic: Family Planning
Subtopic: Gender imbalance, role of community* and individuals to address this
Measurable Objectives: After listening to this episode, the audience will:

KNOW:

- What gender imbalance is
- The root cause of gender imbalance
- Disadvantages of gender imbalance
- How to prevent* gender imbalance

DO:

- Realize the importance of everyone in the community working together to avoid gender imbalance
- Work together to find ways of preventing gender imbalance in the community
- Encourage provision of equal opportunity to both males and females in all areas of life

PURPOSE:

The purposes of this episode are to motivate people to:

- Assume responsibility for encouraging gender balance in all areas of life
- To create awareness of and concern about existing gender imbalance
- To motivate people (especially community* leaders) to initiative discussion and action to overcome gender imbalance
- To sensitize the elders about their role in maintaining gender balance in the community*

CONTENT:

- To motivate the community* to provide equal opportunity to all, including females.
- In UP the sex ratio is 898 females for every 1,000 males.
- This means that in terms of wives and mothers there is a desperate shortage.
- There is ample evidence throughout the world to show that women who are educated not only make better wives and mothers, they can also contribute to the welfare of the family and to the welfare of the community, the state, and the nation.
- The idea that boy children are more valuable than girl children is old-fashioned and foolish. It is time that everyone worked together to destroy this old belief and to accept girls and boys as equally valuable in every way.
- The giving of dowry is illegal throughout India so there is no need for families to worry about how to supply dowry for their daughters. People who expect dowry are out of touch with the modern world and out of touch with the law of India.
- Girls are just as capable of taking care of parents as are boys. There is no basis whatsoever for not recognizing and acknowledging that boys and girls are equal in every way.
- Community leaders and respected members of the community should make it their business to encourage meetings at which these old ideas of inequality are denounced.
- Regular meetings and discussions should be held to motivate everyone to move towards the modern way of thinking and recognize the equality of the sexes.

Episode #16

Topic: Maternal and Child Health
Subtopic: Care during pregnancy
Measurable Objectives: After listening to this episode, the audience will:

KNOW:

- The importance of looking after a pregnant woman
- How the family can provide essential care to her

- How to recognize an emergency during pregnancy
- What to do when an emergency arises

DO:

- Make increased efforts to look after a pregnant woman properly
- Seek immediate help in case a pregnant woman has an emergency

HAVE AN ATTITUDE OF:

- Responsibility towards pregnant women in their families
- Confidence that they can take care of pregnant women correctly and recognize and respond to danger signs appropriately.

PURPOSE:

The purposes of these episodes are:

- To educate families and reinforce* their current knowledge about how to take care of pregnant women
- To educate families about danger signs in pregnancy and how to respond to them
- To motivate all family members to take appropriate care of pregnant women

CONTENT:

- It is a matter of great joy and pride to have a pregnant woman in the family because she is bringing a precious new life into the world. All pregnant women need to be looked after so that they remain healthy and have a better chance of having a healthy baby.
- It is the duty of the woman's husband and all family members to ensure that she is well taken care of. Those husbands who are actively involved in looking after their pregnant wives should be very proud that they are contributing towards the health of their wives and children.
- A pregnant woman needs to eat more food for the growth of the unborn child. Whatever she is eating, she must eat more, including seasonal fruits and vegetables.
- The pregnant woman also needs more rest, so besides sleeping for 8 hours at night, she should also rest for 2 hours during the day.
- The family of the pregnant woman should not allow her to do hard work such as carrying buckets full of water as it can be dangerous for the pregnant woman to carry heavy loads.
- It is also important to keep the pregnant women happy and stress-free.
- The pregnant women should be registered with the ANM so that she is provided antenatal care at the right time.
- In any pregnancy an emergency can sometimes arise suddenly. If a pregnant woman has one of the following symptoms, she should be taken to the hospital immediately as every minute counts.

  ➢ Bleeding from vagina
  ➢ Dirty discharge from vagina

> ➤ Severe pain in abdomen
> ➤ High fever
> ➤ Excessive vomiting
> ➤ Severe swelling in hands/feet
> ➤ Convulsions
> ➤ Baby stops moving in the mother's body
> ➤ Blurring of vision/fainting

- Remember, it is the responsibility of the entire family to take care of the pregnant woman so that she remains healthy and gives birth to a healthy "bundle of joy."
- If you have any questions about pregnancy or about the health of a pregnant woman in your family, you can get the answers you need from your local health service provider* or from the nearest clinic.

Episode #21

Topic: Maternal and Child Health
Subtopic: Breastfeeding
Measurable Objectives: After listening to this episode, the audience will:

KNOW:

- The importance of colostrum (the first milk/*khees*) and breastfeeding for infants' health and growth
- When to start breastfeeding and for how long it must be continued
- The right technique of breast feeding*
- When to supplement breast milk with other foods

DO:

- Start breastfeeding early—within an hour of birth—and give colostrum* to the newborn
- Approach the health service provider* in case of any problem with breastfeeding
- Practice exclusive breastfeeding for 6 months.

HAVE AN ATTITUDE OF:

- Sense of fulfillment, of giving one's best to the child
- Confidence in the correct technique of breastfeeding

PURPOSE:

The purposes of this episode are:

- To provide reaffirmation to the mother that the traditional practice of breastfeeding handed down to her is indeed beneficial to her child
- To remind the mother of correct practices of breastfeeding
- To reinforce* the importance of colostrum* and of exclusive breastfeeding for 6 months.

CONTENT:

- When a baby is born, put the child to the mother's breast as soon as possible.
- Breastfeeding is best started early (within 1 hour of birth of the child).
- The mother's first yellow-colored milk (colostrum*) should be fed to the infant because it contains important nutrients that protect the baby from many diseases. It is important to ensure that the child is given this "first milk."
- The more a mother breastfeeds her newborn, the more is the production of milk.
- All mothers can produce enough milk as per the baby's needs as long as the baby continues suckling, since production of milk is more if the baby suckles more.
- Breast milk is sufficient nutrition for the child till 6 months of age. Even water is not necessary and should not be given.
- It is important to breastfeed as frequently as the child demands.
- In case of any problems with feeding, please contact the health worker to learn about correct ways to breastfeed the baby. The health worker will advise you on what to do.
- Make sure that both breasts are alternately used to feed the child. After feeding, put the baby on the mother's shoulder and pat gently, to make it burp. A burp releases gases and prevents the baby from throwing up the milk.
- The size of the mother's breasts does not matter. Even a woman with small breasts can produce enough milk. Even if a woman has had twins, she can produce enough milk to feed them both.
- For the duration of exclusive breast feeding* (6 months), it also works as a natural contraceptive*.
- While the mother is breast feeding*, she must take a **regular** nutritious* diet and continue to take iron and calcium.
- In case of problems like cracked nipples or painful breasts, contact the health service provider*.
- It is important that the new mother discusses all aspects of breastfeeding with the HSP to ensure that she is doing the right thing both for herself and for her baby.

Episode # 24

Topic: Child Health
Subtopic: Other childhood* diseases
Measurable Objectives: After listening to this episode, the audience will:

KNOW:

- What Vitamin A** deficiency is and how it can be prevented/cured.
- How to prevent* diseases like pneumonia, worms, etc., and when to go to the local health service provider* for help

DO:

- Take the child for Vitamin A** dosage to the nearest health service provider*

- Recognize some basic symptoms of common diseases and seek help from local health service provider*
- Maintain hygiene and cleanliness for all family members.

HAVE AN ATTITUDE OF:

- Confidence among parents to correctly assess the situation and ask for help from the local health service provider* when necessary.
- Ability and willingness in family members (including in-laws) to help identify a problem that requires help from the health service provider* and to seek help for appropriate referral and care during transportation

PURPOSE:

The purposes of this episode are:

- To make parents aware of simple, common illnesses that can be prevented and cured with the help of the local health service provider*
- To help parents realize that if these illnesses are ignored, they could lead to serious diseases and possible death
- To recognize some simple symptoms of diseases
- To motivate parents to seek help from the service provider* at the earliest (for both boys and girls)

CONTENT:

- **Note to the writer:** Please emphasize the need for parents and other family members to seek health services as early as possible for both girl and boy child alike even for simple illnesses, i.e., fever and common cold to prevent* the condition from worsening.

VITAMIN A*

- Vitamin A* is important for the body and lack of Vitamin A* can cause Night Blindness* (*Ratondhi*) in children, which develops into total blindness if not treated in time.
- Vitamin A* deficiency can be prevented and cured by going to the local health service provider*.
- The first vitamin dosage should be given to children at 9 months of age along with measles* vaccination. Four more dosages need to be given until the child is 3 years old. The service provider* will remind parents of the next dosage and provide them free of cost.

PNEUMONIA

- Early symptoms are breathlessness, fever and cough.
- Even a common cough/cold needs to be treated through the local health service provider*, as early as possible.
- It is important to protect your children (especially infants) from cold by keeping them warm in winter.

WORMS

- Worms in children are caused through lack of cleanliness and hygiene (personal and household).
- To prevent* worms:

  ➢ Give clean boiled water to your child.
  ➢ Maintain cleanliness by washing hands.
  ➢ Wash fruits and vegetables thoroughly before use.
  ➢ Keep the children clean.

- Persistent stomachaches and vomiting can be symptoms of worms. If your child shows these symptoms please seek help from the health service provider*.

General Advice:

- In case of high fever, simple precautions like sponging with a wet cloth should be given at home and the local health service provider* should be contacted immediately.
- If a child continues to feel sick for more than a day the local service provider* must be contacted immediately.

All parents are responsible for the good health of their children and it is important that they remain aware and are quick to act in case of common childhood illnesses.*

For the Design Workshop

SAMPLE LETTERS OF INVITATION TO DESIGN WORKSHOP PARTICIPANTS

For Content Specialists

Dear ...,

(Name your organization) in association with (name of sponsoring agency, such as United States Agency for International Development) is preparing to create a radio drama serial to encourage adolescents to live safer, healthier lives (name your topic).

In order to ensure that the messages delivered through the drama serial are accurate and appropriate, we are holding a design workshop at (name the venue) from (opening date) to (closing date). We would very much appreciate your presence as a design team member for the duration of this workshop.

The aim of this workshop is to prepare a design document which will contain the **exact messages** that must be contained in each of the episodes of the drama serial. Your contribution to developing these messages would be very welcome. We would like to have your assurance that you can be with us for the entire duration of the workshop so that we can be sure that all design team members agree on all contents of the design document.

It would be most helpful if you could bring with you any print or other materials relevant to our main topic so that you can share the most up-to-date knowledge with other team members during our small group work.

For Writers

(Name your organization) in association with (name your funding agency) is preparing to create a radio drama serial to encourage adolescents to live safer, healthier lives (name your topic).

In order to ensure that the messages delivered through the drama serial are accurate and appropriate, we are holding a design workshop at (name the venue) from (opening date) to (closing date). We would very much appreciate your presence as a design team member for the duration of this workshop.

The aim of this workshop is to prepare a design document which will contain the **exact messages** that must be contained in each of the episodes of the drama serial. Your contribution to developing these messages would be very welcome. We would like to have your assurance that you can be with us for the entire duration of the workshop so that we can be sure that all design team members agree on all contents of the design document.

In your role as a possible writer for this drama, we believe that you will benefit greatly by being part of the design team and taking part in the determination of the message content. We would hope that by the end of the week, you would have started preparing some possible storylines and character profiles that could be used for the drama serial. We would like to encourage you to think of ways of creating an exciting, culturally appropriate story that would allow our messages to be brought in naturally, gradually, and subtly. You will have the opportunity to meet with representatives of our chosen audience, as well as with the content (or message) specialists. This will help you understand the audience's likes and needs, and also to gain a clear understanding of the messages that are to be incorporated into your story.

The design workshop will open with a dinner on—at—to which you are cordially invited. Then the workshop will run each day from—to—Please see attached agenda.

Board and food will be provided for you throughout the workshop and you will receive a per diem of ....

Sample Message Page

Episode #

Topic:
Sub topic:

Measurable Objectives: After this episode, the audience will:

KNOW:

DO:

HAVE AN ATTITUDE OF:

PURPOSES:

The purposes of this episode are:

CONTENT:

GLOSSARY:

SUGGESTED AGENDA FOR DESIGN WORKSHOP

DAY 1

8:30 AM	Introduction of facilitators and participants
9:00 AM	Introduction to Behavior Change Communication (BCC) radio programming
	Discussion of BCC radio programming in (local country) to date
	Introduction to and overview of the Entertainment–Education approach to Behavior Change Communication
10:30 AM	TEA
11:00 AM	Sample of BCC radio program. This can either be a prerecorded program in the local language (if programs of this nature have been locally done previously) or a group of participants can be invited to present the script on page 255–66 of this book)
12:00 NOON	Introduction to the design approach

- The design team
- The design workshop
- The design document

1:00 PM	LUNCH
2:00 PM	Commencement of the design document (Plenary):

1. Justification: Presentation of findings that clearly demonstrate why the present project is necessary.

Plenary discussion on the findings.

3:30 PM	TEA
4:00 PM	2. Audience: Plenary discussion can determine the audience(s) to be addressed. Small groups can examine the audience(s) with regard to their needs related to the topic(s). Sharing of small-group findings
5: 00 PM	Review of day's work
	CLOSE

DAY 2

9:00 AM	Brief overview of accomplishments of Day 1
	Continuation of design document:

       Justification of chosen medium
       Overall Measurable Objectives
       Overall Purpose(s)

10:30 AM	TEA
11:00 AM	Overall message and emotional focus
	Number of programs and duration of each program
	Topic scope and sequence: Introduction (small-group work)

1:00 PM   LUNCH

2:00 PM   Completion of Topic scope and sequence, including number of programs devoted to each topic

3:30 PM   TEA

4:00 PM   Introduction of message design for individual programs

           Small-group exercise on individual message preparation

           Presentation and discussion of exercise

5:00 PM   Review of day's work

           CLOSE

DAY 3

9:00 AM   Brief overview of accomplishments of Day 2

           Message design: Small-group work

           Message design will continue for the remainder of this day, with lunch and tea breaks at usual times.

5:00 PM   Brief overview of day's achievements

           CLOSE

DAY 4

9:00 AM   Brief review of previous day

9:30 AM   Review of final individual program messages

10:30 AM TEA

11:00 AM Completion of all program messages

           Completion of glossary

1:00 PM   LUNCH

2:00 PM   Part 3 of design document:

           Implementation plans:

           Script review panel

           Support materials

           Promotion plans

           Monitoring and evaluation plans

           Time lines

3:30 PM   TEA

5:00 PM   CLOSE

DAY 5

9:00 AM   Brief review of entire workshop

9:30 AM   Presentation by writers of story ideas

           Quick written evaluation by participants

10:30 AM TEA

11:00 AM Workshop evaluation

           CLOSE

SCRIPT EVALUATION

TITLE: _____

WRITER: _____

1. What is the format of this drama: ☐ Serial ☐ Series
2. How well do you think this program would appeal to our audience(s)?
   ☐ A lot ☐ A bit ☐ Not very much
3. Do you think this program will allow our messages to come in comfortably?
   ☐ Yes ☐ No
   Explain your answer:

   _____
   _____

4. Name or describe TWO of the characters in the program:

   _____
   _____

5. Is there any humour in the program outline? ☐ Yes ☐ No
   If so, which character provides the humour?
6. Briefly explain your opinion of this program outline and why you think it would or would not be suitable for our purposes:

   _____
   _____
   _____
   _____

If you like the outline, but you can see some important changes that should be made, please comment on those in this space.

_____
_____
_____
_____

SIGNATORY PAGE SAMPLE

Radio Communication Project
Distance Education through Radio Communication Project (RCP)
2000–2001

In order to ensure that the fourth phase of radio programs designed for the Distance Education of health workers is in accordance with ministerial policies, in line with the National Reproductive

Health/Family Planning IEC Strategy, 1997–2001, of the Ministry of Health, and is of acceptable educational and cultural standards, this Phase IV Design Document was reviewed by a distinguished panel of specialists during the final stages of its development. As a result of this input, appropriate changes were made to bring the Document to completion.

The signatures below indicate that this Phase IV Design Document, in its final version, has been content-endorsed by the following organizations through their nominated representatives.

Here followed the signatures of leaders of the various organizations who were involved in and responsible for the creation and management of the project.

SAMPLE ·ACTOR'S CONTRACT

MEMORANDUM OF AN AGREEMENT
made and entered into by and between:

JOHNS HOPKINS UNIVERSITY, POPULATION COMMUNICATION SERVICES
(hereinafter known as JHU/PCS)
and

_____
(hereinafter known as "the actor")

Whereas it is agreed that JHU/PCS engages the actor and the actor accepts the engagement to play a role in a Radio Drama Serial (hereinafter known as "the drama") to be produced by JHU/PCS and for the time being entitled "JOURNEY OF LIFE" upon and subject to the following terms and conditions:

1. The actor agrees to be available to JHU/PCS for rehearsal and production on the designated dates and at the designated times between July and November 2001.
2. For these services JHU/PCS shall pay to the actor as compensation the amount of 15 Birr for each minute of the actor's appearance in any episode.
3. The actor shall be paid fortnightly, following submission of an account approved and signed by the Program Manager.
4. In accepting this appointment, the actor agrees to:

   - be available for all rehearsal and recording sessions,
   - be aware of the timetable for rehearsals and recordings and commit to being available at these times,
   - prepare and rehearse the script prior to the rehearsal session with the Program Manager and/or producer,
   - abide by the decisions of the Program Manager with regard to script changes and script interpretation.

5. The actor agrees that for every rehearsal or recording session missed, no payment will be made to the actor. Failure to turn up for more than two recording sessions will result in the actor being removed from the cast.

6. The actor agrees that for every half-hour of late arrival for rehearsal or recording he/she will forfeit 10 percent of due payment for that session. No deductions will be made if the delay in rehearsal or recording is beyond the control of the actor.

7. The actor shall keep JHU/PCS informed well in advance of any recording dates on which he/she will not be available.

8. Rehearsals will be held from 9:00 a.m. to 12 noon on Mondays at Ras Stereo. JHU/PCS will provide transport to and from this address to the Radio Ethiopia Studios on recording days.

9. JHU/PCS agrees to provide the actor with adequate advance notice (at least one week in advance) of the dates on which the actor will be needed for rehearsal and recording.

10. JHU/PCS agrees to provide the artists with scripts at least 2 days in advance of rehearsal and recording date of each episode of the drama in which the actor is to appear.

11. The actor shall not without the written consent of JHU/PCS incur any liabilities or expenses on behalf of JHU/PCS nor pledge JHU/PCS's credit.

12. The actor shall not be entitled to any further payment from JHU/PCS for repeat broadcasts of the drama on Radio Ethiopia or other broadcast networks.

SIGNED at ADDIS ABABA this ＿＿ day of ＿＿ 2001, in the presence of the undersigned witnesses.

<u>AS WITNESS:</u>   <u>AS WITNESS:</u>

....

....

Johns Hopkins University/   ACTOR
Population Communication Services

Design Workshop Question Guide

The following guide provides a statement of the exact intent of each segment of the design document, together with information that should be shared with the design team as they begin discussion of the section, and an explanation of what should be written in the design document. Also provided are questions that can be used to initiate discussion of each section of the design document. The suggested questions should not be seen as the only questions to use, and in some cases not all the questions given here will be necessary. In most cases, it will be important to ask other relevant questions as well as these. These questions are offered only as a guide and suggestion for those who have not run a workshop of this nature previously.

BACKGROUND AND OVERALL DESCRIPTION

1. Justification for and Statement of Desired Change in Behavior

Intent: To be sure that every member of the design team is perfectly clear about, and persuaded by the need for the proposed radio serial drama and the behavior changes it seeks to encourage.

Written requirement for the document: A clear, concise statement of why the project is being undertaken. This will include a summary of research findings and an explanation of why a radio serial drama has been selected as a communication strategy.

Give to the design team before this discussion:

- The names of the sponsoring agencies.
- Information from the research done during the analysis phase.

Include in the justification statement:

- Names of researchers, and dates and places where research was carried out.
- Names of sponsoring agencies and ministries.

If possible, researchers should be asked to make a presentation to help the participants understand the need for this project.

Questions to guide the discussion: Initiating questions to clarify the rationale in the minds of design team members:

- *What factual knowledge do we have to help us understand whether or not our listeners perceive their current behavior as a problem?*
- *What is the cause or what are the causes of current individual behavior and social norms in the area of the desired behavior change?*
- *Is knowledge about the new behavior the only or major need of the audience?*
- *Are the current individual behaviors and social norms influenced by factors such as:*
  - ➤ *fear,*
  - ➤ *lack of resources,*
  - ➤ *tradition, and*
  - ➤ *other, perhaps unidentified, factors?*
- *What do we not know that we should find out about before we complete the statement of rationale?*

2. Information about the Audience or Audiences

Intent: To describe as clearly and precisely as possible the audience or audiences selected as the main recipients of the radio serial drama. Since radio is a universal medium, anyone can listen, but the intention of this section is to make clear that the drama will be designed to appeal especially to specific listeners.

Written requirement for the document: A simple profile of each of the chosen audience(s), together with an explanation of why the chosen audience(s) are likely to want and respond to the suggested behavior change.

Give to the design team before this discussion: A summary of the analysis of audience data obtained during the analysis phase.

Invite audience representatives to give a brief overview of what they know from their own experience about the intended audiences with regard to the recommended behavior change.

Questions:
Information required for structuring the messages:

- *What do we know as fact about the audience's feelings on this topic?*
- *How do we know this?*
- *Is there any part of this topic in which we are ignorant of the audience's true feelings? How can we increase our knowledge in this area?*
- *What do we know about the audience's degree of knowledge on this topic?*
- *What do we know about the availability of necessary resources for our audience?*
- *What is the CAUSE of the current behavior of the audience (ignorance, tradition, religion, disinterest, etc.?)*
- *What change agents are likely to be most influential with this audience?*
  (Change agents can be people, such as figures of authority, sports and entertainment stars, and influential peers, or they can be benefits like increased wealth, higher social standing, and more leisure time.)
- *Will it be necessary to direct the message to more than one audience? If so, who will the other audience(s) be?*
- *Can all audiences be addressed through the same drama, or must we consider other ways of meeting the needs of the other audiences?*

Information required for creating the drama:

- *What information will the writer need about the daily lives of the audience that should be reflected in the drama?*
- *What type of drama or entertainment appeals to the chosen audience(s)?*
  (Some members of the design team—including the audience representative(s)—can set aside some time during the design workshop to put together a detailed audience profile that the writer can use in creating the characters and locations for the serial drama. The writer should assist in the creation of this profile.)

3. Justification of the Chosen Medium

Intent: To be perfectly clear about the reasons for selecting the chosen medium (in this case, radio).

Written requirements for the document: A clear statement of the reasons for selecting *this* medium to deliver *this* message to *this* audience.

Give to the design team before the discussion: Information on the listening habits, program preferences, and the radio ownership of the audience from the analysis phase research.

Questions:

- *Why are we using radio as the main medium, and not some other medium?*
- *What types of radio programs does the audience enjoy? How do we know?*
- *Does the audience usually use the radio for entertainment, or does it use radio only for news, music, and information?*
- *How have members of the audience responded in the past to radio dramas that contain a message? How do we know?*
- *Are they likely to turn off the radio if they discover that the drama contains a message? Would the audience prefer messages to be delivered in a more straightforward manner? How do we know?*
- *Are they likely to believe and trust information delivered through a fictional radio drama? How do we know?*
- *If they are not likely to trust this information, how can we make this format more acceptable to them?*

4. The Overall Measurable Objectives of the Serial as a Whole

Intent:

- To provide a concise overview of exactly what changes in individual behavior and societal norms the radio serial drama hopes to affect.
- To be perfectly sure that these objectives are SMART (see page 41).

Written requirement for the document: A clear, simple statement of the measurable changes in individual knowledge, attitude, and behavior and in societal norms that it is hoped the audience will demonstrate as a result of listening to the serial.

Give to the design team before the discussion: A definition of a SMART objective and some examples of the difference between measurable and non-measurable objectives (see page 38). Explain that what is needed here is a limited number of broad objectives; specific objectives will come up later in the discussion.

Questions:

- *What increase or decrease in certain knowledge and behaviors do we want to see in the audience as a result of this radio serial?*
- *What changes do we want to see in societal norms as a result of this radio serial?*
- *Where do the majority of members of our chosen audience stand on the Steps to Behavior Change? (See page 39). How do we know?*
- *Which of the Steps of Behavior Change must we model in the serial in order to guide the audience toward the desired change?*
- *Are there any possible impediments to our audience members moving up the Steps to Behavior Change?*

- *What do we want to be able to observe our audience believing, doing, and advocating as a result of this serial?*
- *Are our stated objectives SMART? (See page 41)*

5. The Overall Purpose of the Serial as a Whole

Intent:

- To explain the approach that the radio serial drama will have to take in order to make it possible for the audience to want to and be able to make the recommended behavior changes.
- To explain whether the major focus of the serial will be: to educate; to model; to motivate; etc., or whether the drama will need to combine a number of approaches or purposes.

Give to the design team before the discussion: An explanation of what is meant by "purpose" and a list of possible purpose statements as given below.

Written requirement for the document: A simple, clear statement of the main approach or approaches to be used in the radio serial drama so that it can have the best possible effect on audience behavior change.

Questions:

- *Overall, what approaches are we going to take in the serial drama to help the audience reach the desired objectives?*
- *Which of the following approaches will need to be expressed by the drama:*

  ➢ *to educate the audience about____*
  ➢ *to model ____ for the audience____*
  ➢ *to reinforce audience's existing knowledge of____*
  ➢ *to demonstrate how to____*
  ➢ *to motivate audience members to____*

- *Other possible program approaches can be*

  ➢ *to update*
  ➢ *to encourage*
  ➢ *to overcome (fear and misbeliefs)*
  ➢ *to recommend*
  ➢ *to increase awareness of, etc.*

- *If more than one approach is needed, will these approaches be simultaneous or sequential?*
- *If there are several purposes to be approached sequentially, what will the sequence be? In other words, should the serial drama begin by, for example, educating and then move to reinforcing and then to motivating?*

6. The Overall Message and the Main Emotional Focus of the Serial

Intent: To state briefly the overall message that the serial drama must convey throughout. For example:

Good nutrition is the foundation (basis) of good health. All caregivers should know how to feed pregnant women, breastfeeding mothers, and children appropriately to ensure proper growth, development, and good health. They should also know and practice home based management of common childhood illnesses, family planning, personal and environmental hygiene.

Give the design team before the discussion:

- An example of an overall message.
- An example of a main emotional focus, such as, "The audience will have a positive attitude to child health and home based care for childhood illnesses and will be **proud** of being able to keep all family members healthy."

Written requirement for the document: A clear, simple statement of the overall message that the broadcast serial drama will deliver, and a statement and explanation of the emotional focus it will emphasize.

Questions:

Overall message

- *What is the simplest, clearest, least confusing summary statement we can give about what the serial will be conveying to the audience?*

The main emotional focus

- *Will a positive or a negative emotion be more likely to influence our audience in the direction of the desired change?*
- *What is the strongest overall positive feeling or emotion we want the audience to gain and maintain with regard to the desired behavior change as a result of listening to this serial? Some possible emotions:*

Love	*Wisdom*	*Freedom*
Happiness	*Capability*	*Perseverance*
Empowerment	*Self-confidence*	*Personal empowerment*
Togetherness	*Success*	*Other feelings?*

- *Is there any need to instill any negative emotions throughout the serial drama?*
- *If so, what should they be?* (**Note:** *Remember the importance of leaving the audience with a strong positive feeling, even if the drama brings in some negative emotions along the way.*)

7. The Number of Episodes in the Serial

Intent: To determine the number of episodes the serial will contain together with a rationale for the chosen number.

Give to the design team before the discussion: Any information that has been obtained relevant to radio station time availability, budget restrictions, program length to which listeners are accustomed, etc.

Written requirement for the document: A statement of the number of episodes decided upon, together with a statement of the reasons for the chosen number. If this has not been predetermined by the broadcast station, or by special needs of the project, you can ask the questions given below for a better idea:

Questions:

- *Is the audience accustomed to a particular number of episodes in a radio serial drama?*
- *How many episodes will be needed to tell a really exciting story?*
- *How many episodes will be needed to deliver all the message information and provide necessary modeling comfortably without overloading the audience with information?*
- *Are there any constraints on writing and recording time that could affect the number of episodes that can be prepared?*

8. The Duration of Each Episode

Intent: To determine the appropriate broadcast length for each episode of the serial drama.

Give to the design team before the discussion: Any information that has been ascertained relevant to radio station broadcast slots, budget restrictions, etc.

Written requirement for the document: A simple clear statement of the agreed-upon duration of each episode, together with reasons for the determined duration. If this has not already been predetermined by broadcast station policy, ask the following questions.

Questions:

- *How many minutes (at one time) can this audience realistically devote to listening to a drama? (Radio station personnel can help with this decision, based on previous experience with radio dramas.)*
- *How long can this audience listen attentively to a radio drama—even a very good one— without being distracted?*
- *What is the usual length of a radio drama program in this part of the world? What does research indicate about whether this is or is not an acceptable length?*

9. The Topic Scope and Sequence

Intent: To determine the topics and subtopics that must be covered under the main message in order to provide the audience with all necessary knowledge, modeling and motivation. To determine if there is a particular sequence in which the message topics must be presented and/or repeated.

Give to the design team before the discussion: Information from the research done in the analysis phase that might be pertinent to these determinations, such as particular knowledge gaps or strong resistance to particular behaviors. Explain that message scope can be thought of as the chapter headings in a textbook—listing the various subjects or topics that the book will cover. Also explain that "sequence" means the order in which the knowledge must be given. Explain that consideration also must be given to whether some of the topics need more repetition than others.

Written requirement for the document: A listing of all the topics to be covered, in the order in which the topics should be presented.

Questions:

- *Into what main topics can we divide the message information that is to be given to the audience?*
- *Is it necessary to present these topics in a certain order? If so, what should that order be?*
- *Are some of these topics more difficult than others for our audience to understand or to accept?*
- *Should we repeat these topics more than the others?*
- *How should we spread these repeats throughout the entire serial?*
- *In what sequence should these main topics be included in the story so that listeners are led appropriately and comfortably up the steps to behavior change?*
- *Should we keep all the episodes on one topic together in the serial drama, or should we spread them among the episodes?*

10. The Number of Episodes to be Devoted to Each Topic in the Message Scope and Sequence

Intent: To determine if certain aspects of the message need to be expressed more frequently than others throughout the serial.

Give to the design team before the discussion:

- Research data relevant to aspects of the topic which the audience currently seems to have the most trouble understanding or agreeing to undertake.
- A reminder of where the research suggests the audience is with relation to the Steps to Behavior Change. Explain to the design team the importance of distributed learning, which ensures that a topic is not dropped altogether once it has been covered. Distributed learning

allows for a period of concentrated exposure to a topic, followed by continued appropriate reference to that topic from then on throughout the serial drama.

For example: There might be four sequential episodes (14–17) concentrating on the importance of Vitamin A. From then on to the end of the serial (episode 52) the value of vitamin A will be discussed again more casually several times.

Written requirement for the document: A final numerical listing of all episodes showing the topics and indicating the number of episodes being devoted to each topic (see Appendix A, pages 281–82).

Questions:

- *Looking at where our audience stands on the Steps to Behavior Change, should we be putting more emphasis on certain aspects of this subject than on others? Which aspects should have more episodes devoted to them?*
- *How much of the information in each of the topics is new to this audience and may need to be repeated?*
- *Should the repetition be spread throughout the series, or should it be concentrated in the block of episodes devoted to a particular topic?*
- *Should some broadcast slots be set aside for review and for listener questions and comments (rather than for ongoing episodes)? If so, how many and at what intervals?*
- *Will related topics be delivered one after the other, or will they be separated and spread throughout the serial?*

PART 2: INDIVIDUAL EPISODES

11. The Measurable Objectives of Each Episode or Group of Episodes

Intent

To be perfectly clear about the knowledge or behavior change or attitudinal change that the audience will be expected to have as a result of listening to a particular episode or group of episodes.

Give to the design team before the discussion:

- A reminder of what is meant by measurable objectives.
- A reminder that no one episode can be expected to result in enormous changes of attitude and behavior and knowledge, but that each episode should be written to fulfil specific measurable objectives.

Written Requirement for the Document

A simple statement to fill in the following grid for each episode or group of episodes (it is not always necessary to have all three objectives in each episode):

After this episode, the audience will:

KNOW:

DO:

HAVE AN ATTITUDE OF:

Questions:

- *Is each objective stated in a way that leaves no doubt in the writer's mind what changes the episode is to try and achieve in the audience?*
- *Do the stated objectives fit in with the overall objectives for the series?*
- *Are the objectives truly possible to obtain after one episode?*
- *Are the stated objectives SMART? (See page 41)*

12. The Purpose of Each Individual Episode

Intent: To clarify (especially for the writer) the approach the episode should take. For example, an episode that has "to educate" as its purpose needs to present information in a systematic and repeated manner, than does an episode designed to motivate an audience.

Give to the design team before the discussion: A reminder of the need for stating the purpose of the episode or group of episodes. A reminder about possible episode purposes (see Section 5 discussed earlier).

Written requirement for the document: A simple statement for each episode that completes the following sentence:
                         The purpose(s) of this episode is (are)....
         (See samples in Appendix A, Part 2: Individual Program Message Content.)

Questions:

- *What is the real purpose of each episode or group of episodes? Is it to educate, to demonstrate, to motivate, to model, etc.? (Use the list that the team worked out for Section 5 of this guide.)*
- *Does this purpose fit in with the overall purposes of the project? Is it necessary to have more than one purpose for this episode or group of episodes?*

13. The Precise Message Content for Each Episode

Intent: To provide a clear, precise statement of the message content that should be included in the episode.

Give to the design team before they begin group work:

- A reminder that it is *not* the writer's job to determine the message.
- A reminder that every message given in an Enter-Educate serial drama must be: complete, correct, clear, concise, consistent, culturally appropriate and compelling (the 7Cs).
- Share with the design team some samples of well-written content (page 283 onwards).
- Provide each working group with "content pages" on which they can record their determinations about the objective, purpose, and content of each episode or group of episodes.
- Remind design team members to mark all words that should be included in the glossary.

Written requirement for the document: A clear, detailed statement of the precise message information that must be included in each episode or group of episodes, together with a statement of how any technical words or terms are to be listed in the glossary and used consistently by the writer.

Questions:

- *What must be presented in this episode to give the audience the very best chance of achieving the objectives of the episode and of the series as a whole?*
- *How must the drama express the content so that it makes complete sense to everyone in the audience—even those with no previous knowledge of the topic?*
- *Which technical words or phrases need to be reexpressed in language that the audience can accept and understand easily?*
- *Is there enough content? Too much content? Can we simplify the content even further?*
- *Is this message complete, correct, clear, concise, consistent, culturally appropriate, and above all, compelling as it is stated for this episode? Is it consistent with what has been given for other episodes?*

14. Glossary and Acronym List

Intent:

- To determine all words and phrases that need to be expressed (or defined) in a simple and consistent way every time they are used and to provide appropriate definitions.
- To provide the writer with the full and correct names of any organizations, methods, etc., that are usually expressed as acronyms.

Give to the design team before they begin small-group work: A place where they can list all words that should be included in the glossary. This should be a flipchart or board where all members of the design team can see what is being added to the glossary, or where they can add their own contributions. Remind the team of the importance of giving simple explanations and definitions of technical words, and of the importance of using consistent words and phrases when explaining important aspects of the message.

Written requirement for the document: A glossary presented in alphabetical order. Also be sure that design team members mark with an asterisk (*) all words or phrases in their content pages that have definitions in the glossary.

Questions:

Glossary:

- *What is the simplest, clearest explanation we can give of this word or this term that will be understood easily by our audience?*
- *If the design team is working in a language different from that to be used in the scripts, will it be necessary to include a local language translation so the writer will know exactly what words to use?*

Acronyms:

- *Are there acronyms used in the content of the episodes that need to be spelled out (and translated) for the writer's use?*

PART 3: IMPLEMENTATION

15. Script Review Panel and Script Support Team

Intent: To determine which members of the design team should undertake the regular task of reviewing every script of the serial drama as it comes from the writer, together with reviewing the finished design document and support materials. Also, to determine those who are willing to be available for script support. (Information on the precise needs of the script review panel and the script support team are given in Chapter 2.)

Give to the design team before the discussion:

- A reminder of the importance of reviewing every script to ensure that the message adheres to the design document and that the story is well written, suited to the audience, and likely to attract and hold the attention of the audience.

- A reminder of the need for the scriptwriter to have supporters to whom to turn when questions about content arise.

Written requirement for the document: A listing of those who will be on the script review panel and those who will be on the script support team.

Questions:

Review panel:

- *What types of expertise should be represented on the review panel: content specialist, audio director, language specialist, etc.?*
- *How much time will these people need to review each script? How much time can the project allow? Which members of the design team have this time available?*
- *Should each reviewer check the entire script, or should the script be marked up, showing individual reviewers the parts on which they should concentrate?*
- *Will it be necessary to reimburse panel members for review work?*

Support team:

- *Which members of the design team can be available to the writer as a support team?*
- *To fulfill the requirements of the script support team, will it be necessary to recruit people outside the design team? If so, who should these people be?*
- *Will it be necessary to reimburse script support team members for this work?*

16. Support Materials

Intent: To determine what, if any, support materials will be needed to accompany the radio serial drama, bearing in mind that any communication project has an increased chance of success if more than one medium is used.

Give to the design team before the discussion:

- An overview (and copies where applicable) of any existing support materials that should be considered for use with the radio episodes.
- Explain any budgetary limitations that might exist with regard to existing or new support materials.
- Share with the team the guidelines for support materials (see Chapter 6).

Written requirement for the document: A statement of exactly which existing support materials will be used, or what new materials will be developed, together with a brief rationale of why these materials are needed.

Questions:

- *Is there an essential need for support materials with this serial drama? If so, for whom are they essential and what should they be?*

- *Should these be written support materials? Is the literacy level of the audience adequate for written materials?*
- *Are there adequate ways of distributing support materials?*
- *Are there other forms of support materials that could be used with this project?*
- *Are there existing materials that can be used? Is the content of these materials consistent with the messages to be included in the radio serial drama?*
- *How much time will be needed to develop and test new support materials?*
- *How and where will listeners be able to obtain the support materials?*

17. Promotion Plans

Intent: To determine what promotional activities and materials will be needed and developed to bring the radio serial drama and its messages to the attention of the audience.

Give to the design team before the discussion:

- Remind the team of the need for promotion of the communication project, and share with them guidelines for promotional activities.
- Invite the team to consider creation of a logo and a slogan.

Written requirement for the document: Statement of promotional activities and materials to be developed, together with any slogan and logo agreed upon.

Questions:

- *Which media—to which the audience has regular access—could be used for promotional spots or pieces:*

  ➤ *radio?*
  ➤ *schools?*
  ➤ *newspaper?*
  ➤ *clinic posters?*
  ➤ *community groups?*
  ➤ *other?*

- *Are there any popular figures: sports stars, movie stars, etc., who could be used beneficially in promotion?*
- *When should promotion begin? How often should promotional pieces be used before broadcast commences and during regular episode broadcasting?*
- *Should there be a special logo or slogan (or both) which people could associate immediately with the serial and its message?*
- *Will the promotional materials be developed in-house or will an advertising agency be employed to prepare the promotional campaign? Is there a budget for this?*

18. Monitoring and Evaluation Plan

Intent: To devise an effective system of monitoring the outcomes of the radio serial drama while it is being broadcast, and to carry out summative evaluation when the broadcasts are complete.

Give the design team before the discussion: Invite an evaluator to explain to the design team the importance of pilot testing, monitoring, and evaluation. The final details of this plan will most likely be put together by the evaluation specialists who will be hired to carry out the evaluation. Design team members, however, can be asked for ideas about where, when, and how pilot testing, monitoring, and evaluation can be carried out.

Written requirement for the document: A statement of exactly how, when, and where monitoring and evaluation will be undertaken.

Questions:

- *How many pilot episodes should be tested?*
- *How often should audience response to the serial drama be monitored once it is being broadcast regularly?*
- *Where, and in what way, might audience feedback be best compiled?*
- *How will the writer make use of feedback about earlier episodes once writing is underway?*
- *Where, and in what way, might final summative evaluation be undertaken? What should be done with the summative evaluation results so that future projects can benefit from them?*

19. Time Line

Intent: To create a detailed chart showing the dates by which each step in the writing, typing, translating, reviewing, revising, pilot testing, recording, editing, and broadcasting of each episode and all support and promotional materials must be completed.

Give to the design team before the discussion: Explain the vital importance of establishing and maintaining a time line. Provide a template of the activities that need to be included in the time line. Note that the time line cannot be finished during the design workshop, but design team members need the opportunity to give their input and to appreciate its importance.

Written requirement for the document: A full, detailed time line for all activities.

Questions:

- *Will the writer(s) be working full or part time on this project?*
- *What is the realistic number of scripts the writer(s) can complete each week, bearing in mind that it will be necessary sometimes to work on revision of earlier scripts at the same time as writing new ones?*

- *How does the production house or radio station prefer to work: recording one episode a week on a regular basis, or recording blocks of episodes at one time?*
- *How long after the completion of the design workshop can the design document (or at least the writer's brief) be ready for the writer's use?*
- *How long after receiving the design document or writer's brief (in draft form) can the writer deliver the finished story treatment and character profiles?*
- *How long after approval of treatment and profiles can the writer deliver the pilot episodes?*
- *How long will it be between the completion of the pilot scripts and the carrying out of the pilot tests?*
- *How long after the tests before the results are compiled so the writer can commence ongoing script writing?*

20. Story Treatment and Sample Episode

This part of the design document will be prepared by the writers. They will provide a narrative outline or synopsis of the plots for the entertainment side of the drama, indicating how the message will be included naturally, subtly, and gradually.

The story treatment and sample episode will be added to the design document after the design workshop.

Questions:

- *What type of story do members of our chosen audience prefer: adventure, romance, comedy, tradition, etc.?*
- *What type of characters do members of our chosen audience prefer? What should these characters do for a living? Where should they live? How old should they be? What names should they have? What type of personalities should they have? What language should they use: formal or colloquial?*
- *What type of emotional involvement is most likely to appeal to members of our chosen audience: negative or positive emotions? Fear, jealousy, love, pride, compassion, success, etc.?*

The full script of a sample episode—showing the quality of the drama and giving an understanding of how story and message will be blended—will be written for the design document when the writer has been selected and the treatment and character profiles have been approved.

Journey of Life Episode Synopsis

The following pages contain the synopsis of the first three episodes of the Ethiopian radio serial drama, *Journey of Life*, as a sample of how the episode synopsis should be written. Before commencing the scripts, the writer, Almaz Beyene Kahsay, completed the synopsis of all 26 episodes of the serial drama, together with a detailed profile of all main characters. The synopsis and character profiles were approved by the review team before scriptwriting was undertaken.

EPISODE 1

MAIN PLOT

Tilaye (male), Mekdelawit (female), and Eden (female) are talking during rehearsal at the nightclub. Tilaye and Eden are lovers. Mekdelawit is Eden's friend and studies as an extension student at the university. They are asking her about her lessons there. They jokingly tease her about her being a nightclub musician and at the same time a student at the university. During their conversation Eden also talks about her parents, especially about her father's love towards her. Tilaye keeps quiet. Mekdelawit notices his mood and when she questions him about it, there is bridge music.

SUBPLOT A

Bahru's house. Askale (f), Bahru (m), Saba (f), and Teje (f) are talking about Teje's being a wife and mother of a baby. Teje says that she loves her husband very much but she is burning up inside at being the second wife. This makes her happiness at having her own home meaningless. But she thanks God for giving her a family. At this point there is a knock on the door. The door opens and a dog barks. They all laugh when they see Bedlu with a piece of meat he brings to cajole the dog.

SUBPLOT B

Ato Getachew (m), Fanos (f), and Workitu (f) chat with each other. Immediately Workitu shouts at Fanos and orders her to reduce the volume of the tape playing in the room. Getachew stands

Note *that the first episode does not contain any message; it is used to introduce the characters and the story. In subsequent episodes, the writer has clearly marked where the messages will come in.*

by his wife and retorts that his wife has done nothing for Workitu to shout at her like that. Workitu takes it as an insult that they dare to talk to her like that in her parent's house. She gets angry.

SUBPLOT C
Yeshiwork (Tilaye's aunt) comes to the nightclub looking for Tilaye and someone gets him for her from the rehearsal place. He asks her why she has come to look for him. She then tells him that she is very worried because of the bad dream she had the previous night and has come to visit him for this reason. She also makes a remark about his father, saying that she has finally found the address of his father's shop.

EPISODE 2

MAIN PLOT: two weeks later
Mekdelawit and Eden are rehearsing a song at the nightclub while they wait for Tilaye. They talk about his being late. Mekdelawit says that although Tilaye seems happy working at the club as a musician, she always sees him feeling discontented. Eden then says she loves him very much but that she is also worried about his behavior and unusual quietness lately. Tilaye arrives at this point. Eden gets sulky and tells him that she just saw him talking with a new girl while coming to the nightclub.

SUBPLOT A
Teje's house. Bahru, Bedlu, Askale, and Saba are sitting listening to Teje. She tells them that she is in trouble because her husband continues to send money to his wife residing at Wolkitie. Bedlu insists that she ought to convince herself to accept the situation. Besides, he is unhappy at having only one child by her till now. Bahru then tells him the advantages of having a planned family **[EPISODE 2 MESSAGE]**. At this point someone from outside calls Bedlu and he goes out. Teje gets angry, saying that he has probably been called by his first wife's relatives.

SUBPLOT B
Getachew and Fanos are talking in the heat of love. Fanos implores Getachew to pack and leave the house for good because she can no longer tolerate his sister, Workitu. Incidentally, Workitu happens to hear this without them seeing her. Suddenly there comes someone behind her where she is hiding and listening; she lets out a terrified cry. Hearing this, Getachew and Fanos come out. The stranger is Alemayehu, the older half-brother of Workitu and Getachew. He says he is in trouble and threatens Workitu to give him his share of the inheritance from their father. But she retorts that he has already taken his share and there is nothing left for him. Furthermore, the rest of the property he claims is all her mother's. When she warns him to get out or she will call the police, there is bridge music.

SUBPLOT C
Mekdelawit makes a reconciliation between Tilaye and Eden. Then, Tilaye leaves the room called outside by his aunt, Yeshi's wife. She says that she came to ask him for some money because she is in trouble. She couldn't pay the house rent and the liquor she is selling is no more in demand. She then tells him about his father; that he has a big store and asks whether he would like to visit him. He stays quiet and she gets uncomfortable and asks him why he looks so pale.

EPISODE 3

MAIN PLOT

There is a sound of music. Tilaye and Eden are ready to start work. Mekdelawit is late. She hasn't come yet from her university lesson. They agree to get themselves ready and wait. In the mean time, being curious, Eden asks him what he loves most, his music or her. Tilaye says he loves both. She insists that he choose. He says he can't. By way of pursuing the subject, she asks him why he is afraid of introducing her to his parents if he loves her. He says that his father was a singer who is now dead. She then asks about his mother. He simply tells her that his music now is both his father and mother. Eden gets sulky and says he is deliberately hiding his real identity from her. He assures her he himself doesn't know his identity. When she is startled and asks him why, there is bridge music.

SUBPLOT A

Teje cries. Bahru and Askale try to console her. Bedlu is angry because he cannot understand why she is upset and jealous at having learnt that he already had a wife when he married her. Teje says that if she had known he was already married, she would never have married him. Bedlu insists that she will just have to accept the fact that she is his second wife. Bahru interrupts and explains that having two wives at once can be dangerous, because if a man is not faithful to one woman, he exposes himself more easily to HIV/AIDS **[EPISODE 3 MESSAGE]**. Bedlu replies that as long as both his wives are faithful to him, he is safe. Askale taunts him, asking him why he believes his wives will stick to one man if he cannot stick to one woman. Bahru says Bedlu should decide and choose just one of his wives, but Bedlu insists he loves them both.

SUBPLOT B

Workitu and Getachew are talking. Workitu not only loves her brother too much but, she also respects him. She is now telling him about Alemayehu. She gets annoyed that Alemayehu went to her husband's shop last week and quarreled with him. Fanos appears to tell them the coffee is ready and that they should get in. Workitu suddenly notices Fanos' suit and questions her where she intends to go. Fanos says she is going to the university. With a veiled insult, Workitu remarks that it is not good for a woman to be out at such late hour. Alemayehu comes in suddenly. He implores Getachew to make an intercession for him. Getachew, accepting his plea, requests Workitu to make peace with Alemayehu and help him, even though he squandered his share of the money. Workitu refuses pointblank, and orders Alemayehu to get out. Alemayehu shouts threateningly and says that her husband is living in luxury with his father's money and now he will do something about it. He then goes out. Workitu gets alarmed and says look how he goes threatening her.

REFERENCES AND SELECT BIBLIOGRAPHY

Ang, I. 1985. *Watching Dallas*. London: Methuen.

Bandura, A. 1986. *Social Foundations of Thought and Action: A Social Cognitive Theory*. Englewood Cliffs, NJ: Prentice-Hall.

Black, J. 1995. *The Country's Finest Hour: Fifty Years of Rural Broadcasting in Australia*. Australian Broadcasting Corporation.

Bentley, E. 1968. *What is Theatre?*

De Fossard, E., J. Baptiste, C. Corrales, and A. Bosch, (Eds). 1993. *Interactive Radio Instruction*. Washington DC: USAID.

The Johns Hopkins University/Center for Communication Programs (JHU/CCP). 1984. Basic processes and principles for health communication projects. Baltimore, USA.

Morley, J. 1992. *Script Writing for High Impact Videos: Imaginative Approaches to Delivering Factual Information*. Belmont, CA: Wadsworth Publishing Co.

Nariman, Heidi Noel. 1993. *Soap Opera for Social Change*. Westport, CT: Praeger.

Piotrow, P.T., L. Kincaid, J.G. Rimon, W. Rinehart, 1997. *Health Communication: Lessons from Family Planning and Reproductive Health*. Westport, CT: Praeger.

Singhal, Arvind, Michael J. Cody, Everett M. Rogers, and Miguel Sabido, (Eds). 2003. *Entertainment Education and Social Change*. Lawrence Erlbaum, Associates.

About the Author

Esta de Fossard is Senior Communication Advisor at the Johns Hopkins University's Bloomberg School of Public Health, Center for Communication Programs. She previously taught at the universities of Southern California and Ohio, as well as at George Mason University in Virginia. Ms de Fossard has served as an international freelance consultant for numerous projects using radio or television for behavior change or classroom education. Her role involves assisting with curriculum design, training, production, and evaluation of the media campaign. Her practical experience in using media for behavior change spans 60 countries in Asia, Africa, and Latin America. She is also a prolific author with more than 50 books—both for adults and children—to her credit. Ms de Fossard is currently working on two more books in this series, related to the use of television and distance learning for behavior change.